LOVE
THE LAW OF THE ANGELS

A CLASSIC FROM THE PEN OF
GWEN SHAW

End-Time Handmaidens, Inc.
P.O. Box 447
Jasper, Arkansas 72641
U.S.A.

Copyright 1979 by Gwen R. Shaw
End-Time Handmaidens, Inc.
Engeltal
P.O. Box 447
Jasper, Ark. 72641

Printed in the United States of America

ISBN 1-932123-09-1

FOREWORD

"He brought me to the banqueting house, and His banner over me was LOVE" (Song of Solomon 2:4).

Beloved, it is not an accident, nor by chance, that you are holding this particular book in your hands, wondering what it is about and whether it might be of any interest to you. Know this, dearly beloved, that in God's ever-present, all-pervading love, there are NO accidents with God. As our loving Father, He wants only the best for each one of His precious creations. He has led you to be at this very moment holding this book and reading these words.

Because God is, above *all* else, LOVE, and in this all-pervading love, He wants us to sit at His Banqueting Table with Him and enjoy a feast of what surely is closest to His great heart.

The central theme of His written Word, and the essence of Jesus Christ, His Living Word, is LOVE . . . but too few of us know and understand just what this God-love really is. And this sad state of affairs is surely a commentary on the effectiveness of God's mortal and spiritual enemy, Satan, in keeping us blinded to this truth of God by his unloving, destructive, hateful, on-going spiritual warfare against our Almighty God and His images, created in His likeness . . . we human beings of all races, colors and creeds.

So to help us to know and to understand, and thereby to be enabled to experience and enjoy the attributes and power of His very essence, God has raised up and called out, and for many, many years put through training, trials and testings one of His very special Daughters, that she could be able to prepare for us less privileged a rare and unique feast for our betterment and growth in becoming that which He created us in His image to be . . . LOVE, like our Lord Jesus Christ is, always was and always will be!

'Sister' Gwen, as she is affectionately called in the more than fifty nations to whom she has ministered in the past thirty-two years, my very, very precious wife, is this unique one who comes to us now, sharing with us from the depths of her soul that which God the Father, God the Son and God the Holy Ghost has for seeming eons of time been preparing her to share with us from His Banqueting Table. As those who have read or studied any of her many other books and Bible Studies, or been ministered to in music, sermon or personal ministry know full well and appreciate, she is one truly anointed by God and with the beautiful gift of being able to quickly get to the point and clearly enunciate that which God lays on her heart.

Knowing her as I do, and having the same burden on my heart as she, I must hasten to add this note of caution . . . it is with the most sincere prayer of her heart, as you read these words she has written, that you will look past her as being only the willing and obedient instrument and scribe, to see only the actual Author and Finisher, her true Lover, the Bridegroom, the Lord Jesus Christ, God's Son, the Very God, Saviour. And that with her you will lift up your eyes and hands and heart in praise and thanksgiving and worship to our Father God for His infinite and eternal Grace and Goodness to each of us for having prepared and given to us such a beautiful further evidence of His love and His desire that we can know The Law of The Angels and become motivated to live by it and then become that which He is; not just to know and to understand, but to truly BE LOVE.

"Now unto him that is able to keep you from falling, and to present you faultless before the presence of his glory with exceeding joy, To the only wise God our Saviour, be glory and majesty, dominion and power, both now and ever. Amen" (Jude 24, 25).

Lt. Col. James v. D. Shaw
United States Air Force, Retired
3 March, 1979

To My Beloved Husband
Lt. Col. James v. D. Shaw, U.S.A.F. retired

INTRODUCTION

I wish I could say that my own love is perfect, or that I myself had attained unto the high degree of perfection which you will find in the pages of this book. These are truths that God has made known to me and which I have certainly tried to live by. I know that even though I may not have attained this perfection, these truths still stand undaunted and unshaken in spite of my failures and weaknesses.

The bride of Song of Solomon said, "He brought me to the banqueting house, and his banner over me was love" (Song of Solomon 2:4). Every royal family has its own ensign. Our Lord also has His ensign or banner, and that is the Cross of Love. As we look up at that old banner in the hour of our trial and testing, let us take courage from the message it gives us: "GOD LOVES US!" Whatever trials you are going through, look up to the cross and remember it is the banner of love. Remember that cross where our Saviour hung for six long hours on a dark Friday almost 2,000 years ago. Remember again how He loved you and died for you, and know that there has NEVER been a time in your life when He has failed you. He has done everything for you.

Jesus has touched your life and painted it with glory and splendor through His love. God has seen the deepest longings of your heart and He has even given you the things which you have desired. Rejoice in this truth, that GOD IS LOVE, and that HE LOVES YOU. There is no joy on earth that can compare with the joy that comes by knowing that God Loves You.

Every joy we receive on earth comes to us because God loves us, and because He loves us others can love us. And we can give of that love to others, for God will use our hearts to love mankind.

Remember that Jesus said, "It is more blessed to give than to receive." It is more blessed to give love than any gift we are capable of giving. Love lifts you. The love you have in your heart toward God will lift you close to Him. God does not need your love so much as *you* need to love Him. You need to be able to love more than you need any other thing in this world. Love will lift you out of the dark gutter of hopelessness and despair and failure. Love will light the window of your soul. Love will purify, cleanse, renovate, spiritualize, perfect and translate you. Love will make you like God. It is the ONLY thing that will make you like God.

Love will lift you above the laws of the kingdoms of this earth with their limitations, their hopelessness and failures, into the Kingdom of God where the law of the saints and angels stands unchallenged and perfect in love since before time began

TABLE OF CONTENTS

Chapter		Page
1	What Is Love?	1
2	Love Is the Fulfilling of the Law	6
3	Love Makes Provision	16
4	Love Is Powerful	18
5	Love Never Fails	22
6	Love Is Holy	26
7	Love Is the Key to the Mysteries of God	29
8	Love Is Sacrificial	33
9	Love Is Kind	40
10	Love Serves	47
11	The Love-Slave	52
12	Love Is Unity	59
13	Love In Marriage	64
14	Love Is Eternal	77
15	Love Is in the Spirit	88
16	Love Is a Breastplate and Protection	92
17	Love Is in the Blood	105
18	Love Gives	116
19	Love Separates	125
20	Love Is in the Light	130
21	Love Weeps	148
22	Love Washes Feet	155
23	Love Is in the Glory	164
24	Love Obeys	175
25	Love Saves	180
26	Love Qualifies	187
27	Love Makes Great Soldiers and Kings	194
28	Love Disciplines	201
29	Love Communicates	206
30	Love Forgives	215
31	Love, the Key to Knowing God	221
32	Love Heals	236
33	The More Excellent Way	244

Chapter 1
WHAT IS LOVE?

I was running through life
When he stopped me and said,
"I love you."
I looked at him and repeated the words,
"I love you."
He took my hand and we walked,
And while we walked
I tried to fathom this thing
Called Love.

What is Love?
And we walked through springtime...
Does it feel good?
We walked through summer...
Can I touch it?
We walked on through autumn...
Do I see it?
We walked through winter...
I turned and said, "I love you."
And I saw him walking with another,
Laughing and talking about the love *they* shared
And I started to run away...
... Diana

Diana. That is all I know about her. Her name was Diana. She was only seventeen years of age and had tried to take her life because she was running away. She was trying to escape the terrible pain and hurt that comes with great and tender love. But where is there to go? What medicine can heal the heart? What new scene can block out yesterdays? What distance must one travel to escape the suffocating and overwhelming power of love? How many years, or decades must one live to begin to forget the rhapsody and the anguish of love?

What is this thing called LOVE? This is the question that Diana cried out on her hospital bed in Tonawanda, New York when the doctors brought her back to life. She found she had not run far enough to escape the hurt and pain. And yet we ask the question, will death erase the ability to love and the power that it engenders?

What is love? This is a question which many of us ask. Perhaps you can remember someone saying to you that they would love you forever. They vowed to you that they would never stop loving you; and they really meant it. Perhaps you have done the same. But now when you look back, you have to admit that this "forever" was maybe one year, or two or three . . . and that was all. Somewhere, somehow that love died.

What is love? Love is the theme of the universe, the symphony of heaven, the inspiration of life, the power of creation, the life of all we see and know . . . and love is also pain. Paul the apostle so truthfully described it: Love suffers long.

Yes, love must be prepared to suffer. An ancient poet put it like this:

> Love, unspeakable treasure.
> Hast thou more of pain, or pleasure?
> Endless torments dwell around thee
> Yet who would live, and live without thee?

Is that why we see so little love today? Are we becoming afraid to love? Are we afraid of being hurt? Are we running, running, running?

And where can we go to find the answer? What book

can tell us the truth about love? What author has the answer that we need? We need it now. Time is running out. Where is there one who will bring the perfect sacrifice of love and show it to us so that we will understand and know by that life, what the true cost of love really is?

Oh, thank God, there IS ONE, and there is A BOOK, the like of which has never been duplicated, no matter how many have attempted. There are many great philsophies, many ideologies, many prophets and sages, writers of many pages, holy and not so holy, but not one of them can compare to this ONE BOOK. Neither the Vedas of the Hindu nor the Koran of the Moslem, or any other can in any way compare to the grandeur or magnificence of the Love-story called The Holy Bible.

Love is the theme of the Bible, It is the red cord that runs through its pages from Genesis to Revelation. It was in and through Love that God did His mighty work of creation. God IS Love! That is where the secret of His power lies. That is why God had power to create the heavens and the earth, and to work signs and miracles and wonders. Today, man's power is limited by his limited love (unless Satan gives him power). God is the perfect picture of love's power.

And yet all men have asked the question, "What is love?" The world has forgotten that Jesus came down to this earth to be an example of love. The greatest example of love that we have was His love. And He set us an example, that we should walk in the same way in which He walked. He taught us that we must do the same things He did. He gave us the royal rule of Love. In fact, when God created mankind, He made us in His own image. The Bible says, "So God created man in his own image, in the image of God created he him: male and female created he them" (Genesis 1:27). And Genesis 5:3 says, "And Adam lived a hundred and thirty years, and begat a son in his own likeness, after his image; and called his name Seth." We are the descendents of Seth. This whole human race is his descendents, for all others were destroyed in the flood of Noah's time. There is no reason that we too should not have the likeness and image of our forefathers, except that sin has left its mark on us.

Yes, sin has left its mark on us in many ways, but Jesus came and died to give us full redemption and it is time now that we enter into our inheritance and our redemptive rights and attain unto our "So Great A Redemption." The key of our perfection which most of us have tried to ignore is LOVE.

God is love. Adam was created in His likeness and Seth in Adam's likeness and I in Seth's likeness, therefore I must have the resemblance of the fathers or I am unworthy to be called a son or daughter of Adam, much less a son or daughter of God. God created Adam and Eve with the capacity and the virture of loving and responding to each other and to God. They knew ONLY love. That is why Eve was deceived by Satan in the garden. Love knows no guile. But Love must be trained to know the difference between good and evil. Had Eve or Adam obeyed the laws of divine government, "Thou shalt not eat of the tree of the knowledge of good and evil," they would not have fallen. Love also demands obedience to the Law-giver.

Love is life. Adam and Eve and the patriarchs were able to live many centuries. Is the secret of their long life their ability to love? God later told Moses that if man wanted to live a long time on earth he had to love and show respect to his parents. Love is the inspiration of life.

When a man lives without love in his life he is only "existing." He is not really LIVING. Love is the power that should motivate our lives. Love should be more than something we possess. It is something that will possess us and control us and make us do things we would not ordinarily do.

An Indian preacher once said, "Love has no balance sheet." Yes, that is true! Love does not reckon, has no accounts, does things which the natural mind would think foolish.

Love is that strength within you that has been poured into you from God's own supply of Love, and it is beyond all our capacity to understand it. Love is the thing that the world needs now. The lack of love in the world is the thing that is causing the world to lie in the lap of the wicked one and shake and tremble in the hour when God is preparing to pour judgment upon it. Love is the one thing that will save your country, your family and your soul. Love is the greatest thing that we possess today. How strange it is that in spite of the fact that God has created us and given us a capacity to love, we are lacking this virtue even though we profess to be children of God, redeemed from the curse. Yes, we have even been given the Holy Spirit, and yet we must confess that we lack the most important fruit of the Spirit of God, LOVE.

Chapter 2
LOVE IS THE FULFILLING OF THE LAW

If you love someone deeply, you know how they think, you understand their deepest feelings. You are able to "find them in the spirit." When you love God, you can feel His heartbeat. That was the trouble with the religious people of Jesus' day. They did not know God as a Lover. They did not recognize Him even when He came and walked amongst them in the person of His Son. They missed Him completely, even though they were keeping all the rules of the book. We call this pharisaism, and yet it is not outdated. We see the same thing in our churches today. Yes, we even find it amongst our so-called "saved, born-again, converted" Christians. We are missing the great and high calling of God in this crisis hour, . . . even the high-calling of LOVE.

Love is NOT the keeping of laws and traditions of the elders. Love is greater than that. Love is the fulfilling of ALL the laws, even the unwritten ones, the law of the heart, the law that the saints and angels keep, the law of heaven. Let us leave our earthbound thinking and ask God to give us His heavenly understanding. We are citizens of another country and another city, one whose maker and builder is God; let us learn the laws of that future abode and let us learn them NOW. Let us live by them NOW.

Love goes beyond the do's and don't's. Love places in your heart an intense desire to please the one you love, no matter how great a sacrifice you must make. Neither does it matter what difficulty you must go through; love will keep you from hurting and grieving the one you love.

Romans 13:8 says, "Owe no man any thing, but to love one another: for he that loveth another hath fulfilled the law." Love is the fulfilling of the law. If we had perfect love, there would be no need to preach, "Do this. Don't do this!" We would never have to make rules, even God would not have to give us rules and commandments. He only gave us rules and laws because our love was limited. God called Moses up into Mount Sinai and gave him a message from heaven. God gave him a covenant between himself and His people. God was trusting that when Moses would take that covenant down to them, that because of the great deliverance He had given them out of 400 years of terrible slavery and persecution in Egypt, the love that the people would have for God would be so big, so overwhelming, that they would spontaneously, out of the love of their hearts WANT to obey Him and do all that He knew was best for them. And yet we know the record, they broke the laws of that covenant again and again.

Even back at the beginning when God put man in the Garden of Eden, He put one tree in that garden and said, "Don't touch." This was the beginning of law and, like typical people, they immediately broke the law.

Then God gave a new law on the morning that Noah came out of the ark with his family. It was a simple law, which was not difficult to keep, one that most anyone could keep without any difficulty. God said they were not to eat the blood of animals. He gave Noah dominion over all creation. It was a beautiful covenant of love and trust. Time went by and God brought His people, the children of Israel, descendents of Noah through Shem, out of Egypt. He saw that flesh had corrupted itself and mankind had learned sinful living by sinful men. Men had fallen a long way from the days of the ancients which lived before the flood. That is when God took their leader Moses and the seventy elders up into the mountain where, with His own finger, He wrote out His laws for them (Exodus 31:18). He said that the keeping of this commandment would make them the greatest nation on earth because it was the most righteous of all laws known to men (Deuteronomy 4:7, 8). It was on these laws that the American Constitution was built, and as long as we kept these laws we also were the greatest nation on earth. The more we deviate from them by amendments and by-laws, the further we go from our greatness. Today we are fast becoming a fallen nation on the face of this earth. Compromise with evil is NOT love. You see the love of God in each of the commandments that He gave Moses on the Mount.

But man was not satisfied, he changed the laws and added many others which God had not commanded him to do (Deuteronomy 12:32). When Jesus came to earth, man had added so many laws and traditions that mankind was burdened and crushed by the weight of these man-made laws. The tradition of the elders was a great yoke on the necks of God's people (Matthew 15:3 and Mark 7:8). Jesus called them vain traditions. Things which God had NEVER commanded them to observe.

God sent His son Jesus to give us the *perfect* law. When Jesus came He cancelled the old law by making a new *covenant of love.* John 1:17 says, "For the law was given by Moses, but grace and truth came by Jesus Christ." In Hebrews 7:18, 19 we read, "For there is verily a disannulling of the commandment going before, for the weakness and unprofitableness thereof. For the law made nothing perfect, but the bringing in of a better hope did; by the which we draw nigh unto God."

Do you understand what Paul means? He is saying that Christ came and disannulled the old law. He cut off the old commandments. He did this because there was a weakness in them. He said they had proven to be unprofitable, because they had not made man perfect.

How would it make you perfect if you didn't gather sticks on the sabbath (Numbers 15:32-35)? There were many things that men thought would make them perfect, such as the washing of their hands, or cooking certain things in certain pots. All these things they did to be perfect and yet they fought and hated and cheated and lied, they committed adultery and even went so far as to worship many other gods beside Jehovah. Therefore God had to give man a new law.

And that is just exactly what Jesus did. Jesus said, "A new commandment I give unto you, that ye love one another; as I have loved you, that ye also love one another" (John 13:34). Again He said, "Thou shalt love the Lord thy God with all thy heart, and with all thy soul, and with all thy mind. This is the first and great commandment. And the second is like unto it. Thou shalt love thy neighbour as thyself" (Matthew 22:37-39). Jesus did away with the old laws by giving us a better law, a law of glory and perfection. He said that the command to love God . . . was the FIRST law. It was the law of heaven, before we ever came to earth. It was the law that Lucifer broke, and that was the reason he was cast down. Then the SECOND was given to us when God created man . . . that was the command to love our neighbor, or, in other words, mankind.

Jesus taught the commandment of love many times and He lived it ALWAYS. He began His earthly ministry with the Sermon on the Mount, and He closed with the Sermon of Love in the Upper Room. He told us that our love toward each other would be the proof that we are His disciples. "By this shall all men know that ye are my disciples, if ye have love one to another" (John 13:35).

And yet in giving Moses the law, God had tried to teach men the conduct of love. Do you realize that in the Pentateuch, God, at least seven times, told the people of Israel to love Him. Deuteronomy 5:10, 6:5, 10:12, 11:1, 11:13, 19:9 and 30:6 are some of the references. Read them and search the Scriptures. Time and space does not permit me to quote them here. God wanted them to love Him, but how strange they only remembered all the other commandments. They observed and kept rules that were easy to keep, and did not demand the affection of the heart. Are we not guilty today of doing much the same thing? They kept all those laws that were the lesser and omitted the most important one of all, the one that would make them perfect, even the one that would help them to fulfill all the other commandments which they strove so hard to fulfill.

Yes, they missed it. They missed it by so much that when God came down to earth in the person of His Son, they hated Him. Why did they hate Him? Because keeping all the laws is nothing if you don't love God. But if you love God, you will know whom God sends. Jesus said that in rejecting Him they were rejecting the Father. He said that if we love the Father, we will love those whom He sends. He said, "I know you, that ye have not the love of God in you. I am come in my Father's name, and ye received me not" (John 5: 42, 43).

If you love the Father God, you will love those whom God sends. That is why Jesus followed the law of LOVE TO GOD with the law of LOVE TO OUR NEIGHBOR, the second commandment which He said was like unto the first, or linked to the first. "Thou shalt love thy neighbor as thyself." It is absolutely impossible to love your neighbor if you don't love his God. But it is just as impossible to love God and not love those whom God loves. 1 John 4:20, 21: "If a man says, I love God, and hateth his brother, he is a liar: for he that loveth not his brother whom he hath seen, how can he love God whom he hath not seen. And this commandment have we from him, That he who loveth God love his brother also." It is true that if you love God with all your heart, all your soul, all your mind and with all the strength that you have to love, you'll love your neighbor. You can test your love for God right now by asking yourself, "How much do I love my neighbor?" And that neighbor can be in Africa or Russia or China.

Why does God want us to love? Because He knows that anything less than love is harmful. It is dangerous for us not only to hate, but to have disrespect, to sneer, to mock and show disdain or feel or do any act that is unlovely. All these belong to the "Hate family." They do us harm. To give evil is to hurt ourselves. There is only one person that no power of hate can hurt or touch. That is the Almighty God. What is His protection? LOVE! God is Love. Now you know what *your* protection is! Love builds a wall of fire around yourself. It is for your good. It is for your deliverance.

You may say, "I can't love my enemies." If Jesus said you should love them, then you CAN DO IT. He said, "Love your enemies, bless them that curse you, do good to them that hate you, and pray for them which despitefully use you, and persecute you . . . that ye may be the children of your father which is in heaven" (Matthew 5:44, 45). Your Father loves His enemies. He makes the sun to rise on the evil and the rain to fall on the unjust and treats them with the same love as He does the good folks and the just ones. God asks us to be just like He is. We are coming again into His likeness and His image. And we are coming into it through LOVE.

When we take on His image, we will take on us His glory. Yet we cannot have the glory of God until we have the love of God, because the glory is in the love. Jesus said, "The second commandment is like unto the first." The reason is that they are linked together, you can't separate them. They are "married" to each other . . . love to God and love to your neighbor. Don't try to tell God you love Him if you don't love your neighbor. If you love God, love will pour out to your neighbor and your neighbor will feel your love, just like you feel God's love.

This giving and receiving of Love is like an electrified circuit. God is the eternal generator whose supply of love never runs out (even in wrath He remembers to be merciful). He pours His love into your heart, it flows through your heart to your neighbor and directs your neighbor Godward, making him love God more. As his love and worship goes up to God, God returns it back to you again through His own heart. Each time the circuit comes back to you, it comes back multiplied and it is sent forth multiplied and the power of love increases more and more until we become so full of love that love becomes our very nature, and love will shine from our expression and transform every cell of our bodies. Love is the secret of happiness, contentment, good health, long life and even translation. You will become so beautiful in this love of God that people will want to talk with you, and come to you because they will feel the warmth of your love. They will bring you their burdens and their heartaches, because they will feel the drawing power of the greatest magnetism the world has ever known ... LOVE.

It was not in vain that the Lord told us that we should love. When the Lord gave us the Rules of Life in the Sermon on the Mount, He was giving us the pattern for living right here on earth in our earthly flesh, and NOT for when we have our glorified bodies in heaven. These are the ROYAL LAWS OF THE KINGDOM OF GOD. They are beautiful. They are rich in the truths of God.

In James 2:5 we read, "Hearken, my beloved brethren, hath not God chosen the poor of this world rich in faith, and heirs of the kingdom, which He hath promised to them that love him?" God is telling us that HE is doing some choosing! He has that right. It is important for us to know what kind of people God is choosing, so that if we have a chance, we can be included in this number of chosen ones. Let us look at it more closely. First He said that they would be those who are poor in earthly things, but who are rich in faith, and then He said they would be those WHO LOVE HIM.

The greatest of all virtues is LOVE. Paul said, "And now abideth faith, hope charity, these three; but the greatest of these is love." Oh, it's love, it's love, it's love! From Alpha to Omega, from beginning to end, from the highest heaven to the lowest sinner, it's love!

And then we are told in James 2:8, "If ye fulfill the royal law according to the Scripture, THOU SHALT LOVE THY NEIGHBOUR AS THYSELF, ye do well." This is called the *Royal* law because it is the law of the kingdom of God. There *is* a law to keep ... a law so high, a law so holy, that if we keep it, we will become like the One who gave it.

The Law of Moses made no one like God, but the Law

of God given to us through Jesus Christ is perfect in that it is able to perfect us. We can already see this perfect love working in the lives of certain individuals. Love will motivate a person's life. It is the greatest power behind us. It is an inspiration. People who do not love are very uninspired. It is true that hate can sometimes inspire you, but the inspiration that comes from love is pure and strong and everlasting. It is the most powerful weapon on earth.

The Bride of the Song of Solomon said, "Love is strong as death" (8:6). There is nothing that men fear more than death. Of all of the enemies of men, none is more powerful than death. The one unconquerable enemy of all time is death. He comes to the rich man and he comes to the poor, and they all must bow before him. He comes to the strong while in the peak of health, and snaps off his life by an unexpected accident. He comes to the old, and he comes to the infant. Death is one enemy whom nobody has conquered except Jesus, Enoch, Elijah and maybe a few hidden ones.

But in the Song of Solomon we find that there is one thing that is equal to that powerful enemy. Death has found an enemy that is as strong as himself. Oh, thank God, he has met his equal. Now we can shout, "Oh, death, where is your sting! Oh, grave, where is your victory." Hallelujah! We are clothed in love and, because of that, we fear death no longer, for He who loves us takes our hand and leads us safely through the valley of the Shadow of Death. We won't even know we have died. We just walk away with Him. Love is as strong as death!

You have a friend. His name is LOVE. The Bible says God is Love. He is your protection. Let yourself love Him with all your heart. As you read this message from the Lord to you, put your hand in the hand of God. Let His love pour through your heart. Let this poor, crippled, dark, miserable, hating world feel the love of God through your heart.

Remember that teen-aged American girl, Diana, who lay on her bed with a broken heart and asked the question, "What is love?" You go out into the highways and byways of life and show them what love is.

You may say, "How can I love the people?" The answer is in Matthew 22:37 . . . If you love the Lord your God with all your heart, your soul, your mind and your strength, that love that you give to God will bounce back into your heart, like a boomerang, and you will love others. This is the key.

Why has the church of Christ failed to bring the world to God? Not because we didn't work hard enough or keep enough laws. Nor is it because we didn't observe the rules of "the elders." We failed to reach the world because we didn't come like Jesus came. We didn't come in love. They looked at us and said, "What is love?" They didn't see love in us and they didn't see it in our churches. They came into our churches and they felt coldness. And they went out just like they came in. They were disappointed. And they asked themselves again, "What is love?" We gave them tracts, and we testified and preached to them. We showed them how "holy" we were because we didn't smoke and drink and do the "sinful" things they did. We wore our dresses longer when theirs were short, and ours short when theirs were long, to prove to them how "holy" we were, and we wondered why they didn't love our God.

You see, the law of Moses will NEVER point anyone to the cross. You know what the law of Moses did? It crucified Jesus. Do you know that it was on the authority of the law of Moses that the Jews crucified Jesus? John 19:7, "The Jews answered him, We have a law, and by our law he ought to die, because he made himself the Son of God." They were referring to the law recorded in Leviticus 24:16, "He that blasphemeth the name of the Lord, he shall surely be put to death . . ." It was the same law which they used as their ground for stoning Stephen (Acts 7:54-58).

It was the same, fanatical, religious zeal that made a murderer out of Saul. Acts 22:3-5, "And I persecuted this way unto death, binding and delivering into prisons both men and women, . . . and I went to Damascus, to bring them which were there bound unto Jerusalem, for to be punished."

Later in the dark and dreadful past of the church age, the church leaders again persecuted, excommunicated, tortured, imprisoned and cruelly put to death thousands of children of light, thinking they were doing God a favor, because so-called "heretics" were not keeping the laws of the church and were drawing people out of the church by their new-found freedom and liberty in the truths of the Scripture. The Moslem, the Jew and the pagan looked on our inquisition of saints and turned away from our Jesus.

How are we going to win the lost to God? Is it by the law? For four thousand years before Christ the law could not deliver the pagan heart to God, and for another two thousand years since Christ the law has not been able to do it. The law has failed!

What does the world need today? It is LOVE. The Lord is saying to you today, "YOU GO AND LOVE THEM." Don't just love your family, or your friend. Love them . . . the Lost, the Communist, the Murderer, the Lesbian, the Blasphemer. It is a hard commandment, but I cannot change it, so you cannot change it either. God loves all of these, and if God lives in your heart . . . He will love them through your heart. You are a part of the power circuit of God's love to a lost generation, a corrupt generation, and even a blasphemous generation. Let your sun shine on them and let your rain fall on them, and let the Holy Spirit do what He will in their lives.

Yes, and we religious people must love not only the one in our own church, but the one in the church across town, even the one who has split off of our church and started another church. Does not the Lord say, if someone comes in not dressed in the "same kind of coat" as you are, you will love them as yourself? You must love the one you understand and are in the spirit with, and the one who grates on your nerves, whom you cannot understand. You must love the one who has nobody to love him. You must love the one who is ugly and mean . . . because Jesus did.

Love is your protection. Love is your glory. Love is God in your life.

Chapter 3
LOVE MAKES PROVISION

Love provides. It is through love that God performed His great acts. It is a dangerous thing for any being to have power without love. That is what makes Satan so evil. He has limited power and absolutely no love. Let us rejoice that our Eternal Father, Creator and Sustainer of this universe is Love. We can understand this more fully when we remember how the earth was created. The very work of His creation was an act of love, it was the building of a home for the ones He loved. He loved us before He created us. He prepared all things perfectly for us, like a bridegroom prepares a home for his bride. He did not make man first and put him out into space with no place of habitation. He made this beautiful planet, earth. He planted a garden called Eden in it. He made great rivers to flow through it, flowers to give scent and color, beautiful trees to give shade and beauty and homes to the birds. He created animals to be the companions and helpers of man, birds to sing us our lullabys, fish to make our waters sparkle like jewels. Have you ever noticed the many varieties of colorful fish? God filled the world with delightful works of His creation and then He created man and put him in this beautiful world. Isn't this love? Love provides for all that we need. That is why Jesus told us, "Take no thought, saying, What shall we eat? or, What shall we drink? or, Wherewithal shall we be clothed? for your heavenly father knoweth that ye have need of all these things" (Matthew 6:31, 32). He was there creating the world at the beginning. He KNEW the law of provision. Was not one of His names Jehovah Jireh, The Lord Provides?

When a mother loves her family, the Bible says that "She ariseth while it is yet night and prepares food for her family" (Proverbs 31:15). That is love. That is how our Heavenly Father provides for us. Jesus does not want us to be anxious about what we shall eat or drink or wear, for He says our Heavenly Father KNOWS that we have need of all these things. If Father would take the trouble to dress the grass with a beautiful garment, so beautiful that even Solomon in all his glory was not arrayed as one of these, how much more will He give us the same provision because He loves us? Oh, if only man would recognize the greatness of His love and His willingness to provide. Love not only has the power to create, but to provide for the need of what has been created.

God said, "It is not good that the man should be alone," so he provided him with a wife.

God provided a refuge for Noah, a grave for Sarah, a wife for Isaac, a throne for Joseph, a nurse for baby Moses, a deliverer for Israel, manna in the wilderness, a fountain in the wilderness, a long day for Joshua, an army for Gideon, strength for Sampson and a friend for David. Yes, He has provided everything—strength for today and bright hope for tomorrow. Truly we can say, "Great is Thy faithfulness, Lord, unto me."

Chapter 4
LOVE IS POWERFUL

We already mentioned how the writer of the Song of Solomon said, "Love is strong as death." He also said, "Many waters cannot quench love, neither can the floods drown it:" (8:7). Love is like a mighty raging forest fire, a fire so great that any amount of water cannot put it out. It is like the fire that fell from heaven in the days of Elijah. The water was poured on the sacrifice until the trench around the altar was filled with water, but when the fire fell it not only consumed the burnt sacrifice and the wood, but it also burned the stones and the dust and LICKED UP THE WATER THAT WAS IN THE TRENCH (1 Kings 18:38).

True love will climb every mountain of obstacles and swim every torrent of hindrances. It will not accept discouragement or difficulty. What is impossible with man is possible with love. Love is hope and courage and faith. Love does not give up or yield to defeat. Love hangs on when the doctor says, "The case is hopeless"; the father says, "I forbid you to marry him"; the bank account shows there is no money to make that certain sacrifice. Love finds a way, for love is the great force of God in action.

God can fill our hearts so full of His love that it will pour fresh life into us. Yes, love will rejuvenate us, will strengthen us; it will give us a fresh reason for living, a new purpose of life. Many people have been lying in their hospital beds, and they didn't want to live any more because their lives were without love. They felt forsaken, they felt lost and unwanted, rejected and alone; but if someone could have loved them at that moment, they would have wanted to live. Love can pull you back from the grave. Love is a mighty force because love is full of the life of God. When we are possessed of that love of God there will be life within our families, in our homes, in our churches and in our country . . . yes, if we can love, we will even bring life back to this world.

The story is told of how love brought a "miraculous" cure of paralysis. When Siegfried Wiesauer was freed from a Siberian prisoner of war camp in 1951 he began looking for Maria Hartmann, his fiance to whom he had been engaged during the war. After six years in the prison, he had returned to his home in Austria. Until 1970 he searched for Maria. Even the Red Cross helped him, but it seemed it was impossible to find her. He went into such a state of depression that he lost his voice and became partially paralyzed in both legs and his left side. Doctors said that it was a collapse of the nervous system. But his parents knew that their son was pining away for Maria whom he could not find despite hundreds of letters sent to her hometown of Augsburg, Germany. They had given up hope, when suddenly one day there was a telephone call from Augsburg. It was Maria, asking to talk to Siegfried. Of course, he couldn't make himself understood, but he knew that it was Maria. His face lit up, and for the first time in twenty years they began to hope. Red Cross officials had finally found Maria. They had found that Maria had married, her husband had died, and she had begun to draw a pension. Her maiden name was now in the records. She was no longer the twenty-year-old war nurse he had known; now she was forty-five years old. But she hurried to his side and helped to nurse him back to health. She fell in love with him again and he began to regain the use of his voice and limbs and hopes. Love had made a miracle. The last I heard, they were planning on being married.

Love did not come easily to Maria the second time. There were many obstacles to overcome. Siegfried was no longer the strong, healthy, handsome young man she had first loved. He was a broken, crippled, sick, weak wreck of a man.

Maria said, "I did not think that I would, but I did fall completely in love with him again."

You say, how can I love? I'll admit, you may have to work at it sometimes. There are times when you have to put all your attention to it, especially when it comes to loving God. Why is this? Is it because we are not close enough to Him? Is He not near enough to us? If we lack love for God, is it because we don't practice love? Let us talk to Him, love Him. Don't make long prayers! We make such long prayers. We pray so much and love God so little. And it should be the other way around. If we just rest in Him like He said the lilies of the field do! They don't toil or spin, they don't work or fret, or go through all kinds of contortions, and the Heavenly Father clothes them more beautifully than Solomon was clothed in his kingly raiment and earthly glory. What is the secret of the beauty of the lily? The secret of the beauty of the lily is—it exists just to glorify God. And this should be the secret of our beauty: we should live just to glorify God.

Many Christians are full of gloom, misery, sadness, grudges, grievances and unforgiveness. They live in that state constantly. Their minds are always occupied with dark things, fearful things, things by which no child of God should allow his mind to be governed or possessed. And, therefore, there is no peace in their hearts, because the Bible says, "Thou wilt keep him in perfect peace, whose mind is stayed on thee: because he trusteth in thee" (Isaiah 26:3)—and their minds are *not* stayed on the Lord.

And there are those who suffer all kinds of fears because they do not have this perfect love that casteth out all fear, and they do not know that the Bible says, "He that feareth is not made perfect in love" (1 John 4:18).

God wants us to open our hearts to Him and let His love flow through us like a torrential river. When His love flows through us like a river, it will wash away the gloom and sadness and the dark things that have been destroying our lives and making us unhappy. Our minds should be full of the light of God and we should always meditate on the love of God and thus keep the perfect peace of God in our hearts at all times, no matter what happens.

We can live constantly on that higher plane with God. It will elevate us to heavenly places in Christ Jesus, for this is the law that the angels and the redeemed saints of ancient times lived by.

Do you live like that? Or do you live like a mortal, a craven, defeated mortal, chained to the dark dungeon of past failures and hurts? Are you wallowing in the mire of yesterday's bitter experiences, dragging about the chains of sins that Jesus has washed away in His blood? Are you acting as if you have never been redeemed, as if you have never been made a new creature in Christ Jesus? How do you live, my brother, my sister? Do you live what you are, a child of God triumphant, an example to the angels? Or, do you still live without your full measure of love?

Angels are full of love. They come and minister to us, whether we want them to or not. They will stand by a drunkard, a harlot or a murderer. They will fulfill their commission which the Father has given them, even if they are cursed to their faces and hear the name of their God spoken in blasphemy. An angel will never forsake the one to whom they have been sent to minister. An angel will fulfill his place of duty right up until the very hour when that soul departs its body. This is the Love that God wants us to have. We should love as much as the angels love, and I dare to say, we ought to love MORE than angels can love because Jesus said, "To whom much has been forgiven, the same loveth much." I have a right to love God more than Gabriel does, or Michael, because He has done so much MORE for me than He ever did for them. He poured out His blood for me. His blood covered His head, His face, His hands, His feet. Oh, precious blood of Jesus! Each drop was a little drop of the Love of God. The greatest gift ever given to me were those precious Blood drops that fell upon me to wash me whiter than snow, to redeem me and make me His own, an heir equal with Him who even died for me. This is LOVE!

Chapter 5
LOVE NEVER FAILS

The Word of God tells us that God is love. It also says in the writings of Paul, "Love never fails" (1 Corinthians 13:8). It never can perish, it never gives up and therefore because of its power of endurance it is the greatest of all the virtues. It is holy because it comes right from God.

It is true that love can be perverted. Like some of the other gifts of God have been misused, so can the gift of love be misused. There are men who have been given a gift of faith and have perverted that gift of faith and have used it to make themselves great on earth. They have used it to accumulate wealth and power and fame. They seem to have forgotten that some day they shall stand before the judgment and shall have to give an account of the gifts they have misused. The tragedy is that Jesus will have to reject some of our greatest miracle workers. They will say, "Lord, didn't we cast out devils in Thy name? Didn't we do many mighty miracles in Thy name? Surely You know the gifts I have! You know the works I wrought for You! You know how I labored long and hard! I made a good name for You, God, on earth!" And He will say, "Depart from Me, ye workers of iniquity, I never knew you."

Who are these people who will come up for judgment? Some of them are our own Pentecostals. We were the ones who were casting out the demons and doing the healing ministry. The reason they did works which brought them before judgment is because they did them with the wrong motive

It was not the motive of love. We will receive not one bit of eternal reward if we have all the gifts, give our body to be burned, give every penny we have, or preach like Paul and pray like Moses. All these things will not give one ounce of eternal reward. No gift which I have received from God will give me an eternal reward. There is only one thing which will, and that is the fruit of the Spirit in my life. We have got to get back to the facts, even to the foundation of our faith. We have to build on the right foundation. We have built too much on works. We have built too much on gifts and it is time for us to return again, where we will build on the true foundation of the purity of the Spirit of God. Love, joy, peace, longsuffering, gentleness, goodness, faith, meekness, temperance are the true fruits of the Spirit against which there is NO judgment (Galatians 5:22, 23).

When the books are opened, you will want to stand before God with an open face. And in many cases the books are being opened right now! I said, RIGHT NOW! We are all coming up before God for judgment, and we can see this happening one by one. Great men are being removed. In the last decade some of the church's most tremendous men have been called off the scene of their earthly ministry. We all have an appointment with God to stand before judgment. We will want to hear Him say, "Well done, thou good and faithful servant, enter thou into the joy of thy Lord."

Do you know how you are going to accomplish that? It will not be because you are a great preacher, nor because you have given all your tithes and offerings and more. Neither will it be because you have been a missionary on the field for forty years, nor because you have healed the sick, cast out demons or prophesied mightily. You won't get a bit of reward for prophesying. Neither will you get a bit of reward for speaking in tongues. You WILL be rewarded for LOVE. Against such there is no judgment. For your grace, for the mercy you have shown, for the understanding you have given, for your tenderness, and the faith you had to stick by when the going was hard, and believe God no matter how much it seemed impossible. For THIS you will be rewarded.

So you can see that ANYONE can have great rewards. Any woman can have great rewards that will be equal to the greatest woman who ever lived. Doesn't that make it easy for you? Isn't that wonderful? You can have the same reward as Hudson Taylor, Jonathan Goforth, C. T. Studd, David Livingston, Praying Hyde, Florence Nightingale, Amy Carmichael—because you loved as much as they loved. You can love that much if you only let your heart love. But don't seal your heart up into a little hard ball and say, "Oh, I am so afraid that if I will show my love a little bit I am going to get hurt." That is self-preservation. Self-preservation is another form of self-pity and it is the most wicked, cruel enemy you have. It will drive you in the mud and crush you under the feet of an army of demons. It will make you a prisoner of gloom. Self-pity is the one place that the devil drags the suicides into. God's people must rise above that state, and into the plane where they know that in all things they can rejoice and give thanks for THIS is the will of God concerning them . . . even when it seems to be ridiculous. God is so wonderful. He doesn't make any mistakes in your life. If you will rest in His love and rejoice in every circumstance and condition you will be able to find peace and rest in every situation. The hardest rock can become the softest pillow.

When we were arrested on the borders of Russia for bringing Bibles into the country and were held as prisoners for several days, we had such peace in our hearts that we were able to lie down and sleep on the floor as well as we could have in our own comfortable beds at home. Perfect love had taken over in all of our hearts. It had removed the fear and anxiety. We knew that God was in control. It had not been in our plans to get caught, but it had been in His plans and He would work out His purpose in all our lives. If we did not then know what His purpose was, we knew that there would come a time when we would understand and praise Him for it. Perfect love won the final victory, it did not fail us in our desperate hour.

Solomon tells us in the Song of Solomon 3:10 that the chariots of the king are cushioned with love. The bride is talking about the chariot in which she rides along with her king and she tells us that it is cushioned with Love. Sometimes on your journey there will be bumps and there will be hard knocks. Slow traveling will sometimes annoy you, and there will be the mockers on the side of the road who will cast their stones at you and mock and ridicule you and shamefully treat you. But look! The carriage that you are riding to heaven in is cushioned with the Love of God. No matter what the conditions are, the Love of God is right in the middle of every situation and condition of your life. Say, "I LOVE YOU, LORD!"

Chapter 6
LOVE IS HOLY

Because love comes from God and God is holy, love is very holy and pure. It is also the characteristic or gift of the Holy Spirit. The Bible calls it a fruit of the Spirit. I am not speaking of lust, which many call "love." Satan has very subtly deceived this generation into thinking that the mad lust of the flesh for sexual relationship is love. The animals have more affinity for one another than some humans who carry on a sexual relationship. We must not confuse darkness with light, filth with purity, passion with charity. God wants us to have that pure and holy love that comes from Him. Love is like a light. It is the greatest light that shines in this dark world, and its only hope.

When you turn on a light, it drives away the darkness. When the light is removed, darkness reigns. Most of mankind dwells in darkness, but this is not the way God intended it to be. God meant for us to live in love, which means that we will live in light. When we live in light, the light will shine and chase away the darkness. When the light shines, it shows its power by dispersing the darkness. It gets dark at night because the light of heaven, the sun, withdraws itself from one side of the earth. But as soon as the sun comes around in the morning it drives the darkness of the night away. So which is greater? Is it not light? Light is symbolic of the love of God, the radiation of His being. When it flows through us, it will do a miracle of beauty in us. It will purge out all evil and dark memories of the past. We may remember them, but they will not torment us any longer. Love has caused them to lose their power. Isaiah 43:18 says, "Remember ye not the former things, neither consider the things of old."

The NEW THING that God is doing, is that He is sending a spiritual awakening of love. Everyone is wondering what new thing the Lord will do. Most of God's children are praying for a great revival. I am going to tell you what revival God wants to send. It is a revival of love. This is the "more excellent way" that Paul wrote about in 1 Corinthians 12:31. Paul, speaking about the gifts of the Spirit, such as speaking in tongues, said, "But when that which is perfect is come, then that which is in part shall be done away." The day of doing miracles, healings, casting out demons will some day pass away, but one thing will remain, and that is love. Paul said, "But whether there be prophecies, they shall fail . . . whether there be knowledge, it shall vanish away" (1 Corinthians 13:8). All of this phase of the demonstration of power shall one day pass away, but love will last eternally.

Do you know what we need in our nations today? We need a revival, but not a revival of gifts and charisma. That time has passed. It had its day. We need a revival that is beyond denominational boundaries, one that cannot have a name over its church door. We need a revival that will touch the heart and change the life, a revival of love. God began His work of creation in one great act of love and He must also finish His divine plan in one great and tremendous demonstration of love. Until we have love we are not ready to meet the Lord Jesus Christ. Love will take away all the memories of the sorrows of the past. It will forgive, it will heal the broken heart, it will drive out the grief, the hurt and the pain. "There shall be no more sorrow or crying, neither shall there be any more pain, for the former things are passed away" (Revelation 21:4). There will be only love over there, and we will be filled with that love. Let us prepare for it now. Let us bring heaven on earth, through the Holy Spirit in our hearts.

How long do you expect to wait until you get this love? Where will you find this love? Isn't it in the Lord? Don't we have Him living in us NOW? Will you only have Him AFTER you die, or AFTER you go to heaven? Of course not. You have Him NOW. So what *do* you have when you have Him? LOVE! I am so glad that you have love NOW. That makes you the most beautiful person, for when your heart opens up to love, you become beautiful in His love. That love makes you pure and holy. Your beauty is in this true holiness of God, and without holiness no man shall see the Lord (Hebrews 12:14).

Love is the garment of the bride. She may wear the finest gown, but if she is not adorned in love, she is not properly attired for the wedding. Jesus told the parable of the king who made a marriage for his son. Many were invited to that wedding feast. The first group who got the invitations refused to come, so he sent his servants into the highways to gather together as many as they found, both good and bad. When the king came to see the guests, he saw there a man who had not a wedding garment on. He said to him, "Friend, how camest thou in hither not having a wedding garment?" The man had no excuse. "He sat speechless," the Bible says. Then said the king to the servants, "Bind him hand and foot, and take him away, and cast him into outer darkness: there shall be weeping and gnashing of teeth" (Matthew 22:1-14). Then Jesus added in verse 14, "For many are called, but few are chosen."

Remember that these people were not invited because they were "good-living people." There were good and bad in the crowd. But ONE did not have the proper adornment. He did not have the "wedding garment," even the garment of LOVE. There will be a lot of disappointed people on the day of the marriage supper of the Lamb. And some may be "good" people, too. The garment of the "Bride" will be her love. This is her true holiness. It is when she is adorned in this holiness she will be able to see the Lord and be accepted by Him as His bride.

Chapter 7
LOVE IS THE KEY TO THE MYSTERIES OF GOD

Perhaps this is why many of the mysteries of God are still hidden from many of God's children. Jesus said, "Ye search the scripture because you imagine in them to have eternal life: . . . yet you have no desire to come to Me, so that you might have life" (John 5:39, *the Holy Bible in Modern English).* While it is true that the mysteries of God are in the Scriptures, the key to the Scriptures is not "our much study" or "our many teachers," the enlightenment that we have upon the Scriptures comes through the Holy Spirit. The Holy Spirit will not give the secrets of God to the one who is not near to the heart of God. Jesus said, "He shall take of mine, and shall show it unto you" (John 16:15). This He said to His disciples who were very intimate with Him. We can claim it also IF we are as close to Him as His disciples were.

I have met some of God's "mystics" in my life and they are truly God's "peculiar treasures." The crowd does not understand them. But neither did the religious leaders understand Jesus. Some of these saints are hidden away in sick rooms, or hermitages that are seldom frequented by the careless multitude. They are not "big names" in the church's estimation. And yet, they are the treasures of heaven, the salt of the earth.

One such treasure was a saint whom I met when he was eighty-three years old. I met him when I was going through a great trial some time ago. He was indeed one of God's hidden saints. For eleven years he had not left his bedroom. Because of a stroke, his leg was lame and he could not walk. He told me that he was the Lord's prisoner. For twenty-seven years of his life (at the time I met him) he had taken the "nightwatch" in prayer, from 12 midnight until 5:00 a.m. Every night he communed with his Heavenly Father. I had heard about him earlier and I had read some of his writings. When I came to the place where he was, I said in my heart, "Oh, I wish I could meet that man." I asked someone who lived there if he ever came downstairs. They said that he always stayed in his room. So I prayed, "Lord, I'd love to meet that child of Yours." I felt that he could be a blessing to me and help me by teaching me some of the things that he knew. But I didn't feel worthy to ask to come into his presence, so I never said anything.

One Sunday morning, during a meeting, the church asked me to testify. After the service was over, a sister came to me and said, "Brother A. wants to see you upstairs." I had not realized that the service had been relayed to his room and that he had heard me. I was so happy when they told me that he had asked to see me. I remember the sense of awe I had as I went up the stairs; I felt I was going up to meet God. As I came into his room, I saw an elderly man with white hair, wearing a flaming orange figured shirt, sitting in a chair by the bed. I got such a shock! This is not what I had expected. Being of Mennonite background, where our spiritual leaders wore somber colors like black or navy blue, somehow I had expected this man of God to be attired to fit the role of a mystic. He said to me, "Sit down, sister."

I looked at him, and he looked at me. After a moment he said, "I heard what you said and I want to tell you that we welcome you to our home. You can stay as long as you want. Our home is your home."

I got a catch in my throat; the tears came to my eyes. I felt the pure love of God, something one seldom finds anymore on this earth. I said, "Brother, I only came to fast and pray for a few days."

He answered me, "It doesn't matter if you want to stay

a long time, you are welcome here." As we talked, he told me how God had taken him to Israel for seven years to fast and pray for that country. As we shared the end-time revelations, my soul was lifted within me. When I looked at my watch, I found, to my amazement, we had talked for almost three hours. Time had stood still. It had seemed like three minutes. Two days before I left, I again visited him and we talked for four hours. Again it seemed like a few minutes.

Why? Because of the Spirit of the Lord which was in him. We shared the things which God had been showing us. When I discovered that I, this little unworthy handmaiden of the Lord, had received many of the same revelations of the Lord that this great saint had, it thrilled my heart. I know the things which God had revealed to me were truth, for God had revealed them to His servant also. I found that he, too, was expecting the imminent return of the Lord, which would immediately transform the "first-fruits company" and bring them into their glorified state. He knew God in a tremendous way. To know God, you have to know Him by love, and this man loved God. God had given him the most beautiful revelation on the book of Revelation. He had the key to that book of mysteries. Do you want to know what that key was?

Let me give you a clue. Who wrote the book of Revelation? John the Beloved wrote it by the inspiration of the Holy Spirit. Just preceding the book of Revelation are some other writings by John. If you only glance at them for a moment, you will see that the glorious theme of these epistles of John is LOVE. John was the Evangel of Love. That was the key to writing the book of Revelation, and THAT is the key to understanding it! If love could inspire it, then love can interpret it.

Church history tells us that just before John wrote the book of Revelation in the great persecution under the Roman emperor Domitian, he was taken to Rome where he was thrown into a pot of boiling oil, which had no power to hurt him. He was then sent as a slave laborer to the salt mines of Patmos. Why did the boiling oil not harm him? What was his protection? It was love!

Love took the martyrs through death, it gave them courage to stand when the flames were kindled about them. Polycarp said to those who were preparing to tie him to the stake . . . "I have no need of thongs to hold me there. If my love for my Lord is not strong enough to bind me to the stake, then have I served Him all these years in vain." He worshipped the Lord in a rapture of love as the flames burned his limbs. Love made his face to shine with the glory of God.

Nor was it the nails of Rome that held our Saviour to the cross. It was His love. There are no nails so strong as the nails of love. One day as I was going through my own fiery trials, I cried out to God from the anguish of my soul,

> Oh, blessed nails of Calvary
> Secure me to the cross of Christ
> And hold me there . . .
> Lest I should weaken in my love
> And seek to flee from Thee.
>
> Yea, let the blood in crimson red
> Flow from my bleeding heart.
> Pain do not spare . . .
> And let me never cry out, Lord,
> That You should spare the rod.
>
> For I would live as You have lived
> And die as You have died.
> By Thy grace, Lord . . .
> With all my life hid in the One
> Who hung on Golgotha.

Yes, love will either give us the grace to go through our suffering, or it will transfigure our bodies so that we will not feel the pain, or be burned in the fires of it.

Chapter 8
LOVE IS SACRIFICIAL

Love is sacrificial. It is possible to give without love but it is not possible to love without giving. It was because God so loved the world, that He gave His only begotten Son. Love demands that we make a sacrifice. If you say you love and yet you have never made a sacrifice, there is something wrong. Your love could be self-love—a selfish love. You give a little so that you can receive a lot in return. You consume all the love that is given you upon yourself and give nothing back.

That is why it is impossible to love THINGS. I cannot love a building, or a piece of furniture, or an article of clothing, because these things cannot love me in return. Love demands response or it is madness. Love generates love, and God's love shed abroad in our hearts generates a response. The Bible says, "He who would have friends must show himself friendly" (Proverbs 18:24). In other words, if you want someone to love you, you must pour out love and it will return to you. There is no other way, it just has to come back to you again, sooner or later.

Jesus said, "Greater love hath no man than this, that a man lay down his life for his friends." This is the zenith of love. The highest sacrifice one can bring is not earthly things that we possess, which can be bought and traded, but our very life. Jesus was telling these truths to His disciples on the eve of His betrayal. He was trying to reveal to them how great His love was.

One of the greatest stories of love in the Bible is that of Jonathan, the son of King Saul, and David, the shepherd boy from Bethlehem. It says in 1 Samuel 18:1, ". . . The soul of Jonathan was knit with the soul of David, and Jonathan loved him as his own soul."

David had just come into the palace after killing Goliath and he had brought this head of Goliath by the hairs of its head, into the presence of King Saul. Jonathan was a warrior who had been trained in warfare. He was one of the finest in Israel, a man with courage and daring, but he had not had the courage and daring that David had had, even though he had won many victories. When no one would fight, Jonathan and his armor bearer courageously attacked the enemy even when it was a perilous thing to do, and he was at a great disadvantage. He had cleaned out the nest of Philistines and won a great victory in Israel in an hour of crisis. But when Goliath stood before the army of Israel, mocking them and blaspheming God, Jonathan was as helpless and full of fear as the rest of the soldiers of Israel. Because a man has courage one time, does not mean that he will have strength and courage another time. Fear had made him timid. It is fear that will make you timid. But there was something else in Jonathan's life that made him hesitate, and this one qualification David had. David had a great love for God that Jonathan had not had. David had sat on the hills of Bethlehem and had sung the praises of God from the time that he was a little boy. David had been alone with God and that was where he had learned to know God. He had sung the praises of God until the hills shook with his music. He loved God with all his soul and being, and when he saw that Goliath standing there and mocking his God, David forgot that he wasn't a warrior. He forgot that he had never been trained in warfare. He forgot everything but that this man was standing there and defying his God whom he loved with all his heart. He left his belongings which he had brought with him in the care of his brothers who were mocking him; and before the eyes of all of Israel's mighty hosts, he ran to meet the enemy because that enemy was his Lover's enemy. You can fight for your Lover when you have enough love in your heart. I believe that Jonathan was older than David. He had watched David's youthful courage and admired it, and his heart had turned over inside of him. Now, again, as David spoke to Jonathan's father, he was watching. The Bible says that his soul was knit to him and that he loved him as his own soul. A deep love is more than a love of the mind. It is true that you must love the Lord your God with your mind, but a deep love is more than a love of the mind. The soul is involved in a deep love. It touches the spirit of man. If your love for God has not touched your soul, then you do not love as you ought. It took that kind of love for Jonathan to do what he did.

When David left Saul's presence, Johathan took him aside and made a covenant with David. The wedding ring on your hand is a token of a covenant which you made because you love the one with whom you made the covenant. Whenever that covenant is broken, the ring should be removed because it is mockery to wear it after that. Jonathan made a covenant with David which he sealed with gifts.

The first thing that Jonathan gave David was his *robe*. David had just come in from the shepherd's fields wearing a dirty, smelly shepherd's garment. He had walked all the way from Bethlehem, a considerably long journey in those days. He was tired and dusty; he looked like a farmer's boy, because that is what he was. Now he was a friend of a prince, and he had to dress like what he was. Jonathan was going to take him around and show him different things. He was going to introduce him to people and when he looked at David in his little shepherd's tunic he said, "David, I just can't take you around the palace in that. I am going to put a royal robe on you. That smock of the hills will not do around here." You see, the shepherd boys wore a short tunic so they could chase around after the sheep. Jonathan said, "I am going to dress you up." And he stripped himself. Why didn't Jonathan take something out of his wardrobe instead? Why didn't he give David one of his old robes? Or perhaps one of his castoffs, the kind we send to the mission field and give to the poor—something out of style, or which we have outgrown? When you see the missionaries you know they have been dressed from the "missionary barrel." Dresses twenty years old, belts missing, buttons torn off, zippers broken. That is how they love us! That is what they send us, and that is what we wear out there. I know. I have lived on the mission field for many years and I have seen my sisters and brothers. But Jonathan did not do that. He gave David what he himself was wearing. And you can be sure that when Jonathan the prince had dressed himself that day, he was wearing what HE liked . . . it was the best. So he gave his best. Love makes you give generously, not cheaply, not the left-over, or the cast-off, but that which costs you the stripping of yourself. Why don't we love God like that? I want to love Him with all my heart, so that I can be stripped for Him. Only when I am stripped for Him and He has taken all my possessions, will I know that my love has been proven to be worthy of His love.

And then Jonathan gave David his *sword.* That was the sword that he had fought with. It was the most important thing that he owned. It was with this that he had won victory after victory. A warrior will prize his own sword more than any other great possessions. It reminded him of past battles. Every time he looked at the sword he could remember how his life had been saved through the sharpness of that sword, and how his people of Israel had been delivered. It was a valuable sword for swords were very few in number in those days (1 Samuel 13:22). But when he saw that David didn't have a sword, and that all David had was a sling, somehow he knew that sling did not fit with that new robe David was standing in. God had a new future for David and the sling would not fit with it. He needed a new weapon. It is alright to use the "slingshot" until you come to that new place in your life. Then when you come to the place when the "slingshot" days are over the Lord will give you a sword. This is the trouble with many of God's people. They are still using the slingshot when the should be using the sword. God wants us to progress in warfare. The slingshot was alright for bears and lions, but David would soon be the captain of the hosts of Israel, a mighty warrior, the greatest soldier since the days of Joshua, and perhaps the greatest the world has ever known. There is no record of David ever losing a battle. The sword of the prince of Israel was put in his hand as a token from God that he would stand in the place of the prince of Israel and do battle in the place of the prince of Israel. It was not only a preparation of great days ahead but it was also prophetic of what was to come in his life.

After this, Jonathan gave him his *bow*. Jonathan was famous for his ability to handle the bow and arrow. He had taught archery to many in Israel. The Bible says, "He bade them teach the children of Judah the use of the bow" (2 Samuel 1:18). David did not know how to use the bow and arrow when Jonathan put it in his hand. It was the finest bow in Israel, for the master of archery owned it.

When Jonathan looked at David with his new robe, the sword in his hand and the bow at his side he said, "There is something missing." And he gave him his *girdle*. The girdle was a princely, beautiful piece of raiment. I can see it with its golden filigree work on it and jewels inset, as he ties it around the breast of David. "Now you look just like me. In fact, the folks wouldn't even be able to tell the difference."

That is what Jesus did for us. He robed us in His robe of righteousness, He put the sword in our hand; He put the arrow of deliverance in our other hand and then He enveloped us in the girdle of His love and tenderness, His mercy and kindness, and now when the people look at us they cannot tell who is Jesus, for they see Him in us. That is what God wants to do. He wants to adorn you in His own likeness so that no one will be able to tell the difference, for you will be a joint-heir with Jesus Christ, a prince in Israel and co-ruler of the new kingdom. You are not a shepherd boy forever. You are a future prince of Israel. Remember who you are. It was the love of your Heavenly Jonathan that gave you this authority.

Then came another great challenge in Jonathan's life, a time to prove his love in even a greater way. David was so loved by the people, that Saul became jealous of him. The more the people loved David, the more jealous Saul became, until he sought to kill David and David had to flee into the wilderness to hide from the anger of Saul. Have you ever had anyone hate you? One who goes out of his way to destroy you? It seems like their heart is filled with madness. They will do everything they can to destroy you. That is how Saul hated David. Jonathan, knowing his father's hatred for David, went out into the wilderness to comfort and strengthen David's hand in God. The greatest strength you can give to someone is a word of encouragement, a word of comfort, a word of challenge. It will lift the soul because words have power. We do not use our words to help people like we should. Too often we use our words in a negative way and therefore we do not strengthen the hand of our brother in God like Jonathan did. He said, "Fear not . . . for the hand of Saul my father shall not find thee." Oh, what splendid faith! Saul had thousands of soldiers out looking for David. They were constantly searching the hills. And now Jonathan tells David, "Don't worry . . . my father will not be able to find you." He must have prayed through and known the truth because that is what happened.

What an encouragement it must have been for David when he was in the heat of the battle and his fears were at their worst! There must have been many times when David wondered as he hid in the wilderness, "Does Jonathan still love me?" He had every reason to believe that Saul had turned Jonathan against him. He wondered if he remembered the covenant they had made. And then, one day Jonathan came to him. He did not bring him garments, robes, swords, bows, and girdles, but he brought him something much greater, his loyalty. It was not easy for Jonathan. He was torn between two great loves. His father Saul loved him and had only one ambition, that Jonathan would be king of Israel one day. They had fought side by side in battle. The Bible says they were beautiful together. And then one day the Holy Spirit whispered into Jonathan's heart the divine plan of God and Jonathan knew it was different than the one that his father had. The Lord had said, "Jonathan, give David ONE thing more."

What else was there left to give? It was his rightful place on the throne. So he came to the wilderness to find David and to tell him. There in that Judean desert he said to David, "Thou shalt be king over Israel." This is the deepest story of love you can read anywhere. It meant that Jonathan was stepping down from the throne, and he was letting David ascend to the throne and be the next king over Israel.

In the same way, our Lord and Saviour Jesus left his mansion above and came for a lifetime down to this world that we may take our place of rulership in the eternal kingdom of God. Oh, such love, such wondrous love!

Chapter 9
LOVE IS KIND

Too many people find it hard to be kind to others. This is because there is not enough love in their hearts to go out of their way to help another who is in need. The true love of God will always make you concerned about others. You will not be able to rest in peace while others are suffering. You will want to help. This kindness will not only be extended to friends, but it will also touch the lives of your enemies.

Do not think for one moment that you love your brother when you do not show him kindness. You cannot push him out of the seat of honor and grab first place for yourself. Love does not push its way to the head of the crowd or the front of the line. Love stands back. Love pays a price; love makes a sacrifice; love looks for something more to bring. Love will encourage and inspire you to give everything, it pays a debt it does not owe. It makes you want to bring that royal position that is yours and lay it at the feet of another and take the second place like Jonathan did. Love is kind. Love does not give nasty digs, or fling out hurting insults. Love has no sneaky acts. It doesn't take the biggest part of the apple, the extra scoop of ice cream. It doesn't cheat its neighbor. Love never has to go to court to win a court case. Love gives the coat when the cloak has been taken. Love offers the second cheek when the first has been smitten. Love walks that second mile, because love is kind. Love returns good for evil. When you have Jesus you have His qualifications.

This is "angel law." This is the way the angels live. IF you are a child of God you will rule angels some day, for you were created higher than the angels; you are of a higher order. Your position is higher and therefore your responsibility and your life and love must be higher than the angels. Love doesn't talk about his neighbor and criticize. It doesn't spread gossip, even if it is true, because love covers a multitude of sins.

That is how David loved Saul. No matter how Saul treated him, or how much he had suffered at the hand of Saul, David did not fight back or seek revenge. Sometimes he suffered so grievously, so unreasonably, for Saul was like a madman after him. When the news that Jonathan and Saul had been slain in battle was brought to David, he sorrowed greatly. Do you know what many of us would have done? We would have run around with our arms in the air shouting, "Ha, ha, did you hear what happened to Saul? He sure had it coming! I knew that God was going to judge him one of these days. I was waiting for it to happen." We would spread the news about with a cruel gladness in our hearts. But not David. He was not like that. When he heard the news of Saul and Jonathan's deaths, he knew what that news meant. He knew that now he was free to be king and that all the hindrances were, in one moment of time, removed. Not only was Saul taken, but Jonathan, the crown prince was also dead. All that remained was for David to step on the throne. You would have thought that he would have been glad about it. We would even understand why he was glad, because now he would not have to be a fugitive in the wilderness and fear for his life. Now he could go back home and look for his wife Michal, whom he had not seen for many years.

But this was not true of David. He loved with a kind heart. In 2 Samuel 1:19 we read his words, "The beauty of Israel is slain." This hard, cruel, mean, hateful, treacherous Saul, who wanted to kill him, who had made one last trip into the wilderness to destroy him, David called "the beauty of Israel." This man who had taken the javelin and thrown it into the wall, trying to kill David, this man who had been so possessed with demons that at times he was even ridiculous (and no one had seen him in his madness more than David, for David used to be called in at these times to play and sing for him). Now he says, "The beauty of Israel." Oh, God, give us a heart like David, that can look past the mistakes, the cruelties of others, their hatefulness and let us always see the beauty that is somewhere hidden in them, for in the worst of creatures there is still some beauty.

I have seen it wherever I have gone. When I ministered in the great Bilibid prison of Manila, Philippines with Olga Robertson, I have seen it amongst these men, too. Some of them are serving life imprisonment. If you go there ten years from now, they will still be there. There are men who have murdered one, two and more people. Yet these are such beautiful men. I can say this because I know them. I have prayed with them. As I put my hand on their shoulders, I have seen the tears of these murderers drop on the floor in little puddles and that was when I saw a beauty in them from God. Yes, even in the hearts of some of the hardest of them. Beloved, how do you see beauty in others? Only through the heart of kindness and love. That is the kind of a heart that David had. That is why David could say, "Tell it not in Gath, publish it not in Askelon: let not the daughters of the uncircumcised triumph." David did not want the sinners to rejoice. Oh, if only we would have this heart of kindness!

In Proverbs 17:9 we read, "He that covereth a transgression seeketh love. But he that repeateth a matter separateth chief friends." In other words, it says that he who loves will cover up another person's mistakes. He won't broadcast it. In the Song of Mourning which David composed and sang for Saul, he never once mentioned any of Saul's failures or weaknesses. Instead he said, "Saul and Jonathan were lovely and pleasant in their lives." He said that that wicked man Saul was beautiful. That is love! Perhaps this is the reason that David was a man after God's own heart. Certainly it was not because he had kept all the commandments. For we know he did not keep them all. He made some of the most terrible mistakes. No man of God in the whole Bible fell as far in sin as David, and yet hundreds of years later, under the anointing of the Holy Spirit God calls him, "A man after HIS own heart." What was the key? How can a man make such mistakes and still be loved? If we found a man making those mistakes in our churches we would throw him out. We would call a meeting of the elders and talk it over and then we would force him to make a public confession. And when he did, we would still despise him and talk about it to everyone and it would be "beneath us" to have fellowship with him. It would be the gossip in every home of the church membership for weeks. The telephone lines would be busy, we even would not mind paying long-distance then. But David didn't do that. David covered Saul's mistakes, because he knew that he would need his own sins covered someday. Jesus said, "Judge not, that ye be not judged, for with what judgment ye judge, ye shall be judged" (Matthew 7:1, 2). Do you know how I am going to be judged on the day of judgment? In the same way as I judged my sister, my brother. It will be in exactly the same degree of hardness and severity. Where I was hard, God will be hard with me. Many of us do not forgive as much as we have been forgiven. Remember the story of the unjust steward (Matthew 18:23-35).

How many of us are like that! After God has so mercifully forgiven us all our sins and paid all our debts we look around at those who owe us something and we judge them. "This brother here owes me 20 pennies, and that sister here, she owes me 95 pennies." The master in the story which Jesus told was angry with the unjust servant. He said, "Bring him to me. I was kind to him. I was merciful. I didn't judge him like he should have been judged. But because he was not merciful, now I will step in. Now I will judge him like he judged someone else. I gave him love and mercy, but he gave no love and mercy in return. So now my mercy and my love will be taken from him."

That is why you do not dare to pass judgment. Someday

you will need mercy and God will judge you in exactly the same way that you are judging others. "Whatsoever a man soweth, that shall he also reap" (Galatians 6:7). Watch it happen even in this life. The one who has judged too harshly will find that the same tragedy will happen even in this lifetime

So David was speaking wisdom when he said, "Don't tell it. Don't publish it." He not only sang this beautiful "Song of Mourning," he taught it to the children of Judah. In it, he reminded the people how Jonathan had taught them how to use the bow and arrow. It was Jonathan who had also taught David the use of the bow. Every time David let his bow fly, he would remember the one who had taught him how to use it. Even after many years, he would remember how Jonathan had said, "Just draw it so tight . . . and it will shoot so far. Draw it tighter and it will shoot that much farther. Draw it even tighter and it will shoot even farther." David remembered these lessons, for these lessons had saved his own life many times.

David also said, "They were swifter than eagles, They were stronger than lions." Isn't that beautiful! He compared these two men to the eagle that soars the sky and the lion in his majesty. This horrible, angry, jealous, demon-possessed Saul, David compared him to an eagle that soars. Then, he likened him unto a lion. In the Bible the lion is called the mightiest among the beasts which neither fears nor turns back before any of the beasts (Proverbs 30:30).

In 1 Samuel 24 we read how God delivered Saul into David's hands and David had the opportunity to do what he wanted to do with him. "And the men of David said unto him, Behold the day of which the Lord said unto thee, 'Behold, I will deliver thine enemy into thine hand, that thou mayest do to him as it shall seem good unto thee.' " God gave David the right to kill Saul. He had God's permission, because God was going to kill him anyway, but God was testing the love of David's heart. God was testing his power to forgive, his kindness, his mercy and his worthiness of the throne of Israel. I am glad that David did not kill Saul, because later on David needed mercy from God when he killed somebody else and if he had not been merciful to Saul, God would not have been merciful to him. His soldiers encouraged him, "Kill him, kill him," for they all wanted to leave this life of wandering and go home. They knew that as soon as Saul, the troubler, was out of the way they could freely return to their families. They put the sword into David's hands and said, "Kill him!" This was the greatest test in David's life up until that time.

Do you know that the highest test of your life is when God delivers your enemy into your hands. When at last you have something to use against him. When he has ruined your reputation, torn your work down, done everything he could against you, when he has hated you and killed your "image," and now you have some "weapon of revenge," some juicy piece of gossip that you know will destroy him because you know it's true, what are you going to do? Are you going to drag his "dirt" before the people? Are you going to spread it around and ruin his name, like he ruined yours?

God has given me this power. There is one person who has tried to destroy everything I ever did for God. Everywhere I went, this person has written letters against me. Everywhere they tried to destroy my reputation. I felt their hate from one end of the world to another. And now that person is living in deep sin. I have the power to reveal it and destroy that person. I have the proof of what they are doing. I am standing where David stood. Here lies my enemy in my hands. All I have to do is take this proof and tell it abroad. This will clear my name and show what they are. But the Holy Spirit says to me, "You do as it pleaseth you," and I must do what David did because I want to be a woman after the heart of God.

All David did was to cut off a piece of Saul's skirt as he lay sleeping, exposed to danger that night in the wilderness; but even so David's heart smote him. He said, "God forbid that I should do this thing to my master, the Lord's anointed, to stretch forth my hand against him, because he is the anointed of the Lord." David remembered the anointing Saul had received. David remembered that the same prophet of God, Samuel, who had anointed him had also anointed Saul.

That one who tries to destroy me was also once anointed of God. But they lost that anointing a long time ago. I know there was a day when they were anointed, and the One who anointed that one, anointed me. It is not my task to use the knife of judgment. I will put that one in the hands of God. I raise my hand to God and pray that I may never use the knife of judgment to cut off the skirts of my anointed brothers and sisters, or to ever use my tongue as a knife to cut off their skirts and show their shame. It is better by far that in my own short life on earth, I bear *all* the shame and take *all* the blame, than that I should try to do the works of a judge. For You alone, Lord, are the Judge and I lay those who have judged me into Thine hands and I pray that You may be merciful and kind to them. For in the hardest and cruelest of them I see beauty. I pray that their wings will heal again, and that those eagles will fly one more time. I pray that they may be "king" again, and live and reign in the power and anointing that once was theirs. I cannot be judge, oh God! I put the knife back into Your hands. I cannot use it, my God, because I know that You said, "He that taketh the sword, shall perish by the sword." So I give it to You, for I know there is coming a day when I will need the mercy of God and as I have shown mercy, You will show mercy to me, for You said, "Forgive, as it has been forgiven you." Let the love of God that poured through the heart of David, pour through my heart in the name of Jesus

Chapter 10
LOVE SERVES

The love of God is wonderful. It is our life. We could have no life on this earth without the Love of God. I am so glad that the love of God is not determined by the condition of man. No matter how wicked man is, or how many mistakes he makes, the love of God reaches out beyond all of his mistakes. The love of God sent His Son Jesus to die. And the love of God is going to visit this world one more time. Yes, God is going to visit this world one more time, and that time has come. The last time He visited this world through His Son of Love. This time He will visit it through His "sons of love." Many people think and hope that they are the "sons of God." But if they are not sons of love, they are NOT sons of God. It is through those who are full of the love of God, that God is going to visit the world. As you have read these words, your heart has begun to burn with the love of God. That is wonderful! Treasure this experience of love. Let it grow in your heart and change and perfect you until you become like the One who is touching you. When you lay down this book, carry this love with you wherever you go.

There is much in the Bible about love, and God is beginning to teach us these truths so that we can come into maturity. He is perfecting His sons. The Word of God says that a servant does not abide in his master's house forever, but the son does, and becomes the master eventually. That is why God is teaching us love. Jesus said, "I called you servants until now, but now I call you friends." He promoted us to friendship. He was making us co-heirs with Him. In other words, we became co-equal with Him; and in order to be co-equal with Him we must have the same characteristics as He has.

Many times we have heard it preached that we are co-heirs with Him and we said, "Oh, how wonderful! Now we have a home in heaven and a beautiful palace. We can walk on those golden streets and eat the delicious fruit of heaven." But these are just the least of the things that will be included in our inheritance. When we read the description of Christ, as God revealed Him to John on the Isle of Patmos, we see Him coming as King of kings and Lord of lords. We see Him accompanied by the armies of heaven as He descends to become the Ruler of this planet earth. Then He tells us that there will be thrones and we shall reign together with Him on these thrones. But how will we arrive to this degree of magnificence? What will the qualifications be? Don't think for a minute that every person who calls himself a Christian will be ruling with Christ. There IS a ruling-people, but if all were rulers, who would they rule? There must be those who will be ruled. Therefore, there will be those who will be chosen from the multitudes of redeemed to be rulers. This is the heritage of the mature sons of God. But the qualifications will be fulfilled only by those who are like Jesus: "He who was with God and thought it not robbery to be equal with God, but made himself of no reputation, and took upon him the form of a servant, and was made in the likeness of men: And being found in fashion as a man, he humbled himself, and became obedient unto death, even the death of the cross" (Philippians 2:6-8). Christ our King became our Servant, to make us to be kings with Him. What were the qualifications? What do you see in Him? What was His power? Love. Only LOVE. Love will govern your every action. Let love be the motive of everything you do, and you will never make a mistake. You will never transgress a law of God. You will not grieve anyone, you will never have fear, for perfect love casteth out all fear. That is what you need. Then you will not know fear, because love gives you the strength to "go to the gallows."

I love the story of Madam Guyon, the beautiful French woman of God who lived 300 years ago, during the reign of King Louis XIV of France. She had some of the greatest revelations of God ever given to man. She was a devout Roman Catholic but the church persecuted her. When she was two-and-a-half years old her parents put her in a convent where she was raised by nuns and taught to love God. As a little child of four years of age she said she would die for Jesus. She announced to all her little friends in the school that she was ready to be a martyr for God. So some of the older girls thought they would test her. They took this child and brought her in a room and said, "The Lord has accepted your offer and He will now give you the honor of being a martyr. First you must confess all your sins." So she went and prayed her last prayer and they laid a cloth on the floor on which they said her blood would fall. One of the older girls appeared with a large cutlass, with which she said she was going to cut off her head. At that moment, while she was kneeling on the floor, she was suddenly overcome by fears that were greater than her faith and she cried out, "I cannot die without my father's permission." The girls laughed at her and said that it was only an excuse and that she really was not ready to be a martyr like she had professed to be.

Deep in her heart she felt she had failed God. Even for years after she felt terrible because she had come to the hour of testing and had failed. That was why she determined that she would never fail God another time. Once she had been "weighed in the balance" and found wanting, and she never wanted that to happen again. Almost from the beginning of her ministry she began to suffer persecution. Her suffering increased as more and more enemies came up against her, until she was cast into Bastille prison, the great, terrible French prison in Paris. She, who was one of France's greatest saints, whose life had brought blessing to multitudes, was condemned as though she were one of the world's worst criminals. She was put in the prison tower whose walls were twelve feet thick at the top and increased in thickness as they approached the bottom. The prisoners were known by numbers. Everything was taken from them, except such clothing as was absolutely necessary. The cells were exceedingly cold in winter because they were unheated and in summer they were stifling hot. Iron cages and other instruments of torture were kept in reserve for those who were refractory. It was here that Madame Guyon was shut up for four years in solitary confinement. Shut out from the world, from her friends, from the pleasant light of the sun, she had nothing to do but to bow in silence and acquiescence of trust in her God. She was not allowed to see her friends or even allowed to write to them. She had been permitted to write letters up until she was put in the Bastille. In one of these she said, "I feel no anxiety in view of what my enemies will do to me. I have no fear of anything, but of being left to myself. So long as God is with me, neither imprisonment nor death will have any terrors. Fear not! If they should proceed to the extremities and should put me to death, COME AND SEE ME DIE. Do what Mary Magdalene did, who never left Him who had taught her pure love."

Madame Guyon had a maid-servant who shared in her burden and revelation of truth. She accompanied her in much of her wanderings and also her suffering. When Madame Guyon was imprisoned her maid-servant was also imprisoned. This faithful, pious woman whose principles of consecration and faith gave her the courage to stand by her mistress even until imprisonment could say,

> "Oh! cease, my wandering soul,
> On restless wing to roam;
> All this wide world, to either pole,
> Has not for thee a home."

She was able to bear her imprisonment because of her state of mind. She accepted all her sufferings from the hand of God. She was an intelligent and refined woman, but she did not wish to be anything greater than a handmaiden to the handmaiden of the Lord. She knew this was her call from God and she had only one aim, and that was to be a servant to her mistress. She has long since entered into her rewards and heaven holds the secret.

One wonders how a woman like Madame Guyon, who had been known for her beauty, married to one of the wealthiest men of France, could so completely dedicate her life to God that she would pay such a terrible price. She lived in a time when France was full of hate and intrigue. She had one message for the people of France. That message was PURE LOVE. They hated her for that. They hounded her from city to city. Wherever she went, they sent their messengers after her and warned the people to watch out for "that woman." She was hated, threatened and finally imprisoned by the church that she served, yet her impact was felt in the palaces of Versailles and the kingdom of France. There is nothing so powerful as love. That is the same lesson that God is trying to teach a dying world today. May God raise up a multitude of women like Madame Guyon who will take this message of LOVE like a flaming fire across the towns, cities and nations of this world!

Chapter 11
THE LOVE - SLAVE

Love will make a slave out of you. It will bind you to someone for all of your life. It will put you in a place of servitude, not grudgingly but joyfully. You will want to serve those you love, for it will be in this that you will be fulfilled

In India a wife is expected to serve her husband in ways that most western women would never be willing to do. She gets up at 5 o'clock in the morning to prepare his tea. Because most of the women living in villages do not have electricity or electric stoves, she must first make a little fire; this she does by using the dry cow-dung that she has collected previously. When he returns home in the evening she has already prepared his supper, had a bath, put on a clean sari and is waiting at the door to meet him. It is a picture of loving servitude which is only found in countries like India or Japan. A woman will care for her husband at great sacrifice to her own self. I have lived in many Indian homes and I have often noticed that the wife will cook the meal, serve the meal to her husband first, and when he is finished she will eat what he has left over.

This is what love alone will do. She doesn't think it a sacrifice. I have seen the love these women have for their husbands. And yet most of them didn't love their husbands when they married them because their marriages were arranged. This was something I found hard to understand when I first went to India. I said, "Oh, this is terrible, to think I could not marry someone whom I know I love." And yet, in home after home that I was in, I saw a beautiful love between husband and wife and I thought, "Surely, these two couldn't have had an arranged marriage! They must have loved each other before they were married." And I would ask, "Brother Daniel, how did you meet your wife?" He answered me, "I didn't meet her until our wedding day." And when I asked him more, he said, "My father was a godly man and he prayed that God would help him find a good wife for me and God heard his prayer. I have the best wife in the world." I saw such devotion and love towards each other and in all the pastors' homes where I visited. I cannot think of one home where there was not this beautiful loyal love between husband and wife. I never heard one talking against the other. I am talking about the Christian homes, where the fathers prayed, like Abraham did for a wife for Isaac, his son. Love is a growing thing; and when it stops growing, it dies. If your love for your brother, neighbor, family or God stops growing, it is dying at the roots and if you don't do something about it quickly you will find that there is nothing left but dead stock.

There is nothing a man prizes more than his freedom. Take away his freedom where he hasn't got the right to speak, the right to act upon his own inspiration, the right to buy or the right to sell, the right to come or go, and a man will often lose his will to live. Yet in the Bible we read one of the greatest stories of love where a man is tested to the utmost of endurance in the test of freedom.

It is the test of the love-slave in Exodus 21:2-6. God made a difference between the Hebrew slave and the slaves that were of another nation. God wanted the people to always remember that the Hebrews were a chosen people. After six years of servitude they had the privilege of being able to go out free. For six years they were the same as any other slave. They had to do the same dirty work and live in humble obedience to every command of their master. The Hebrew with his white skin worked alongside the Negro with his black skin. Both of them carried the same burden, both were in the same bondage. But there was a difference. Something that you couldn't see, but something that you could FEEL. The Hebrew knew that after six years he was a free man and the black man knew that he had been purchased to be a slave all of his life. The Hebrew slave could count off the years. He lived for the day when the master would say to him, "Here is your certificate of freedom." And he would take that document of liberty and go out into the world and be a master himself. For six years, neither the black man nor the white one got any pay. They sat together at the same slaves' table and ate the same slaves' food. Both worked under the same hot sun, both of them had to suffer the same cold winter wind, but ONE had a hope!

Oh, praise the Lord, that even though we cannot see a difference between the sons of God and the sons of man, there is a deep difference. One has a hope. They know that the "six years" are almost finished. Peter said, "Know ye not that a thousand years are as one day with the Lord" (2 Peter 3:8). Do you realize that at the close of this century this world is coming to the end of 6,000 years? Do you know that OUR "sixth day" has almost ended? One of these days we will get our "certificate of redemption" and enter into our "Christ-purchased liberty."

Yes, the Hebrew slave had this hope of freedom, but there was a condition to his freedom which no man could overlook. If he had come in by himself, he had to go out by himself, and if he was married when he came in, his wife went out with him, but if his master had given him a wife and she had borne him sons or daughters, the wife and her children belonged to the master and the slave had to go out alone. Can you pause for a moment and picture this man in the hour of his terrible testing?

The six years had been fulfilled. Tomorrow he could go out free. But he had a wife who still belonged to the master. What is he going to do? Is he going to forsake her, and let her remain a slave forever? Perhaps the thought would come to him, "There are a lot of other women. She is nothing special, she is weak and sickly. There are others more beautiful. I will find another. I am still young. I will forget about her. Oh, maybe I will miss her a few days, but I want to be free! If I stay with her, I will always be a slave."

Can you see what terrible predicament that man was in? He had to make a decision. He could not take her with him. That was absolutely impossible. He had to make up his mind: Did he love her enough to be a slave together with her for the rest of his life? He knew that if he stayed, he must stay until death. At night he slept on his bed. He rolled back and forth. His wife lay beside him. She knew what he was thinking. She knew he had to make a decision. She looked at him in the daytime. She said to him, "Abiah, don't let me hinder you. Take your freedom and go. Don't remain a slave because of me. It is true I will love you forever, but don't stay in bondage because of me. Go! Be a free man!"

From the depths of his soul he cried, "How can I leave you, Sherah? I have learned to love you. How can I live without you!"

Can you see how this poor man is pulled between two great desires . . . one for his freedom and liberty, and the other toward the woman he loves and his children? Every man wants his freedom. Most men would give their lives for it. Like others before him, he has to decide. What will he do? Shall he take his freedom and go out free, or shall he stay a bond-slave for the rest of his life?

The Word of God said, "If the slave shall plainly say, 'I love my master, my wife, and my children; I will not go out free: Then his master shall bring him unto the judges; he shall also bring him to the door, or unto the door post; and his master shall bore his ear through with an aul; and he shall serve him for ever" (Exodus 21:5, 6).

I am sure many of those slaves didn't know until the last day what their final decision would be. Many were not sure until they stood before their master and gave their final decision. I can feel the struggle that they went through, until in the end, LOVE won.

If love cannot win the victory in your life, you are a

failure to yourself. It is better to be a slave all your life, and to be filled with love, than to be free and go through life without having known true love, because then you will become a slave of self. Many are slaves of self, slaves of their own ego, or their own pride and fleshly desires. But for those who chose the pure way of love, the master brought them before the judges where they had to testify and make open confession before all these witnesses that they had chosen the way of love. After that, he was brought to the door of his house, where the master bored through his ear with an awl. From then on he was a lifetime slave of the master.

Can you picture the scene? There he comes! His wife is watching. His children are watching. Daddy has decided he is going to stay with them. Up until then they did not know what he would do. Can you feel their heartbeat, their anxiety? But now they see him coming to the door and the ear is placed against the door. The master takes the red hot awl that was waiting, ready. With one quick thrust, the ear is pierced. One instant of pain! The pain that made him a slave until death. What gave him the strength to bear this blow of heat and hurt? . . . LOVE.

I like the chorus we learned to sing in Australia:
>Make me a love-slave,
>Make me a love-slave,
>How I love this Master that I serve!
>Put my ear up to the door;
>I don't want to leave here anymore;
>Make me a love-slave forever to my Lord.

Love will give you the strength to go through what you have to. It is true that we are coming to the close of the "sixth day," and a new day of liberty is dawning. We are coming into our kingdom rights. And the world is waiting for the manifestation of God's mature sons. But the qualifications will not only be love; there will be the ability to suffer pain, separation, rejection and criticism. God's anointed ones are going to go through these things. It is going to cost us something. We are going to be marked people, a people who will be hated by Satan and his own. We will be brought before their "synagogues." Babylon will hate us because we will make them uncomfortable. It may even cost us our lives. That is the price the slave of love had to pay and that is what it cost Madame Guyon and multitudes of others who are living in the Iron Curtain countries of the world today. The prisons and slave-camps are full of men and women who are Jesus' love-slaves. Beloved, you must determine in your heart to go through with Jesus! Do you love the Master enough for this?

Remember our Saviour, how on the last night before He died, He girded himself about with the towel and knelt down and washed the feet of His servants. He said, "He who is greatest shall be servant." Why? Because it takes love to wash feet and to wait on others. I grew up in a church that had foot-washing services. I love foot-washing services. I think that the church that has this ritual is a beautiful church if they do it with love. But if it only becomes a ritual it will not help them to grow in the graces of God. A great work of grace is always done in MY life when I wash someone's feet and an ever greater work when someone else washes my feet. Many healings of differences are brought about and sins forgiven in a good, old-fashioned foot-washing service. It is what some churches and religious organizations and family-fellowships need to bring healing and the washing away of bitter feelings. Jesus not only washed His disciples' feet, an act of a slave, but He became a slave unto death, even the death of the cross. It was only then that He was able to reign in power. You and I must go the same way. Every time the Lord looks at us, He is looking to see if we have the scar of obedience on us. Even as when the master looked on his love-slave and saw the hole in his ear, and it reminded him that this slave was there because he had chosen to be, and that the mark of ownership was there by his own choice, the master knew that he could trust him above all the other slaves. This one had paid the price. He would not run away.

When God looks at you, does He see the mark of love

on you? What did Paul say? "I wish to God that you were as I am . . . except for these chains." Paul also said, "I am a bondsman of Jesus Christ." These chains were Paul's glory. Don't be afraid to walk the path of suffering with God. When you are God's slave you are walking in the footpath of His Son.

> I'm but a slave;
> I have no freedom of my own.
> I cannot choose the smallest thing.
> Not e'en my way.
> I'm a slave.
> Kept to do the bidding of my Master.
> He can call me, night or day.
> Were I a servant, I could claim wages, freedom
> Sometimes, anyway.
>
> But I was bought.
> Love was the price my Master paid for me,
> And I am now His slave
> And evermore shall be.
>
> He takes me here, He takes me there
> And tells me what to do,
> I just obey. That's all,
> And trust Him, too. . . .

Chapter 12
LOVE IS UNITY

There can be no unity where there is no love. That is why the Communists end up destroying each other. The prisons of Russia and China and other communistic countries have as many Communists in them as there are Christians and so-called "dissidents." Some of the most prominent Communists have ended their lives in slave-camps and dungeons. They serve a god that cannot show mercy. This is the god of materialism and power over the lives of other men.

We must be careful in Christendom lest we serve the same "god." Even in our ranks there is division and strife. My brethren, this ought not to be! In Colossians 2:2 Paul, speaking to the church of Colosse, said that he prayed for them to be knit together in love. He pictures love as a "knitting together," a unity, a oneness, a joining together that is absolutely inseparable. Love will unite us. That is the ONLY thing in the world that can unite us. Today the religious leaders of the world are trying to unite the churches and we hear much about the unity of the church, the One-world Church and the Ecumenical Council, as they gather together around the table of man's organization. But nothing except confusion and darkness is coming out of it. The National Council of Churches has just approved a new plan which they say will bring many churches together. Their latest plans are to open the door so wide that the Roman Catholic church will be able to join. They hope that the whole world will be able to accept their new Bible. They hope that this new Bible will be able to replace all the Bibles of the Protestant and Roman Catholic church. It is called THE NEW WORLD BIBLE. In this Bible the divinity of Jesus is taken away. He is only a teacher and a historical figure who was a reformer who met death as a young man at the hands of the Roman political power. No more will the story of the crucifixion be tolerated. This is the new church that men are trying to organize. The Bible student knows that this is the beginning of the end, the time when we will have one World church, one World government and one World banking system. Beloved, we are near the end and there is going to be a joining together of all churches and people who do not hear the voice of the Lord. "Babylon" will be rebuilt. I am afraid that some who claim to be Spirit-filled will be in that group. But, thank God, there will also be the joining together of those little children of the Lord, that "little flock" to whom the Lord said, "Fear not little flock, it is your Father's good pleasure to give you the kingdom" (Luke 12:32). They will be the despised ones, the outcast ones who knew the voice of the Spirit and knew how to follow Him and were not tricked by the evil one. Oh, let us be united together in love! The Lord said, "The house divided against itself cannot stand."

We are living in a time of great division. Countries are divided. There are two Germanys, two Koreas, two Chinas, two Berlins, two Americas—white and black—and two Canadas—French and English. There should not be any rejection of one another because of ideologies or colors of skin, for the Bible says, "God has made of one blood all nations of men for to dwell on all the face of the earth, and hath determined the times before appointed, and the bounds of their habitation" (Acts 17:26). The same blood pours through my brother's body as pours through mine. That is what my Bible says. But here in America we have a "black America" and a "white America." In Canada we have a French Canada and an English-speaking Canada. We are living in the end-time when nations are divided, families are divided, friends are divided, churches are divided. You cannot be sure any longer that the one who was your friend last year is your friend this year. There is a spirit of separation that is coming from hell. Beloved, we must stick together. Neither the Treaty of Rome, the Salt Agreement, nor any other will unite us. Brother will betray brother and nation will betray nation. The agreements that were signed between nations yesterday will be disregarded tomorrow. We cannot trust governments or politicians. There is only one way that we can be united and that is through the workings of the Holy Spirit in all of our hearts. It is only as we are knit together in LOVE that we can be an undivided nation.

The differences in the color of our skin and our ethnic background should make us MORE beautiful. One of my favorite types of knitting is the fair-aisle stitch which is so popular in England. They use a half dozen colors of wool and knit all these colors together. It is a real art, because if you don't do it exactly right you have a little hole every time you change color. If you work the threads correctly there will be no space between colors. This is what God does with us. One is white, another is brown, another is yellow and another is black. God knows how to knit us together into a beautiful design as we are submissive to Him. There will be no separation between us if we let Him weave our strands together.

Paul was greatly burdened for the church of Laodicea when he wrote those words in Colossians. He said, "For I would that ye knew what great conflict I have for you, and for them at Laodicea. . . . that their hearts might be comforted, being knit together in love. . . ." (2:1, 2). Did Paul see that the church of Laodicea was going to fall? The Lord, speaking to them through His servant John on the Isle of Patmos, said, "I know thy works, that thou art neither cold nor hot: I would thou wert cold or hot. So then because thou art lukewarm, and neither cold nor hot, I will spue thee out of my mouth" (Revelation 3:15, 16). The church of Laodicea was later to become an object of scorn to Christendom throughout 2,000 years of church history. They never heeded

Paul's warning. They did not strive to be knit together in love. They didn't take heed when the prophet of God warned them. They went on their own way, and the little holes came in here and there, until in the days of John's writing on the Isle of Patmos the Lord had to say to them, "You are wretched, and miserable, and poor, and blind, and naked, and I will spue you out of My mouth." What a shame! Their many works could not save them because they did not have love. I would rather have five strands knit together in a church than have 500 all full of holes, because God can do something with a healthy situation.

In Colossians 2:2 Paul said that if they were knit together in love it would bring them into all riches of the full assurance and understanding, to the acknowledgment of the mystery of God, and of the Father and of Christ, in whom are hid all the treasures of wisdom and knowledge. He was telling them that there are hidden treasures of knowledge and wisdom which one will not find until they are full of love. Love is the key to the deep secrets of God. It opens up the mystery realm. There are mysteries that Paul never could share with the people. In Hebrews 5:11, 12 he said that the saints were dull of hearing and could not receive the strong meat. Jesus said to His disciples, "I have yet many things to say unto you, but ye cannot bear them now" (John 16:12). They could not be taught these deeper truths because their minds were not able to receive them. It was not because they had a limited education, but because they were incapable of receiving the deep things of God which are only understood by deep love. A deep love will unveil the mysteries of God to you, and you will probably understand and see in a flash things that you did not see in many years of Christian living. As we yield ourselves to God, He will pour His heart's love into our hearts and in that love will be the fullness of the revelation of God for mankind. These are the days when God is revealing things that have been kept hidden from the foundation of the earth.

In Philippians 2:2 Paul says, "Fulfil ye my joy, that ye

be likeminded, having the same love, being of one accord, of one mind." When you are of one accord, you can pull together. That is why God said, "Thou shalt not plow with an ox and an ass together" (Deuteronomy 22:10). God had created these animals; He knew that the ox has one mind and the ass has another. God says we have to have the SAME mind. He said through His prophet Amos, "Can two walk together, except they be agreed?" (Amos 3:3). The Holy Spirit knows that if we try to hitch different minds together there is going to be trouble. We must have the same mind.

Paul tells us what mind we should have: "Let this mind be in you, which was also in Christ Jesus" (Philippians 2:5). And then he pictures Christ to us as the One who came down from glory and humbled himself and became submissive unto the shameful death of the cross.

It doesn't matter how much people say they love each other, if they do not have the same mind, even the mind of Christ which is one of humility and obedience to the Father, they cannot work together in harmony. It is only as ALL are submitted to the Father that the sweet spirit of unity can flow amongst God's children.

Chapter 13
LOVE IN MARRIAGE

Marriage is "two lives that are lived together until death." It is begun when two people who love each other are united in holy wedlock. But the marriage license that is given to them is no guarantee of love. The license is only a piece of paper. It has no power to bind. There is only one thing that can bind that couple together, and that is love. Love is the great cohesive power of the universe that binds together atoms and substance. It holds families together, friends together, a nation together and a marriage together. If love were withdrawn, all things would fall apart and disintegrate. When a person begins to leave out love in his life, he too falls apart. If love were not eternal, every atom that God has created would have disintegrated a long time ago.

The unity that holds a marriage together must be more than a sexual attraction, or an appreciation for the same things. It must be the kind of unity that comes through love, pure, God-given, eternal love. We need this unity today. There never has been a time when mankind needed it more than right now. We need it in our husband-and-wife relationships, our family relationships. The situation is desperate. Somewhere there must be a pattern for men and women to be able to live by, so that families and husband-and-wife relationships can be saved. And, thank God, there is a pattern. It is not in psychiatric counseling, but in the Word of God.

Many are chafed at the words that Paul writes for the

husband and wife in Ephesians, chapter five, because they hit one pretty hard. But one must study the entire admonition of Paul in order to have balance. If we pick out only a part of it, that places the responsibility on one member of the marriage. Paul speaks to the wives, and he speaks to the husbands. It is like the balancing of the scales. No marriage can work out if both parties do not play their role as God inspired Paul to write it for the church. Let us study it.

In Ephesians 5:22 Paul starts right out by saying, "Wives, submit yourselves unto your own husbands, as unto the Lord. For the husband is the head of the wife, even as Christ is the head of the church: and he is the saviour [or guardian] of her body. Therefore as the church is subject to Christ, so let the wives be to their own husbands in every thing." In Colossians 3:18 Paul, in speaking on this subject, clarifies it more by saying, "Wives, submit yourselves unto your own husbands, as it is fit [right] in the Lord."

Paul is speaking to the husbands and wives in the church. He gives us a rule by which we can live in peace and happiness. It is one of divine order. He is saying that as Christ is the Head of the church, so the husband is head of the wife and the family. God gave this plan so that the family could have order. The husband and wife are one body. It is absolutely impossible for one body to have two heads. It would be a "freak." The husband is the symbol of God.

When God created man, He created Adam in the image of God. There is something about a man that is more like God in some aspects than the woman. Man was created to bear the responsibility of the family. He was to be the priest of the household. He was to bear the burden of caring for his family and providing for it. He was to protect his wife and children. He was created with more muscular strength to enable him to fulfill this role in life. As priest of the family, he was the one who was to represent God to his wife and family. Men need to know their importance in the plan of God. They have been given great honor and responsibility. When a woman tries to take a man's place, she cannot bear it. I know that because of circumstances many women have had to assume the role of both mother and father, but God has said that she is "the weaker vessel." As such, she is carrying a burden that she was never created to carry. It is only through the infinite strength of God that she is able to fulfil it in any capacity at all. Many of my sisters have raised their families and have done a good job of it with the Lord's help, but God did not want to put this burden on them. I respect and honor my sisters who have done a valiant job in bringing up their fatherless children. Often they were not to blame for the role they had to play. They became innocent partners in divorce cases which left them helpless in situations that were too big for them to cope with until God came down and gave them supernatural help. But God did not decree this from the beginning. He made them male and female (Genesis 1:27).

When God created Adam, God put him in charge of the garden. The Bible says, "to dress it and to keep it" (Genesis 2:15). The first man that God created was a "farmer." God brought the animals unto Adam to see what he would name them, and whatsoever Adam called every living creature, that was the name thereof. Adam gave names to all cattle, and to the fowl of the air, and to every beast of the field" (Genesis 2:19, 20).

Adam had a relationship of affection for those animals, and an understanding of their spirit. No man loved his dog more than Adam loved the beasts that he named. But still he was lonely. He lacked the relationship that comes of kindred minds, for the mind of the dog and that of Adam was not the same mind, they were of a different order. So God said, "It is not good that man should be alone; I will make him an helpmeet for him" (Genesis 2:18). The Holy Bible in Modern English translates it, "It is not good for the man to be in solitude: I will make a comforter to live with him." She was not created to be his *slave,* but his *comforter.* A man needs comfort as much as a woman. He faces the hard world every day, while she lives in the protection of her home, surrounded by those who love her. When he returns from his "battle-field," be it the office, factory or the farmyard, he needs the comfort that only she can give him. Sometimes he is like a "little boy who needs his mother." It's all right to "mother him" sometimes. The Indians say that the perfect love of a wife will be four-fold: 1) The love of a mother, 2) The love of a sister, 3) The love of a friend, 4) And the love of a lover. Only in loving in these four different ways is her love for her husband complete.

God caused a "deep sleep" to come upon Adam. This was the first anesthetic that was ever given on earth. While Adam was sleeping, God performed an operation. The King James version says, "God took a rib out of Adam." But some of the early translations say, "God took a cell out of Adam." A "cell" is defined as: "A small compartment or bounded area which is part of a whole." One might also translate this Scripture as reading, "God took a womb out of Adam," for the definition of womb is parallel to that of a "cell" in some respects. Webster defines the womb as "a cavity or space where something is generated." We can understand from this that God took the "cell" or the "womb" out of Adam and with that created the "womb-man" or "woman."

This will not seem strange to us when we fully understand what the Bible means when it says that God created man in His image. God is not only "male," He is "female." One of His names is El-Shaddai, which means "Mother-God." We see the completeness of God only as we realize this truth. He is both male and female, and possesses both mother-love and father-love. So when God created Adam, He made him like himself, creating in him the male and female characteristics. When God created Adam's help-meet, He had to take something out of Adam's own being, something that he would be able to identify with so that there would be perfect harmony and understanding. It would be the closest unity that any two creatures on earth could have. Because of this, man should be more closely united with his wife than others of God's creation. No animal and its mate has this God-created and God-planned bond. That is why a dog can mate a different dog every year, and so can any other animal. Only man was to be joined permanently with his mate because God made them "male and female" at the beginning. When He created you, He created your mate. Way back there in antiquity, in the origin of time, far beyond your known history or ability to recall, you were in the plan of God. You are an eternal living spirit. Your body is loaned to you for only a season of sojourn on earth. As an eternal being, you are without beginning or ending. And back there, hidden in the midst of a million forgotten eons of time we stood in His glory, being part of His Spirit, fashioned even then in His likeness, as He planned for us. There He created us male and female. Isaiah captures this truth in 34:16 when he says, "Consult the Lord's record and read, Not one of them shall want her mate, For His mouth gives command, and His Spirit collects. Himself casts their lot; has apportioned their fate" (Holy Bible in Modern English). This is what Jesus meant when He said, "Have you not read, that he which made them at the beginning made them male and female, and for this cause shall a man leave father and mother, and shall cleave to his wife: and they twain shall be one flesh? Therefore they are no more twain, but one flesh. What therefore God hath joined together, let not man put asunder" (Matthew 19:4-6).

God did not ordain that a man or woman should live all their lives without their mate or, as one translation says, "in solitude," but sin has destroyed much of the pattern of God. Wars, crime, moral decay, abortion, sickness and many other tragedies that are the result of man's disobedience to God have smitten down those whom God had created or planned to be the mates for those who never found their life's companion. As a result, many have spent their lives in loneliness and longing, unrequited and discontent.

Neither is celibacy God's highest plan for mankind. God created Adam that He might have a companion, one with whom He could walk and talk. He wanted Adam to share with Him in the dominion of His creative works. It was out of the depths of God's own need for intimate relationship with a living being, who would preside over the earth and all that is in it, that God created Adam. Because Adam was fashioned in God's image and likeness, he too had the same need for companionship. That is why God said, "It is not good that man should be alone." Even as God needed a companion of the heart and mind, so Adam needed one also. As Adam was made for God's comfort, so Eve was made for Adam's comfort. As Eve was a help-meet for Adam, Adam was to be a help-meet for God. Until man fulfils that high calling, he lives without purpose; his creation was in vain.

Had God not created a companion for Adam, His creative work would have been incomplete. Adam and Eve together complete the works of God. Adam alone is only half of God's creative plan, and the same would be true if God had only created Eve without Adam, which He could have done just as easily. Let us describe it like a circle. A man alone is a half-circle and a woman alone is a half-circle. Being of opposite sex, they are the positive and the negative. It takes the joining of the two to make a complete circle. That is why it says, "One shall put a thousand to flight and two, ten thousand." The difference is that in the joining of the two there is protection. There is no defense when half a circle stands alone. God ordained that we should stand two-by-two.

God created two-by-two when He created Adam and Eve. When Noah and his wife and their three sons and their three wives were delivered in the flood, God spared them two-by-two to re-populate the world. God sent Moses and his brother Aaron to deliver the children of Israel from Egypt. Jesus sent out His disciples two-by-two and Paul never worked without a companion on his many missionary adventures. There is a mighty strength that comes through the uniting of two hearts in one vision and one purpose. Satan knows that, and that is why he has tried since Adam and Eve to destroy the marriage relationship. He attends every wedding ceremony. He commands his demons, "Look at that happy couple. I order you, trouble-making spirit, to go take their happiness away. You must get the wedge in between them.

Start working to make trouble between them. Sow the seed of discord." The demons work day and night to try to destroy and pull down the greatest institution that ever was created, the institution of THE FAMILY.

There is an interesting parallel in Genesis. It says, "And God . . . brought them [the creatures He had created] to Adam" (2:19), and then it says, "And God brought the woman unto the man [Adam]" (2:22). Even as Adam named all the animals, he also named his wife. "And Adam said, 'This is now bone of my bones, and flesh of my flesh: she shall be called 'woman,' because she was taken out of man." It was only after the fall that he called her EVE. "And Adam called his wife's name Eve; because she was the mother of all living" (Genesis 3:20). Eve means the "container of life." It is a beautiful title, but can you see how Adam and Eve's relationship is growing further apart? First, he calls her "woman," i.e., "part of my body" and then he calls her "Eve." Already the fall had begun to separate them.

Let us look at the word "wife" a little longer. In the Hindi language, much of which comes from the Sanskrit (one of the oldest languages known to man), the word *woman* is *Ardh-hang-ani*. I am separating it purposely so you can see the three syllables, each of which mean something. *Ardh* means HALF, *hang* means BODY, *ani* means TAKEN OUT. So the word for wife in Hindi is "Half of the body taken out." That word is thousands of years old. It dates back into the great forgotten past. Every wife needs to realize her identity. She is the half that has been taken out of the man. She has been taken out of his innermost being, out of the seat of his passions, out of the center of his spirit. That is why a man should love his wife as his own body, for she is a part of him.

Paul said, "Therefore as the church is subject unto Christ, so let the wives be to their own husbands in everything" (Ephesians 2:24). This brings us to the question, "Does the wife have to obey her husband when he is wrong, when his mind has been perverted by sin and he is controlled by demons? Does she have to give her body to be used by him in repulsive acts that are just plain orgy?" NEVER. Paul also said, "Wives submit unto your husbands as IS FIT IN THE LORD" (Colossians 3:18). No good man would want to be responsible for bringing his wife under condemnation or sending her soul to hell. If there is any good in him at all, he will protect her from doing what would destroy her. He may send his own soul to hell, that is his prerogative, but surely if there is one ounce of good in him, he will want to spare his wife from disobeying God. If he does cause her to sin and she loses her own soul, on the day of judgment he will be given even a greater punishment, and those who taught him that he had power over her to cause her to do evil will be judged together with him.

There is a spirit of overbearing domination in the land in these last days. Man is seeking to gain mastery and predominance over others of God's creation. They have taken the teachings of God's Word out of context and have used it to rule over and crush the spirits of those who are not strong enough to withstand them, or learned enough in the Scriptures to oppose them. Pretending to be "teachers of the Word" they exert power over the weaker ones, bringing them into subordination and mental slavery.

Personally, I cannot understand why any woman would submit to this spirit of dictatorship, especially when she lives in a free land where it is not forced upon her by a tyrannical government. I can understand that, for the woman who is too weak to resist temptation because of her lack of dedication to God or love for Him, it is a good "cop-out." She can readily make excuse for herself when her husband wants her to join him for a weekend of gambling in Las Vegas, a few drinks at the bar, a night at the porno movie, or what-have-you. Her religious teachers have said she MUST obey her husband. She can do these things and not feel guilty. If the Holy Spirit convicts her, she runs to her religious instructors and they comfort her by brainwashing her still further.

I want to ask you a question: "How far can I sin and still not receive the curse that comes with sinning? When do the seeds I sow not reap a harvest?" NEVER!

In India and China where I lived for many years, if a woman is saved she will refuse to bow down before the demon-gods of her people. For this she is often beaten and sometimes even worse. Would the religious teachers that teach this doctrine of domination dare to say, "Woman, if your husband commands you to bow before devils, you must! God will forgive you!" Where in the Bible have we authority for such blasphemy? NOWHERE! And yet men have taught our women that they must "bow" before demons of lust, uncleanness, bestiality and rebellion towards God. If the daughters of the faith are not taught now to stand up for purity, holiness, godliness and obedience to God, how will they stand when they pass through the fires?

Why are women who know God's Word not submitting? Because they don't see God in their husbands. When a godly woman sees God in her husband, she can't help but love him and honor him and obey him, and be submissive to him, for she will know that he is hearing from God and he will do the thing that is right for her soul and for her physical happiness and good. The Hindu woman has been taught to believe since childhood that there is no "salvation" for her as a woman. Her only salvation is through her husband, he is therefore her "god." Her salvation depends on him. It seems to me that lately we have incorporated a little Hinduism into Christianity. God no doubt intended that Adam should bear His image but, sad to say, most men have lost their original glory of God. How can a husband be looked upon as "God" if he lives like "the devil?" It is impossible. And the woman, in trying to fill the role of a submissive wife becomes frustrated because she WAS created to submit to a man whom she can honor and respect and love. Woman was made to stand at the side of man and not to lead him, but if he will not be led by God, what shall she do? Shall she stand still because her husband rebels against God? Shall she go to hell because she is married to a man who is going there? NEVER!

I have seen more confusion on this subject in America

than on the mission fields. We have so much head knowledge and so little heart knowledge. Oh, that we would be led by the Spirit of God! I do not mean that women should rule their husbands or rebel against them, or lord it over them because their husbands are spiritually weak. But a woman must take her stand for God, that by her godly behavior she can win her husband. How will you be able to save someone out of the mire and the swamp if you jump into it with him? You must stand on the firm ground and pull him out.

The other side of the subject is just as important: "HUSBANDS LOVE YOUR WIVES, even as Christ also loved the church and gave himself for it" (Ephesians 5:25). This is the Scripture the women love. We have been reading how the woman should submit to her husband, and this is all that the Bible asks a woman to do. Do you know, it is strange that Paul never tells a woman to LOVE her husband? He only tells her to submit to him. A great command is given to the husband when he is told to LOVE his wife like Christ loved the church and gave himself for it. When a woman has a husband who loves her like that, she will gladly be his "love-slave." She will do everything for him. If women could find husbands who love them like Christ loves the church they would be overwhelmed by this kind of love. I know there are many men who truly love their wives, but the kind of love Paul is writing about is beyond the natural love. It is the love that Christ has for the church, that great overwhelming, sacrificial love of a bridegroom for his bride. Oh, how Christ longs for and yearns over His bride! This is the love that husbands are commanded to have for their wives. It is the love of protection, provision and of sharing everything he has with her.

The last part of verse 25 says, "Husbands, love your wives as Christ gave himself for the church." The husband must "give himself" for his wife. He must give up some of himself too, some of his own ideas, his own will, his time for self, his money, etc. He cannot hold on to his stubborn will, his greedy, selfish, egocentric desires and hope to have a happy marriage. He must even share his bank account. That is the way the Lord shares with us. The Lord doesn't say, "The bank account of heaven belongs to ME alone, and *you* cannot write any checks on it." Oh no! My heavenly Bridegroom says, "Whatsoever you ask in My name, that will I do." I have written many checks on the Bank of Heaven and on my heavenly Bridegroom's account and He has acknowledged them all according to His riches in glory by Christ Jesus. Hallelujah!

Then Paul says to the husbands, "Husbands, love your wives, even as Christ also loved the church, and gave himself that he might sanctify and cleanse it." Even as Christ sanctified His bride, the church, through His priestly ministry, the husband is called upon to bear his responsibility to be the priest of the family, the intercessor before the throne of God, and the one who brings the sacrifice on behalf of the family. Like Job offered sacrifices for his family, so should a husband do the same. "Job sent and sanctified them, and rose up early in the morning and offered burnt offerings according to the number of them all: for Job said, It may be that my sons have sinned and cursed God in their hearts. Thus did Job continually" (Job 1:5). Our fathers are not travailing for the souls of their sons and daughters like they should be. Most of the time they have left the praying to the wife. God is calling the men of God to rise up and accept their place of responsibility and to help their wives to live a pure and holy life before God.

Many men feel they are competing with God for their wife's attention. This need not be. Every wife must have her sacred time alone with God and also with her husband. Sad to say that very seldom do the husbands take their wives by the hand and say, "Honey, let's pray together." Too seldom do they open the Bible and say, "Listen, I read something I would love to share with you." Most of the time the wife rarely sees her husband with his Bible open before him and almost never on his knees. No time is taken for family prayer. They have forgotten that the family that prays together, stays together. Most prayers have become a hurried, sleepy good-night prayer, and the husband only awakens in the morning to "make love" to his wife and not to his God. Because the wife is the more sensitive of the two, she soon begins to feel that strange "far from God" feeling. Her soul reaches out to commune with God and, because of her subordination, she waits for her husband to take the lead, but when he doesn't do it she feels unfulfilled. Within her is an emptiness, a discontent, and slowly she loses her respect for her priest-husband. For he is not a priest, he is only a bedmate, a slave who works to feed and clothe her. Unless the husband takes his official, God-given place as spiritual head, leading the wife as best he knows how towards the things of God, there can be no ideal marriage. To be a priest, one must offer sacrifices. God needs husbands who will be ready to make sacrifices before God and for God for the welfare and the blessings of his family.

Paul continues his exhortation to husbands by saying, "So ought men to love their wives as their own bodies. For he that loveth his wife, loveth himself. For no man ever yet hated his own flesh; but nourisheth and cherisheth it, even as the Lord the church" (Ephesians 5:28, 29). The gentleness that a man gives his own flesh, the way he protects it from hunger and harm, from heat and cold, from any kind of discomfort; the way he dresses it and perfumes it, the way he cares for it and feeds it the most delicious food, is the exact way he should care for his wife. When he buys her a lovely dress, he is buying it for himself. When he puts a diamond on her finger, he is putting it on his own. When he buys her a steak, he is feeding himself. When he protects her from a cruel tongue or a sharp criticism, he is protecting himself. She is him. When she is hurt, he is hurt. When she suffers, he suffers. This is love. She is an extension of himself.

Paul concludes his message, "For this cause shall a man leave his father and mother, and shall be joined unto his wife, and they two shall be one flesh; let everyone of you in particular so love his wife, even as himself: and the wife see that she reverence her husband" (5:31, 33). Paul is saying that a man has to break the "apron strings" with his mother. He must seek his comfort in his wife. Sure, he must still respect and honor his mother, and he can no doubt have many times of wonderful fellowship with her, but his full attention shall be towards his wife, for she is now a part of him. She is his Eve, his Woman, his "comforter." Many husband-wife relationships are destroyed because the husband cannot make that final break with his mother. The wife is irritated because of mother-in-law interference. The marriage begins to disintegrate.

Marriage is the building of a new relationship. Each family is an institution in itself. It will take all the love and effort that we can give it. Many sacrifices will have to be made. Marriage is like a mighty oak tree that grows from a sapling that has been planted on the wedding day. It takes time for it to grow into beauty and strength. The sun shines upon it and the winter snows fall on it. Sometimes it is covered in sheets of ice and a branch may break off, even a strong bough may give under its weight. A stroke of lightning may strike it, but by the grace and goodness of God it becomes more beautiful with age. The birds rest in it and the children play under it. The lovers romance in its shade. The roots grow deeper with time and its grandeur is spoken of by all who pass by. This is what a marriage of love should be. It should grow more precious and beautiful with every passing year. It was planted by God, this institution of marriage, in the Garden of Eden when God created Woman out of the innermost being of Adam and brought her to him on that first wedding day. "The mountains and the hills broke forth before them into singing and all the trees of the field clapped their hands," as creation joined in worship and praise in that FIRST GRAND WEDDING MARCH.

Chapter 14
LOVE IS ETERNAL

If you are wearing a wedding ring, take it off your finger and look at it for a moment. It does not have a beginning or end; it portrays "eternal" love. There is LIFE in love.

John, in 1 John 3:14 says, "We know that we have passed from death unto life, because we love the brethren. He that loveth not his brother abideth in death." This is a beautiful Scripture. It gives us the key to everlasting life. Love is LIFE. We are under the sentence of death because of sin. John says, however, that if we have love the sentence of death is cancelled and we have passed from the state of death sentence into the state of eternal life. He also says that if we don't have love we are still under the law of death. We may say we are saved and declare that we are born again and brag about our eternal life, but if we don't have love we do not have life, because LOVE and LIFE are linked together and can never ever be separated. As long as we don't have love, we are living under the sentence of death. When we have entered into eternal life, we have that eternal circle that never stops. That is why you wear a wedding ring. It is the token of a never-ending love, the symbol of eternal love. Love is eternal because it flows out of an eternal God whose love is eternal.

Love is not only a virtue of God, it is the very essence of God. God is love. God is the very demonstration of love. Everything God does is motivated by love. God is everlasting because God is love and love is eternal . . . without beginning and without ending. The more you grow into the likeness and image of God, the more love you will have. You will not only have love, you will become love. In that love is the secret of the eternal life of God. It is also the secret of your own eternal life in God.

But you say, "I thought I had love when I became converted." Friend, we haven't done more than just *begun* to love when we were saved. The little bit of love we felt is like the love which a newborn baby has for its mother, whom it cannot even recognize. The love of the child for its mother must be cultivated with trust and love from the mother. It was created to love, but the mother has the power to make that love grow or to destroy it. Not only can the mother have the power to make that child's love grow towards her, the father and those who influence its life can train a child to hate its mother.

As we grow into love we come into a state of maturity and perfection that will resemble the heavenly state. This is what that full immersion of love will do in our lives. That is the reason Jesus came to earth; He came to immerse us in LOVE, to baptize us into His love. Someone said there are three baptisms: The baptism in water, as a testimony of our experience of the new birth; the baptism of the Holy Spirit and the baptism of love. We preached the *Baptism of Water;* it was the revelation given to the Anabaptists of Switzerland, and for this they suffered great tribulation. Then, at the turn of the twentieth century the truth of the *Baptism of the Holy Spirit* was renewed and the ones who followed this truth became known as Pentecostals. We are NOW ready for the *Baptism of Love.* When that which is PERFECT is come, then there is a strong possibility that it will be followed by the *Baptism of Fire!*

Love is eternal. Love hangs on! It hangs on and doesn't let go because it has the touch of God. God said to Ephraim when they were backslidden, "Oh Ephraim, how shall I give thee up?" One translation gives it, "How can I leave you, Ephraim? How can I abandon you Israel?" (Hosea 11:8).

Ephraim had made mistakes, Israel had slipped back and begun to worship idols, forsaking their God. The Almighty God cried, "I can't let you go!" He still loved them. No matter how much they had turned away from Him, He could not give them up. He could not bear the thought of losing the ones He had had such high hopes for. It was as if they were tearing out a chunk of His heart.

Have you ever loved like that? Have you ever loved with a love so great that no matter how you were treated or how many times your heart had been broken or you had been rejected, hurt, disappointed, you still couldn't let go? Then you will understand how the heart of God feels for the backslider. I am so glad that God is married to the backslider. He said in Jeremiah 3:14, "Turn, O blacksliding children, saith the Lord; for I am married unto you." God loves the one who has drifted away.

Do you have a loved one who has gone away from God? Do you have a child who once loved God, who is chasing around after the beggarly elements of the world looking for fulfilment in its filth? I want you to know there is a love that won't let go. Hallelujah for that love, that almighty love, that eternal love, that unchanging love, that love that NEVER lets go! This is the love that God wants to pour into our hearts. If we could love the world like God loves it (and that is God's plan), we could love nations to the throne of God and sinners to the foot of the cross.

What do we lack in the churches? One thing: LOVE!—the MORE EXCELLENT WAY. Our miracles have not brought the multitudes to God. It is time for us to wake up and realize that miracles have failed to bring the world to Christ. Something is missing. We must be honest. If we think we have it all, we deceive ourselves and are fools. Let us be honest with ourselves that we might reach out for the perfection that is to be found in Christ's pure love. May God give us the love that will give us the strength to not let go until the last harvest has been brought in. This was the kind of love that Ruth had.

It was love in the heart of that beautiful Moabitish woman that compelled her to say some of the most beautiful words ever spoken, "Intreat me not to leave thee, or to return from following after thee: for whither thou goest, I will go: and where thou lodgest, I will lodge: thy people shall be my people, and thy God my God: Where thou diest, will I die, and there will I be buried: the Lord do so to me, and more also, if ought but death part thee and me" (Ruth 1:16, 17).

Ruth knew nothing about the laws of the love-slave. She had been born in a land where she worshipped idols. But the laws of the love-slave were written upon the walls of her heart. And there on the road to Judea as she was standing and trying to take leave of her mother-in-law, Naomi, and watching her sister-in-law, Orpah, turning and going back to her home, she faced the greatest decision of her life. Naomi was saying, "Ruth, you might as well go home to your people. I don't have anything to offer you. I don't have anything to give you. I am only a beggar. That is all I will ever be, and when I get back to Bethlehem, I will have to beg. The family has died; there is nobody to take care of me. I cannot give you a husband or a home. I cannot guarantee you a pension or a ministry. I will have to sleep by the side of the road." There was no rosy-tinted security with possibilities of advancement. There was only shame, disgrace and failure. She knew that the people who had known her would shake their heads at her and mock her. The way of obedience is the HARD road, but it is the RIGHT road. For if we do not OBEY the Holy Spirit, we will GRIEVE the Holy Spirit because we are not LED by the Holy Spirit and we will miss HIM forever.

I can see Ruth standing there at the crossroads of decision that day. Oh, how many times I have had to stand at the crossroads where I, too, have had to make up my mind! It is not easy. It is hard. In that hour only the greatest LOVE can win. You will follow the ONE you love the most. I hope that ONE is God!

Here is this young woman who has a love which is not

natural. If it had been the love of a woman for her husband or her own mother, it would be easier to understand; but this was her mother-in-law. She did not need to feel any sense of responsibility toward her. There were no blood relationships such as the commandment of God, "Honour thy father and mother." But she had a love for her that was not after the law. It was a love after the SPIRIT of God . . . a love that was put in her heart by the Holy Spirit because HE was going to bring her into a new land and into a new life. He was going to make her the possessor of the line and lineage of Jesus Christ —one of the ancestors of the Lord.

How did she come into this honor and glory, this little heathen woman who had prayed to idols all her life? How did she come into such great honor and glory? *Love* made her worthy—a love that wouldn't permit her to let go, a love that didn't fail, that hung on, a love that gave her the strength to leave her family, her people and her country to go into a new and strange land from which she could never return, and live with a new people whose ways and customs were completely different from hers. Love sent her out and love qualified her to the glory of a high and holy calling; and if God does not promote you, no one can.

"Intreat me not to leave thee, or to return from following after thee: for whither thou goest, I will go." I can picture that young woman. All she could see in front of her was days and weeks and years of wandering. "Whither thou goest, I will go! Where thou lodgest, I will lodge: Your people shall be my people." It wasn't easy, because the Moabites and Israelites were deadly enemies. Their customs were different, their ways of thinking were different, everything was different. But love gave her the strength to make the change. God's grace is only given to you according to the Love that is in your heart. You cannot become a devoted servant to God and leave all the things you love behind unless you love Him with all your heart.

Sixteen years ago I had to make that decision in my life. I had been a missionary all my adult life, but I had never made many sacrifices. As far as comforts are concerned, I had it pretty easy. I had a nice apartment, furniture, a new piano, a hi-fi, a comfortable bed and an air conditioner. I even had a nice, new car. Besides that I had three precious sons. And . . . I had the call of God, that strange, unexplainable call that I had been born to fulfil. I was like Ruth, standing at the crossroads of my life. I knew I had to fulfil the purpose of my birth.

Night after night I didn't go to bed. I lay on the hardwood floor and cried out to God until the early morning hours. I fasted and wept. It was not hard to lose the furniture or the apartment, and not even the car and beautiful new piano; but the thing that was hard, was to know that there would be times I would have to be separated from my children. Tommy the youngest was almost four years of age. Danny was seven and David was nine. I loved my sons. I had waited ten years for the first one. They were *real special.* Only my God knows of the terrible struggle, the agony of the soul, the hot tears, the aching heart. . . . Heaven has kept the record, I cannot go into the depths of it. This is not the time to tell it all. I tried to reason it out the natural way. I said, "No! I can't leave my sons; I have waited ten years for them. They are MY boys. They need ME. They are MY responsibility. God has given them to ME. *I* have to bring them up." And God was patient, even though the time was running out.

One day as I was drying the dishes God asked me, "Gwen, are you willing to let your sons go to hell?" It was such a shocking question that I stopped what I was doing and cried out to God, "No, God! Never! I love my boys! How can You ask me such a terrible question?" God answered me, "My child, do you think I want to see My sons and daughters around the world go to hell?" It was as if I saw the heart of God. But still I could not make that total surrender that I knew God was waiting for, and more time was running out.

Every Saturday I used to "play" with my boys. I took them to the beach or to some special playground. We packed a lunch and climbed a high mountain, or drove around the island. It was our fun-time together. One Saturday as I was at the beach with them and we had come to the close of the day, I called them to come out of the water and took Tommy to a little shelter to dress him. Suddenly some Chinese boys who were playing there came running to me crying, "Your son is drowned." I felt my legs turn weak. As fast as possible I ran to where they were pointing. I was told to climb the lookout tower where the life guards who are stationed at the beach sit and watch the swimmers. I remember how my legs felt paralyzed and didn't want to climb up the stairs. My heart was panting. I did not even know which boy it was who had drowned—David or Danny—until I saw David running towards me. Then I knew it was my Danny-boy. For a certain reason he has always been special to me. From the time he was only two years old, if he saw me crying he cried with me. If because of grieving I could not eat, he didn't want to eat either. I used to sit and play and sing, "Oh, Danny-boy, the pipes, the pipes are calling, . . ." that beautiful Scottish song with the Londonderry tune, and the tears rolled down my cheeks. And now, my Danny boy, five years old, they told me was drowned.

When I reached the top of the tower, I saw him lying there, rolled in a brown army blanket. He was stiff and still, his skin was the color of death. I fell on my knees beside him and cried out, "Oh, God!" It was as if that cry reached the throne room of God, Danny opened his eyes and looked at me with his cute little crooked smile. God had been merciful. He had given my Danny back to me. I said, "Lord, I'll do Your work." And I did—for three months. And then I changed my mind and said, "I cannot go again!" and I stayed with my boys, and still more time was running out.

And then God spoke again.

One Sunday afternoon I was standing and preaching in one of our churches in the country area of the British colony of Hong Kong. There was a river behind the church. It was a dirty, filthy thing that had not flowed for over a year because we had suffered severe drought for almost a year. The entire river had become stagnant. There was a toilet built out over it and this was used by over one hundred school children who attended the school we had in the church building. Besides that, all the dead pigs and chickens were thrown into it. I had noticed the river that day in a special way because I had brought my youngest son Tommy with me, and the thought flashed into my mind that he could fall into the river. But there was a page-wire fence between the yard and the river, so I believed that this would keep him out of danger. While I was preaching, he sat on the front seat and I had my eyes on him. After a while he got tired and wandered out of the building and over to the swings. I continued preaching, keeping my eye out the window, seeing him playing at the swing. As I continued into the message I forgot about him for a while. The Chinese pastor had a lot of children and I was sure they would watch out for him.

Then, suddenly some of them came running into the church excitedly yelling my name and screaming, "Tommy is drowning!" I remember the sinking feeling as I laid my Bible on the pulpit and together with the whole church ran out to the river. There he was! All I could see in the black filth and the green slime was his little face, covered with stinking filth. His blonde hair was black. He was looking at me with big, blue desperate eyes, his hands trying to reach out to us. I screamed to the pastor, "Save him!" in Chinese. The pastor jumped into the river, shoes on and all. He grabbed hold of one of those outstretched hands and pulled him to the shore. I grabbed hold of Tommy and hugged him. My white preaching frock that I always wore was covered with the smelly filth, but I didn't care. One of the sisters said, "We must pray for him. If he has swallowed any of that stuff, he will die." We began to pray and call on God. I had heard many stories of other Chinese children falling into that kind of cesspool and they had almost always died, or else they had spinal meningitis, or some other terrible disease that had crippled them for life. One such boy who had the same accident about the same time and was saved out alive, immediately developed a fever and became deaf and dumb and blind and crippled permanently.

God had saved Tommy that far. We gave him two baths, the pastor's wife gave me some of her children's clean clothes to put on him. We got in the car and started back home. Before we ever reached the city of Kowloon, he already had a fever. I laid him on the bed and prayed for him. I tried to give him a bowl of soup to eat, but he couldn't eat it. That night he was a very sick little boy. My Chinese servant said, "Call a doctor." But I cast myself on God and fell at his bed and prayed. "Oh, God, Why? Why? Why?" It was a prayer I didn't need to pray. But I did, and God spoke again. He spoke with another question, "Now, My daughter, do you still insist on taking care of your children, or will you let ME do it?" I knew that time had run out. This was my last chance. If I did not surrender to God and commit my family into His care, if I did not put my hand to the plow and stop looking back, I myself would cause the death of my children. But if I would let God have His way, He would care for them like He had cared for Samuel in his childhood and He would be responsible for their every need. It was not easy. Sometimes I had to leave them for many months. I was criticized by Christians and by missionaries. I was lied about by those who were even closer to me than a brother or neighbor. But I knew that if I did ever look back, I would pay a greater price. Time *had* run out. There was no turning back! God had to have first place in my heart!

I will always remember one time when I again had to leave them to go for a preaching tour. It was extra hard that time. I knew I would be staying away longer than usual. That day I happened to read the writings of India's great poet, Rabindranath Tagore:

> I am only waiting for love to give myself up
> at last into His hands. That is why it is so late
> and why I have been guilty of such omissions.
>
> They come with their laws and their codes
> to bind me fast; but I evade them ever, for I

am only waiting for love to give myself up at last into His hands.

As I read those words, I knew God was speaking to me. He was telling me that I, too, needed that GREATER love for Him. It was only as I loved Him in a GREATER way than I loved my children, that I could fulfil this call. I knelt by my bed and prayed with tears running down my cheeks, "Oh, God, help me to love You more; for only in the strength of that love can I accept this cross." And He met my need.

It is only as you have that GREATER LOVE for God that you can serve Him perfectly. Anything less than that is only another vocation in life. This is the love that will take you through when the going gets hard, when your family calls you to come back home, when the devil is sending his messengers to buffet and hinder you, and everyone says you are wrong. It is the love that will take you through prison for Christ and fire for God. It will be there when you stand all alone, unloved and unwanted by mortals who cannot understand your burden or vision. It will drive you out of a comfortable house unto a lonely hut on some missionary field. It is a love greater than the love of mortals. George Matteson captured the depths of this great love after the woman he loved and was engaged to be married to gave him up. He had been blinded through some misfortune and he said to her, "Beloved, when you promised to marry me, I could see. But now I have lost my eyes, and I want to let you have the opportunity of withdrawing from your promise to marry me." She accepted this offer. His heart was broken, but he turned to God and in the hour of his agony he wrote the great words of this immortal hymn:

OH, LOVE THAT WILT NOT LET ME GO

> O Love that wilt not let me go,
> I rest my weary soul in Thee;
> I give Thee back the life I owe,
> That in Thine ocean depths its flow
> May richer, fuller be.

O Light that followest all my way,
I yield my flickering torch to Thee;
My heart restores its borrowed ray,
That in Thy sunshine's blaze its day
May brighter, fairer be.

O Joy that seekest me through pain,
I cannot close my heart to Thee;
I trace the rainbow through the rain,
And feel the promise is not vain
That morn shall tearless be.

O Cross that liftest up my head,
I dare not ask to fly from Thee;
I lay in dust life's glory dead,
And from the ground there blossoms red
Life that shall endless be.

This is the wonderful love of God that won't let go, that holds on tight and even when our ways do not always please Him, loves us still. Yes, He loves us still because it is that eternal love.

Chapter 15
LOVE IS IN THE SPIRIT

"The love of God is shed abroad in our hearts by the Holy Ghost which is given unto us" (Romans 5:5). The Living Word says, "God has given us the Holy Spirit to fill our hearts with His love."

That is why we need the Holy Spirit. We need all of the Holy Spirit, in full measure. There is God-love, brotherly love and sexual love. Brother love is God-given and godly love is eternal. The God-love will go on into eternity. You possessed it back in the beginning before you were born. This eternal God-love will continue on forever. You will never lose it. After you leave this mortal life it still goes right on. The other love, the sexual love, which is God's gift to us temporarily — while we are here on earth — is a beautiful thing and a very powerful thing. It sometimes is more overwhelming than any other love. But it will have to be left behind with our bodies. Our spiritual body cannot take that love with us into the regions of tomorrow. Therefore it is so important that we understand how we should love. We must be careful to not be overwhelmed with a temporary love which we will discard with the decaying of our flesh. Let us make sure that the love we have for another is the eternal love that will keep on through eternity because it is that love that lives forever. No matter how we are treated, that love will continue to be shed abroad in our hearts.

Colossians 1:8, "Who have also declared unto us your love in the Spirit." Because love is a spiritual thing it cannot die, for it belongs to the spiritual realm. When you love someone with the love of God, no matter how they treat you, you will go on loving them just like God goes on loving you, no matter how you have treated Him. Can God stop loving you? No matter how you act, He will go right on loving you. You haven't been worthy of His love. You have mistreated it, abused it, discarded it, rejected it; you have dragged God's love through the muck and mire and God goes right on loving you and saying, "How can I let you go?" His heart is still wedded in love to the one who is backslidden and has drifted away. No matter how men have treated Him, He has loved them. And if HE can do that, then we can do it when He is living in our heart.

I want to warn you to never let one tiny fleck of hatred come into your heart. For hatred is satanic. Love is godly and holy. You must give God a heart that is pure and clean. He looks right through your heart and He sees everything that is in it: malice, grudges, bitterness. It would be an unworthy thing to give a heart with any darkness in it to Jesus. Give Him a perfect heart, a gift that is perfected through love.

I have been amazed at the love in some people's hearts. How strong it is! No matter how they have been scoffed at, or discouraged, they still go on loving that same person day after day and year after year. And that love doesn't make them bitter, it makes them more beautiful because love is something that makes you beautiful, for it comes from God. It is a stream flowing through you. It is a current from heaven, and that is why it is beautiful. It makes an ugly person beautiful and it makes an old person feel young again.

Why? Because God is eternally youthful and God is love. When God flows His love through you it takes the lines out of your face; it gives you a glow! The inspiration of a new love makes you radiant. It makes a seventy-seven-year-old man feel like he is twenty-seven years old. It has happened many times and the world looks on and snickers because it does not understand.

How can love rejuvenate? Because there is youth in love.

And why is there youth in love? Because there is life in love, and life gives life. God doesn't get old. It is true He has lived the longest of us all, but He is eternally young. God has the secret of youth within himself, the secret that mankind has searched for through the centuries of the past, which has eluded him because he thought to find it externally when all the time it lies within. God is love. That is the secret of youth. It is in love that we are reborn, renewed, rejuvenated.

And yet so many are afraid to love because they once loved and were hurt. And as they put that cold, hard shell around their hearts they say, "I will not love again. Not me! I have learned my lesson! This is the last time! I'm not going to be a fool again! No other woman is going to hurt me!" Oh yes, we have done things to protect ourselves and we have harmed our own soul. It is wrong NOT to love, because you were *created* by a God of *love* in an *act* of love, to be an *object* of love and a *vehicle* of love.

Love must be more than physical attraction. Physical attraction will pass with the passing of time. The body loses its shape, the hair grows thin and the teeth fall out. The skin begins to wrinkle and the twinkling eyes are covered with glasses. Yet, love that is born of the spirit lives on. Death claims your beloved and the grave covers him; all you have left is a memory and still love lives on, because love is born of the spirit. Neither old age nor sickness or loss of youth and death can interrupt or destroy that great gift of love. The harmony still remains between the spirits, though one is in heaven and the other is on earth. And prayer brings them together at the throne of God where they can meet.

Oh, the beautiful harmony of love! It is the duet of the soul, the celestial song of the Spirit. "For they shall see eye to eye ... break forth into joy, sing together" (Isaiah 52:8, 9). Love is the melody of heaven. You do not need to say a word, you don't need to put a tune to it, it is already a song. And the music flows out of the heart that is full of love. When we are knit together we have perfect, beautiful harmony in a song that knows no barrier of time or space.

Years ago I was in a fine restaurant having dinner one evening. I looked across at a table near me and saw something that brought tears to my eyes. There were a man and woman sitting at the table whom I would have guessed must have been in their thirties. The man's fingers were all missing. I saw how she had to help him with his food and serve him. But what fascinated me was the tremendous look of love in their eyes for each other. He was trying to hold hands with her, but he had no hands. He was touching her hands with the stub of his hand, and she was caressing the stub of his hand. I had to bow my head and look away. It was too sacred a scene for mortal eyes to gaze upon. I think he might have lost his hands in Vietnam, they looked like they might have been shot off. Later, as we stood up to leave, I went to their table and put one hand on each of their shoulders and said, "You are a beautiful couple. It is a very lovely thing to see the wonderful love that you have for each other. Don't ever lose it." They looked at me and smiled, "Thank you." Then he stood up and added, "What a beautiful thing for you to come and say to us." As I was walking back to the car, I knew that I had "heard" the most beautiful love song, for love is music. Love is harmony. Love is beautiful, even though the hands are shot off and the fingers are missing. There is a caress of love that can be felt even through the stub of a hand.

Chapter 16
LOVE IS A BREASTPLATE AND PROTECTION

1 Thessalonians 5:8, "Let us, who are of the day, be sober, putting on the breastplate of faith and love." Notice how the Holy Spirit dovetails faith and love together! If a man has love for his wife, she will have faith in him. She will not worry because he has to take Mrs. Jones home from church. She knows that he is going to finally deliver all the ladies in the neighborhood home from church and then come straight home to her. She has absolute faith in him. She will love. If she doubts his love, then faith gets pretty shaky. And love and faith are woven together to make a breastplate.

What is a breastplate for? Webster's dictionary defines it as "a metal plate worn as defensive armor for the breast, a vestment worn in ancient times by a Jewish high priest and with twelve stones bearing the names of the tribes of Israel; thirdly it is a piece against which the workman presses his breast in operating a breast-drill or similar tool." So you see the breastplate has many uses.

Worn over the flowing robes of yesterday's styles, it held the garment in. It gives a good, firm grip around the heart. It lifts your heart up and makes you feel secure and strong. It is a source of strength from within. Faith and love also are a source of strength from within.

When worn by the priest over his heart, it was a constant reminder of the twelve tribes of Israel for which he was responsible. He could never get them off his heart. Love is a breastplate that constantly reminds us to be faithful in love to those whom God has put in our care. Wherever we go, we carry them in our hearts. We bear the responsibility of not only our family and loved ones, but the nations of the world. I carry in my heart many nations.

Then, the breastplate is a protection from attacks that come from without the body. There are all kinds of attacks that Satan would try to put upon your beautiful heart. But the one who has love carries the breastplate over his heart, and the man who loves his wife completely won't even be tempted to fall in love with the most beautiful woman in the world, for he is wearing a shield over his heart. This is the shield of the love that he and his wife have for each other. But just let that shield fall away and any "Delilah" could trip him up. That is why no third person can easily "break up a marriage." If the wife mistreats her husband continually and the love is lost, then it is easy for him to fall in love with somebody else. Or if the husband constantly mistreats his wife and she begins to lose hope and faith in her husband, then she might fall in love with somebody else, for the heart is made to love. But NO third person can come between a love where the two are knit together because both carry a shield over their hearts.

The breastplate is an armor of defense. Paul calls us to put on the breastplate of FAITH AND LOVE. It will protect the heart from all dangerous weapons of destruction that are aimed against us. We need to understand more fully the protection that is ours through love. We live in a fallen world. It is fallen because it is full of hate. It will never be restored by miracles. It will only be restored by love. When love again covers the earth it will be the restoration of all things. Beloved, we are living in an earth that is full of hate. Every sin is a selfish act. It is an act either of hate or of self-love, and so we need protection every moment. There is only one protection from the spirit of hate and that protection is LOVE. It was for this reason that Jesus told us in Matthew 5:43, 44, "Ye have heard that it hath been said, Thou shalt love thy neighbour, and hate thine enemy. But I say unto you, Love your enemies, bless them that curse you, do good to them that hate you, and pray for them which despitefully use you, and persecute you."

The Lord knew that we needed protection from hate Hate, even when it is not spoken out, sends out arrows of evil. You can feel hate from a distance halfway around the world. I have felt the hate that has been directed against me by people on the other side of the globe. They didn't need to write me any letters to tell me how they felt about me. I could feel it. How terrible it felt! Then, how much more terrible and strong are these arrows when they are within our reach, when they are right in our home or our churches. How terrible it is when one sister hates the other sister who is sitting across the aisle from her, and all through the worship service she sends her arrows of hate in her direction. Or an elder or deacon hates the pastor and directs those demonic vibrations of hate towards the man of God while he is ministering. Is it any wonder that our churches are dead and dying in many parts of the world? It is a dangerous thing to give yourself to strife and anger or hate, because just as there is a Creator of LOVE, there is a creator of these negative spirits that can possess a man's soul. The Creator of LOVE is God and the creator of hate and all negations is Satan.

We cannot allow any hate to come into our hearts. Not even the tiniest black, wicked seed of it, because when we do, we have a seed of Satan in us and every seed will bear its fruit. Do not be deceived! For when you have this seed of evil in your heart, not only will that sister suffer but you yourself will become a messenger of evil, and you yourself will suffer more than she. Not only will you suffer, but by feeding your thoughts of hate to someone else you can cause their destruction and death. I know a woman who had been a dear friend to me. She had helped me by opening doors of ministry to me. But through the influence of someone who strongly hated me, she turned against me and began to speak openly against me. It was a shock, but I left her with God who is my Judge. Not long after that she died of cancer. The one who hated me could live with hate, but not the one that had been stirred up against me and turned against me. It killed her.

When you have this seed of hate in your heart, you are giving Satan fertile ground to plant the awful tares of destruction that are destroying the world, churches, families and friends. Do not be an agent of the evil one. Refuse to be used by the devil! When you give the Lord your heart, you must give Him the kind of heart that He will accept. The only kind of heart that He can accept is a pure, clean heart. He cannot make His home in an evil abode. Many times I have prayed and wept before God, when I have heard that evil had been spoken against me. All I can say is this, that I have had to cover my heart from those terrible arrows of destruction with love. That is the only protection I have, because the evil that comes from the enemy comes from Satan, and the only breastplate I have is the breastplate of FAITH AND LOVE. If I try to fight hate with hate I would be as evil as they. Often I have wept before God, "Lord, give me a perfect heart! One that is perfect and clean and full of love. Oh, God, let no hate take root in my heart!"

I know it is only love that can keep my heart pure and wash all hate away. It is His Blood that covers my sins, and His love that makes me clean, and it is love that keeps me clean. We must have the weapon of the breastplate of FAITH AND LOVE constantly over our hearts.

This is a day when evil will increase. Those whom God sees are worthy will be chosen out as the elect, and then they will be hated by those who are not in the elect; and if we are not careful we will take the weapons of law, which Jesus referred to in Matthew 5:43 ("Thou shalt hate thine enemy") and think we are doing the will of God. Do you realize that many Christians live by this law? They actually *hate* their enemy! You cannot get into the Kingdom like that. When you hate like that, your heart is unprotected and the evil darts of hate will pierce your heart and you will start to hate back and fall to the low level of your enemy.

When you love, you carry a shield—a breastplate—at ALL times. The arrows of hate will strike your shield and turn right around and return with twice the force to the one who sent them out. That is why God says, "He that hateth his brother abideth in death" (1 John 3:14). When you send out hate, you are putting the arrow of death in your own heart.

Exodus 23:4, 5 says, "If thou meet thine enemy's ox or ass going astray, thou shalt surely bring it back to him. If thou see the ass of him that hateth thee lying under his burden, and wouldst forbear to help him, thou shalt surely help with him." If God would have been speaking to this generation, He would have said, "If you notice your enemy is having car trouble or a flat tire, you should surely help him fix his flat." Most of us would say, "Ha, ha, that serves him right! God is judging him!" God wants us to serve those who hate us. If we live like that we will be living by the law of the angels.

Everyone has an angel, even the most wicked person on earth; the blasphemer, the one who mocks God or denies His existence, has an angel. Hitler had an angel; Mao Tse Tung, Stalin, Judas, Haman (and we could name a few of our day) all had a guardian angel. The angel was dispatched to them at birth and left them at death. Sadhu Sundar Singh and other great saints have seen visions of how the angels of man have fought with demons who came to take the souls of those whom the angels have accompanied in their life's pilgrimage, and how that soul could rightfully be claimed by the demons because that person had served them in his life. He saw how the angels had to stand back, weeping, and allow the demons to carry that soul to hell's everlasting judgment. And the angel was helpless. Oh, how the angel loved that vile and cruel and wicked man! He wept as he saw it going to judgment. Such wonderful love! Do you think it is easy for the angel to stand in attendance by these dark, filthy souls, to behold their bestiality and sexual orgies as perverse demons take control of their bodies to the dishonoring of their own bodies.

How do you think the angels feel when they see the unclean spirits of today possessing two men or two women who burn in lust one toward another, committing shameful acts? How the angels must grieve when they see God giving these, whom they have loved since their baby-innocence, over to a reprobate mind! And can you picture for a moment the angels of these men raping little boys and girls and then murdering them? You say, "Why doesn't the angel kill him then and there?" Because they have not been given the authority to kill, only to love. Neither have we been given the authority to kill . . . only to LOVE.

There *are* the angels of destruction, and there *is* the angel of death. He went out through Egypt on Passover night, and they will work their work only at God's command. Many are now standing in readiness to attack this evil generation and may God have mercy on us on that day! But until that day, those guardian angels of love never fail to stand by the soul of the one that they have been appointed by God to watch over. Moreover, that angel never fails to love that one. That is why, when we were still in sin and living in wickedness, the angels continued to protect us. Some of you know that you would no longer be alive had an angel not protected you. If someone would have said to you in those days of your evil life, "An angel is watching over you," you would have mocked and said, "What is an angel?" Some of you may even have said, "I'd rather have a devil!" So low had you sunk; yet the angel never left you. The angel was never rewarded for the good they did for you. They never even got a "thank-you" from the one they protected; instead they were reviled and grieved, but their ministry continued on and on. That is why God says, "Help your enemy when he is in trouble."

If you have an enemy, you are blessed because you now have an opportunity to prove what you REALLY are. Many have enemies. Jesus had many! Let us ask God to show us some good things we can do for our enemy. This will have a good effect.

Proverbs 24:17 says, "Rejoice not when thine enemy

falleth, and let not thine heart be glad when he stumbleth [is overthrown]." It is possible to get a fiendish delight out of seeing God allow someone to be destroyed. Look at David! He did not rejoice when his enemy was destroyed in battle. That is why David's son Solomon could write these words of wisdom. He had been taught by a wise and godly father. They are passed on to us for our admonition. If your enemy is sick in the hospital, visit that one, bringing them flowers. God will honour you for it. If you cannot visit them, send them a card. Show mercy in the hour when God judges, unless God has commanded you to silence! Then all you can do is pray and send your unspoken love to them.

Proverbs 25:21, 22 says, "If thine enemy be hungry, give him bread to eat; and if he be thirsty, give him water to drink: for thou shalt heap coals of fire upon his head, and the Lord shall reward thee." Isn't that a beautiful Scripture! You may say, "But my enemy is richer than I. He doesn't need bread." But there is some "bread" which you can give him which he doesn't have, or he wouldn't hate you. There is some water he doesn't have—even the waters of life and love. He hasn't eaten the bread of love, which is the bread of life, nor drunk the water of life, which is the water of love. There must be some way you can reach your enemy. God told us to do it. Pray and ask the Lord, for there is a special blessing upon you promised by God if you will obey this law of love. The best thing to do is to obey the law of love. The most perfect way of destroying your enemy is to make him your friend. But if this is not possible and he will not be changed, then keep out of his way but love him, always love him, for love always conquers. Do you know that some of the greatest battles on earth were lost because they were fought with hate? Hitler had the power to take the world, but he went to battle without love. That is why the multitudes of Germany's fine young men died in vain—they followed a Führer who did not have pure love.

In Pakistan when the war broke out against India, the people shouted, "We will destroy India!" I myself remember seeing signs all over West Pakistan when I was there a little earlier that read, "CRUSH INDIA!" I felt the hatred which Pakistan had for India, their brother. Once they had been one nation, and so they still are brothers. Their relatives live just across the border a few miles away. It is like East and West Germany. When the war started there was so much anger and hatred. I had also been in India about the same time. While there, I had not felt this same demonic spirit of hate toward Pakistan. I marvelled at the difference. India is largely Hindu, and Pakistan is Moslem. I wondered if that made the difference.

I remember one day while in Delhi I went to the Pakistani embassy. Something very special was happening there and I wanted to find out what was going on. One of the men working for the Pakistani embassy had been sympathetic toward East Pakistan, which was now being called Bangladesh. Because of his sympathy, he and his wife and children were going to walk out of the embassy. He had just got out when they grabbed him and pulled him back in. They seized his wife and daughters by the hair; they too were pulled in, screaming. Two of his boys escaped. They began to beat this man, his wife, and girls. This was publicized all over India by the newspapers and radio. The people clamored for the man to be permitted his freedom. Great crowds gathered around the embassy. They carried banners and shouted, "We are living in a free world, let that man and family go free!" In the midst of all this confusion, I noticed an Indian holy man sitting and praying. I asked him, "What are you doing here?"

He answered, "I have no political opinions, but my heart is full of pity for this man. He is a man like myself, and his children are crying for their parents, and so I am fasting and praying outside the gate for this man." He was a Hindu. What was his motive? Love. How many of us Christians have that much love in our hearts?

I saw a wonderful thing happen in Hindu India. I saw them doing the works of Jesus. Bangladesh (formerly known as East Pakistan) had also been their enemy. They, too, had hated India, but when the war between West and East Pakistan broke out, the people of East Pakistan were in danger of being annihilated. Their suffering was beyond all description. In their desperation they fled to their "enemy" India for refuge. And India took them in, all ten million of them. When they saw their need and that they were being killed by the West Pakistani soldiers, they had mercy on them and opened their land to them and made a home for them and even fed them, in spite of the fact that India herself was poor and had not enough for her own. A Hindu nation did the works of Jesus Christ, while America stood in the Bay of Bengal with her naval fleet ready to go to war but slow to give mercy.

"When the Son of man shall come in his glory, and all the holy angels with him, then shall he sit upon the throne of his glory: And before him shall be gathered all nations: and he shall separate them one from another, as a shepherd divideth his sheep from the goats: And he shall set the sheep on his right hand, but the goats on the left. Then shall the King say unto them on his right hand, Come, ye blessed of my Father, inherit the kingdom prepared for you from the foundation of the world: FOR I WAS AN HUNGRED, AND YE GAVE ME MEAT: I WAS THIRSTY, AND YE GAVE ME DRINK: I WAS A STRANGER, AND YE TOOK ME IN: NAKED AND YE CLOTHED ME: I WAS SICK AND YE VISITED ME: I WAS IN PRISON, AND YE CAME UNTO ME. . . . INASMUCH AS YE HAVE DONE IT UNTO ONE OF THE LEAST OF THESE MY BRETHREN, YE HAVE DONE IT UNTO ME" (Matthew 25:31-36, 40b).

God blessed India so mightily for the deed she had done when she took in those refugees, that when she had to go to war with Pakistan she won a tremendous victory. In thirteen days she completely defeated Pakistan and took 94 thousand Pakistani soldiers captive. The final soldiers she captured were the great warriors of the Pathan tribes, which no man could conquer. Even Alexander the Great could hardly defeat them. And not only that, but in the following year, India had a bounteous crop and harvest like never before. She said, "We can feed our own people now."

God's Word is true; if you bless your enemy you will be blessed. If you want a blessing, then turn and bless the man who hates you. How can you bless them? By loving them in return for hate. When those vibrations of hate come toward you, just open your heart to the Holy Spirit and let Him fill it with the Love of God. Worship the Lord and say, "I love You, Lord. I love you, my enemy. I bless you, my enemy. I pray for you." You will bring down the glory of God on yourself. That glory is your protection. It will save you from all the fiery darts of the evil one.

Psalm 145:20 says, "The Lord preserveth all them that love him." Here we see that preservation of life is promised to those who have love. If we look back into history we not only see men like Hitler and those of Pakistan lose wars, we also see men who had great power defeated by a holy woman who knew how to fast and pray: Esther.

Haman was known for his wickedness. His hard heart was not only filled with hatred to Mordecai who refused to bow to him, but to all of the Jews; and he sought to destroy all the Jews who were throughout the whole kingdom of Ahasuerus because they were the people of Mordecai. He had the authority of the king behind him. He was the mightiest man in the Media-Persian Empire. But his heart was hate-controlled, while Esther's heart was full of love. She loved her people so much that she was ready to die for them. She not only fasted and prayed for three days, but she said, "If I perish, I perish." Jesus said that if we have love, we will be ready to lay down our lives for our friends. "Greater love hath no man than this, that a man lay down his life for his friends" (John 15:13).

Esther had that kind of love. She was not only willing to lose her throne but also to be killed in her attempt to save her people. In the courts of the Medes and Persians there was a great and mighty conflict going on between two tremendous powers. The one was the power of hate in that demon-possessed Haman (and hate always murders; you can't hate anyone without having murder in your heart). John said, "Whosoever hateth his brother is a murderer:" (1 John 3:15). For the fruit of hate is murder. The other power that was evident in the mighty empire was love. The love in the heart of one young woman, the love that meant grief and pain and heartache for her nation, the love that was so great she pushed her food away to fast, was a love that wouldn't let go. It was a sacrificial love that enabled her to risk her life for her people.

Do you know what your nation needs? It needs ONE HEART as full of love as Esther's. ONE PERSON who wears the breastplate of faith and love. Just ONE. Not a great miracle-worker or multitudes who profess, but ONE who possesses. Love is our greatest protection from hate.

The *Bild Zeitung* of Germany had a story in its December 4, 1973 edition that I will never forget. It read, "MAN KILLS HIMSELF WITH A HEAVY HAMMER."

"Zurich 4. Dezember: When a woman in Zurich told her angry, raging husband that she had had enough of his ranting and raving and that she was going to leave him with her three children, he struck her with a heavy sledge-hammer, knocking her down. When he wanted to strike her again, he brought the hammer back up with such a mighty force that it struck him on the forehead, cracking his skull. He was immediately dead."

This is what hate and uncontrolled anger will do. It will destroy the very one who gives himself over to that evil power.

Pater Pio

Out of Italy comes the amazing story of Pater Pio, a holy

priest, who for forty-nine years bore on his body the marks of crucifixion. During these years people came from all over the world to be prayed for by this man of God, for the Lord had given him a ministry of healing the sick and the brokenhearted.

Not only did multitudes love and revere him, he also had a large number of enemies. From the story of his life, written by Karl Wagner, Vienna, Austria, I would like to include the following, which I have translated from its original German:

"Every person has friends and enemies. Pater Pio also had many enemies. What evil had he ever done? None! And still he was hated and persecuted, and the evil and wickedness of men nailed him to the cross. He lived his life, blessing all upon this world, and still he was persecuted and hated because he reproached sin so strongly, and did not let people live just any old way they wanted. Being convicted of their sins through this man, they wanted to get him out of their way and remove him off the earth.

"One day a taxi driver was bringing a passenger along the road opposite the hill where the church and clinic which Pater Pio had built from the gifts of the devout were located.

" 'What are those big buildings over there on the hill?' asked the passenger.

" 'Those are the buildings of the cloister of Pater Pio,' answered the driver.

"Irritably the man answered, 'Has the old capuchin so much money that he can put up buildings like that?'

"The taxi driver answered, 'My dear man, that is not the case. There in the cloister is where the priest lives who has in his body the exact same wounds of crucifixion that our Lord had when He was on the cross. The people say that he is a holy man. And here in this church, and wherever people are who believe, miracles happen. Pater Pio does not take any glory for the miracles, or credit. He says, 'Freely I have received, and freely I must give.' He does not accept any gifts for the miracles God gives when he prays for the sick. You will see when we come into the town, the many cars and busses that bring the pilgrims from all countries here. They come speaking every kind of language and praying for all kinds of miracles. Sometimes they return to give God thanks also. And although Pater Pio does not accept money, people give and it is from these gifts that the buildings were erected to house the pilgrims and the sick. They are for the people who gave. Pater Pio is no egotist nor selfish. He wants nothing for himself. He lives a lonely life and his whole life is for God and mankind.

"To this, the angry, God-hating man began to speak words against Pater Pio. He mocked and swore and, at the end, he put a curse on him. After a small pause, he said with a sneering smile, 'In a few days the people will celebrate Pater Pio's funeral here and then the whole thing will be over.'

"Just then they arrived at the place where he was supposed to get out of the taxi. The taxi stopped and the man got out of the car. He was about thirty to thirty-three years old. The moment his feet touched the ground, he fell over dead on the spot. It created a great disturbance. People came running to see what had happened. They asked the taxi driver if he had had an argument with the man or hit him. 'No,' he said, 'we were only talking.' And then he told them the story of what the man had said.

"A man standing there who had witnessed the whole thing went immediately to Pater Pio who was in the cloister, to tell him what had happened. Pater Pio met him with the words, 'You do not have to tell me anything. I know all about it.' The man thought that someone had already told the priest. But then Pater Pio added these shocking words, 'In the instant when this man spoke the curse on me and wished my death, I was right in God. The curse could not touch me, it rebounded and struck the man on the spot. So in a couple of days they will have his funeral.'

"The results of this incident you can imagine. From this example we can see that God does not permit man to mock Him or His saints or His works; also that we should never curse anyone because the curse can return on us."

Chapter 17
LOVE IS IN THE BLOOD

Oh, how I would that the angels could give you this message instead of me. I feel that my capabilities are too limited to bring out all that is in my heart and which I see through the Holy Spirit's enlightenment.

For years I have praised God for the Blood of Jesus and I have preached many messages on the blood. I have written a Bible study on it also, called *The Power of the Precious Blood.** In the many countries where I have preached, I would always preach at least one message on the Blood of Jesus. But now it seems that I see more in that truth than ever before.

I want to ask you a question which is based on that Scripture, 1 John 1:7, "The blood of Jesus Christ cleanseth us from all sin." Why does the *Blood* of Jesus Christ have power to take away our sins? Why not some other part of His body? Why not the heart, or the stomach, or the gall? Why does it have to be the blood which has this power?

There is something very strange about blood. From the beginning of time, as it is recorded in the Scriptures, God was revealing to us in part the significance of blood. When Noah came out of the ark, God gave him a set of rules to live by. They were very few in number. He didn't have as many rules and laws as we have in our churches today. But there

---

**The Power of the Precious Blood* by Gwen R. Shaw. (See order form in the back of the book.)

was one law which I would like to draw to your attention.

Genesis 9:4-6, "But flesh with the life thereof, which is the blood thereof, shall ye not eat. And surely your blood of your lives will I require: at the hand of every beast will I require it, and at the hand of man; at the hand of every man's brother will I require the life of man. Whoso sheddeth man's blood, by man shall his blood be shed: for in the image of God made he man." Why did God say this? What is in the blood of man that God should say, "If you shed it, your blood will be shed?" Why was it that God said, "Life for life and blood for blood?" It was God who said it, and not Noah or Moses or any other Old Testament writer. Why was blood so important that if I poured out another's blood, my own blood must be poured out in exchange for it?

The answer is found in two Scriptures. *First*—Leviticus 17:11, "For the life of the flesh is in the blood: and I have given it to you upon the altar to make an atonement for your souls: for it is the blood that maketh an atonement for the soul." God was trying to teach man that blood was a living substance. There is life in blood. If you would ask a scientist what blood is, you might get many answers. Scientists lately have been making an extensive study about blood because they saw there is something peculiar and supernatural about blood. They have come to this conclusion: that blood is congealed light. It is light that has become solidified. In other words, in the body of man there are veins and these veins are flowing with a red substance which is none other than light. Light that has mystically become congealed. How did our blood become congealed light? What was man's original state in his first creation? When God first created Adam, what gave him the power of eternal life in the garden? In the veins of my father Adam and my mother Eve was not congealed light, or blood like mine, but I believe that in the perfection with which they were created there was the very light of God that flowed through their veins and this is what gave them eternal life. This is that glory that they lost when they sinned and a curse fell on the human race. From then on all human flesh began to lose that river of light through generation after generation, as man in his fallen nature fell further and further away from God's purity of holiness, and our blood changed with each generation as iniquity increased more and more, so that in our day we have turned to destroying our very own flesh and blood, the innocent babies that are created within us. We were created to be "gods" ruling over the universe as joint-heirs with Christ, but instead we have become destroyers of that creation. So today that river of light and life is under the sentence of death. The light is still there, but it is so densely congealed that it does not have the power in itself to cleanse our bodies from its defilement and weakness. We need a transfusion from innocent blood, one that will work life into our dying bloodstream. For the life-line of the human race is in the blood. "For the life of the flesh is in the blood" (Leviticus 17:11).

The *second* Scripture is found right in Genesis 9:6, "Whoso sheddeth man's blood, by man shall his blood be shed: for in the image of God made he man." Even as there flowed in God's being a life-line of eternal existence that would always transcend death, so the same was in Adam when God created him in God's likeness and image. That is one reason Adam did not immediately die when he sinned. He still lived hundreds of years and so did Eve and many of his descendents. The veins of these great progenitors of the human race were still filled with a purer degree of light. Man was made in the image of God. The blood was the very life of God in man. To shed that blood was to strike at the "God" within a man. The ONLY reason that man could shed blood was in payment of a debt, even the debt of murder. A life for a life. Blood for blood. The life and the identity of the father is in the blood.

Remember when Adam's son Cain killed Abel, he hid his brother's body because he thought nobody knew anything about it. But God stepped on the scene and said, "What have you done?" And then He added another thing which has been hard for us to understand. "The voice of thy brother's blood crieth unto me from the ground" (Genesis 4:10). In other words, there was life in that blood which had been poured out. There was a voice crying out from that blood, a vibration that reached up to where God in heaven heard that poured-out blood speaking. A thing that is dead, like a table or chair, cannot speak; but there must have been life in that blood so that God could hear it speak. "Blood speaketh!" In Hebrews 12 we read, "Ye are come unto . . . Jesus the mediator of the new covenant, and to the blood of sprinkling, that speaketh better things than that of Abel" (verse 24). Four thousand years after the shed blood of Abel spoke, God said that the blood of Jesus His Son, the Mediator between God and sinner-man, was speaking better things than the blood of Abel. Today, two thousand years still later, Jesus' blood is speaking to us because there is LIFE in it. His blood was not just some powerless fluid that dropped on the foot of the cross and dried up, leaving us only the memory of it. No, no. If the words I speak have life and send out their vibrations to the ends of the earth bringing good or evil, how much more that life-line called the Blood of Jesus!

There is life in every man's blood, but in the Blood of Jesus there is abundant life. There is a life that comes right from the throne of God. Oh, praise God for the Blood of Jesus! And praise God for the life in the Blood of Jesus!

Not only does man know there is life in the blood, the devil knows it also. On the eve of the Passover when the destroyer went out over the land of Egypt he, too, had to recognize this truth. Many people think that this angel was a good angel, but the Bible calls him a destroyer (Exodus 12: 23). The Bible says that the thief (referring to the evil one) came to steal and to kill and to destroy. This destroyer was not an angel from heaven, but a messenger from darkness. He was given the right of God to do his work. No devil or demon can touch you without God's permission. God is still in supreme control of death and life. God is still in control of every devil and demon. That night, because of the sins of the people, God released the destroyer and he went out through the land of Egypt with a limited amount of liberty to kill. God had instructed him that he could only touch and take the life of the firstborn and he could not go beyond God's permitted will. If there were twins born in a family, he could only take the first one that came out of the mother's womb. He could not trespass this permissive will of God.

As he went out over the land he had another limited power. There was a sign that God had commanded the people of the Lord to put on their door. A sign of Blood. And the destroyer knew that the blood was more than just red paint. He knew that the sign of life was in that blood and that wherever that blood was, God has promised life in exchange for it. Yes, there was the sign of life in that blood, and Satan knows who is trusting in the Blood. Life is in the blood, and when you are marked with the blood the sign of eternal life has been put upon you. And God will not transgress His own laws. Neither will He allow Satan, the destroyer. He said, "When I see the blood, I will pass over you" (Exodus 12:13). He also said, "I will not allow the destroyer to come in unto your houses to smite you" (Exodus 12:23). I want to draw your attention to one thing. Blood speaks and, though this was not the blood of Jesus nor the blood of man, it was only the blood of a small creation of God—a little lamb that could not even speak. All it could say was, "Baaa"; still it spoke life to the devil. It was the blood of a lamb and yet it had such power that Satan's power was broken by its very message of life.

We go down through the years and we stand there at Golgotha, at the foot of the cross, that day where Jesus has just offered up His spirit to the Father. And we hear Him say, "Father, into thy hands I commend my spirit:" (Luke 23:46). In that moment His spirit is lifted from His body and a Roman soldier comes back and taking his spear drives it through the side of Jesus; and out of this wound pours blood and water. We see our Saviour hanging there on the cross, pouring out His blood for the redemption of the world. We stand under that flow for a moment and all of our sins are washed away. Just slip under that Blood for a moment now! Just let all of your sins be washed away now! That beautiful Blood of Jesus. Let it flow through your life, through your family, through your church, through your land. *Let it wash away the sin of everyone who reads these words, dear Lord! Let not the destroyer use them or have power against them.*

I want to ask you a question. If you had stood for a moment under the dripping blood of one of the thieves who were also crucified and hung up next to Jesus, would you have felt the same cleansing power? Or would the blood of Peter or John or your pastor have set you free? NO! Then what is the difference between the power of the Blood of Jesus and that in the blood of any other man on earth? Why does the Blood of Jesus speak better things than the blood of Abel?

Remember on the night before Jesus was crucified He poured out the wine, which was only a symbol, and He said, "This is my blood of the new testament, which is shed for many for the remission of sins" (Matthew 26:28). Remember also some time earlier as He was ministering He said, "Except ye eat the flesh of the Son of man, and drink his blood, ye have no life in you. Whoso eateth my flesh, and drinketh my blood, hath eternal life: and I will raise him up at the last day" (John 6:53, 54). Then He added, "He that eateth my flesh and drinketh my blood, dwelleth in me, and I in him." What was Jesus talking about here? Why was His body more powerful broken bread than any other man's and why was His Blood more powerful than any other man's?

To get the answer we need to go back to the garden. We have to go back there one more time. The secret of everything lies in the garden. A couple of years ago God took me in a vision to the garden of Eden and I stood there and saw my mother Eve as she had sinned before God. I heard her crying as she reproached herself for what she had done. And the cry of Eve has gone up to God down through the years. Why did Eve our mother cry? Because she saw the terrible curse she had brought on us. Her love for her children was greater than any mother's living today, because Eve was closer to the creation of God than you or I today. I don't believe in evolution. I believe that the first man and woman whom God created were more perfect than any man living today. I don't believe we have become more perfect, but rather we have fallen away from our former glory. And I saw how Eve's heart was broken because she saw what untold, limitless suffering she had brought upon her race. I saw how through the centuries, even after her transition, she had wept and cried to God the Father to be merciful to her sons and daughters. She had interceded for our release and had been permitted to see that her prayers had not been in vain, her intercession had accomplished its goal and she had prayed through. God is going to begin to show His glory to Eve's children. We have finished drinking the cup of our iniquity, our day of redemption is here now. That is the reason God is using us handmaidens. Somehow God is going to allow us to make up for our mother's failure. We not only want to bless and help our brothers return to the lost paradise, we want to return ourselves. Oh, God help us! Brothers, help us! We need you and you need us! We went out together and we must return together!

Paul said, "The woman shall be saved in childbearing" (1 Timothy 2:15). God does not mean that she shall be saved just through bearing a child, because many sinful women bear children, and some live good lives but still are lost. The Holy Spirit is speaking of something different. He was speaking of spiritual childbearing. As women travail and intercede, they will be used by the Lord to restore all that has been lost through the fall. I want to tell you women that the highest calling you can have is not to stand behind the pulpit and teach and preach God's Word, but to be called to the ministry of prayer. I have cried out to God, "Let me go into a corner and bury myself in prayer"; but I keep hearing in me, "Woe is me, if I preach not the gospel." I preach because I have to preach, but the highest call which lies on each one of you "Eves" is to cry and weep before God, that you may bring forth the sons of God in this generation, for God promised Eve that her seed would bruise the serpent's head. Let us travail that the sons of God will be born in this generation; for when they shall come forth, then our redemption will be complete. Yea, the world waiteth for the revelation of the sons of God!

Jesus poured out His Blood. Why couldn't a mortal man pour out his blood? Because on mortal man came the curse. In my veins runs the blood of my forefathers. Many of my forefathers were godly men. I came from a line of martyrs, but still there is a curse on my blood. There is sin in it. I battle this sin every day. All the sin of my forefathers is in it . . . all the way back to Noah and Adam. The Lord said He would visit ". . . the iniquity of the fathers upon the children, and upon the children's children, unto the third and to the fourth generation" (Exodus 34:7). This is because the wickedness that is in the fathers came right into the bloodstream of the present generation. Our bloodstream should be holy and pure, but it has been defiled by the sins of our forefathers. God will not accept defilement, so God had to look for an atonement. The curse was upon all—Roman, Greek, Gentile, Jew, bond, free, male and female. So He came! He came! Emmanuel . . . God with us! He stepped down and became a baby. Don't ask me to explain the mystery of incarnation. It is too great for my mind. All I know is that the great Creator suddenly became the created one. Miracle of miracles! He had no earthly father, and on that day when His blood poured from His veins it had the power to wash away the sins of the world.

Every child inherits his blood type from both of the parents. We read of paternal lawsuits in which a woman tries to prove that some movie star or big-name person is the father of her child. They use the evidence of the blood to prove this. But Jesus had no earthly father. He was born of a virgin. What type of blood flowed through His veins? Who did He say His father was? He said, "My father in heaven." He had the blood of His father flowing through His veins, the

Blood of God . . . that same life-line that flowed in the first Adam, except that Jesus also had His mother's blood type, and she was of the line and lineage of David and Adam. She was a virgin, but she was not sinless, for if she had been sinless she would never have had the need of a Saviour, and yet she said, "My soul doth magnify the Lord, and my spirit hath rejoiced in God my Saviour." In Jesus' blood was a mixture of deity and humanity, light and darkness, life and death, and love and hate. Oh, glory to God, that though He was tempted in all points like as we are, He overcame all darkness, death, hate and humanity. The God within Him overcame the curse that had come on humanity through sin.

Oh, what a fountain of love that flowed through the veins of Jesus! *That is what made the Blood of Jesus pure.* It was the essence of love flowing in His human body. It was love liquified that flowed from His many wounds, starting a fountain of cleansing that would bring redemption to a fallen planet. Behold that stream of everlasting life! That is why it is almighty. That is why it has a never-dying power. That is why, two thousand years after it was shed, it still has the power to take men's sins away. It still has the power to change a cruel, hard, evil man into a man of kindness; because in that bloodstream flows the very love of God. That is why the Blood of Jesus is the Love of Jesus.

The Lord wants to give you a blood transfusion from Calvary. Your life is in that Blood. He wants to pour that river of healing, cleansing, purifying love through your body. When that happens, God will accomplish in you what must be accomplished in order to have everlasting life.

Jesus said, "Except you drink my blood you have no life in you." What did He mean? He didn't mean that we are to drink blood. In fact, in the New Testament one of the few laws given to the new church was that they were to abstain from eating blood (Acts 15:20). What Jesus meant was that we must partake of His life-giving stream of love. Unless we have His love we do not have His life. "He that eateth and drinketh of my blood dwelleth in me, and I in him." These were the words of Jesus. Or as John says, "If we have love, God dwelleth in us" (1 John 4:12).

Jesus also said we are to eat of His body. What did He mean? His body was broken. That means we are to partake with Him in His broken body. This means that we must have a broken heart like He has. It takes a heart that is broken open to receive. Our hearts are like sealed jars. It takes a swift blow of pain to break them open; but when it is opened up, we experience a communion with God like no ordinary circumstances can bring about. Paul said, "That I may know him in the fellowship of his sufferings, being made conformable unto his death" (Philippians 3:10). Only when our hearts are broken can we partake of His broken body. We are sharing in the breaking of self.

That is why we take the bread BEFORE we take the cup. That is what Holy Communion really means. We have taken it for years and not fully understood its meaning. When we take it we are saying to the Lord, "Take my heart and break it, and out of my life make a broken sacrifice for Yourself." When we take the cup and drink, we are communing with Him and feasting from His love and drinking from that life-giving stream. How sacred and holy is that sacrament! God wants us to partake of His holy body. All the things you have suffered, all your aches and griefs have made you either closer to God, or harder.

Too many have closed their hearts and said, "Nothing will hurt me again." As soon as you do that, your heart becomes like a little hard nut which cannot feel anything any more. This has happened to thousands of God's people. Oh, we have been so afraid to be hurt. Jesus says, "Except ye eat my body [unless you have fellowship with Me in a broken heart], you have no part in me."

God will send a revival. This will be the last revival and it will be the greatest that this world has ever had. Sons of God will be born out of the womb of the church, for the church has been weeping and travailing through thousands of years, and just as the FIRST SON was born so shall the

End-Time Sons be born. As the FIRST SON came in His perfection and was a manifestion of God, so the first among many brethren is a picture of the many sons who shall be brought forth from the womb of the church, perfect in the holiness and the glory of their God. They shall manifest the life and the love of the FIRST SON. They shall be children of eternity. This is the message of tomorrow. We are only hearing a little bit of it ahead of time. This is the hope of the children of God, but we can't have it without the Blood of Jesus. The Blood of Jesus is the manifestation of the Love of God.

The Blood of Jesus is going to become more powerful in the end time. More powerful than in the day it poured from His veins, until it will touch our very bodies, and not only will our spirits be changed, but our bodies will be changed. Not only will our spirits have eternal life, but our very bodies will be quickened to live forever as we stand in the presence of the Lord. That is the power of the message of the BLOOD.

Chapter 18
LOVE GIVES

The greatest Giver on earth said, "It is more blessed to give than to receive" (Acts 20:35). We have heard these words spoken since we were a child and dropped our pennies in the Sunday school offering. As we grew older and the pastor taught us the truths of giving our tithes and offerings, we again were taught the truths of the law of giving. It was used by unscrupulous men who "stole the widow's raiment and ox for a pledge" and consumed it on their own flesh. We have been deluged with begging letters from organizations that have "bought" our names from computerized mailing lists; we have been given every sob-story to stir up our sympathy; and we have been threatened about the dreadful results and the curses that will come on us if we don't give, until we are sick and tired of the whole thing and cry, "Forget about it! I don't want to hear any more about it!" But still the truth remains, "It is more blessed to give than to receive," and because it comes from the lips of Jesus, we can receive it.

We are coming into a time when we will have to know this truth and understand it in order to be able to survive. The Holy Spirit wants to teach us why God said it and what He really meant. God is the GREAT GIVER—He gives all the time—and when we give, we become like Him. It makes us the head and not the tail. It lifts our station in life. To be able to give takes me from the beggarly, receiving end and puts me on the rich and giving end. To receive identifies me as the needy one, and to give as the possessor.

To give is an act of love. You do not need love to be able to receive. Anyone can receive. We live in a nation that is filled with people on welfare, and most of them despise this government and talk against those whose taxes go to feed them and clothe them and give them their welfare check. I have seen the nations that America has fed and financed turn against America and call us the "Ugly Americans." Sometimes it seems like the more we gave, the more they hated us. Was this because they felt indebted to us and wanted to justify themselves for the guilt complex that comes with being poor? But even though they hate us for giving, we must not shut up our bowels of compassion and turn away from the needy, for then God will judge us. Do they not hate Him, even though He giveth and giveth and giveth again?

To receive you do not need love; an enemy can receive. But to give is an act of a friend. To give a handshake is an act of friendship. To give an open home is an act of hospitality. To give time is a sacrifice of yourself. These are the bigger and better things that you can give, and yet they cost so little. When we do these things we are pleasing God because we are obeying the first and great commandment, we are loving our neighbor. When you love, you will give. That is why Jesus said it is better to give than to receive, because He knew that when you give, you are the one who has the love. It is the one who loves who has the blessing.

God has sent us into the world with one message, the message of love. Because His love is so unlimited, He always has something new and wonderful for this world; and He needs people of love who will identify with His compassion and be vehicles that He can use to pour His love upon this world. As He uses the sun to give sunshine and the clouds to give rain, He wants to use us, His creation, to bless this world, be it good or evil. God does not stop giving even though we are unworthy. It is His GOODNESS that leadeth us to repentance. Love is the greatest message that ever was preached to sinful man. But we cannot preach it unless we possess it.

I was a missionary for years and did not possess this great love as I should have, and then God took me through a valley of suffering and to the place where I was rejected; and there in the valley of weeping, when the tears were falling from my eyes, as my friends turned their backs on me, I knew who my ONE TRUE FRIEND was, and what HIS name was, and I fell in love with Jesus all over again. I also learned to know my Heavenly Father in a wonderful, new way.

With this new, wonderful love that came to me in a most unexpected moment of my life, everything was changed. I felt love, breathed love, thought love, became love. God took me to Germany with this message of love and for over a year it was the ONLY message I could preach. It is from those truths that this book is being created. I was there! He visited me and it changed my life. And I know it will change yours when He visits you also.

Every time I preached on love, I could feel His love flowing through me. Sometimes it became so overwhelming that I felt I could take the whole world into my arms, including my enemies. At times it was so glorious that I could hardly keep body and soul together. The love was so tremendous that I felt I could be translated. It was this great love that God poured into my heart which took me over one of the great bridges of my life.

Love is the theme of the Bible. Without love, there would be no Bible. God is love, and if you want to know God you must fall in love with Him. He wants our eyes to be on Him. As long as we follow evangelists, preachers, prophets or any other mortal, we are following the follower. Our love is perfected only as we follow the Christ. If we follow mortals our hearts will be broken as they disappoint us. But now we must learn the perfect love from the One who is perfect, and as He puts His wings out over us we hear His beckoning call, "Come and learn MY love." Oh, beloved, the Lord is returning soon for His bride and she must be filled with love so she will be ready. If she does not have love, she cannot be His bride. If our hearts are sealed against love and we cannot give, we will not qualify as His bride. We must have the spirit of Jonathan, the beautiful giver of the Old Testament.

Jesus told us how we should give. He said we should give as we have received: "Freely ye have received, freely give" (Matthew 10:8). He gave generously; we must give generously. He was not sparing or stingy in His giving and neither can we be. Some people find it hard to give love. They can be gracious and friendly, they know all the manners and etiquette of society, they give honor, respect and praise, but they don't give love. They entertain those who are to their advantage or who interest them, but they never send one bowl of rice to a refugee fleeing from Vietnam. They buy every new translation of the Bible that comes out in print, but never send one to a brother in a Russian prison camp or a pastor who has prayed for forty years in Siberia to own a whole Bible. And then they think they have love. The offering plate comes around when the missionary has spoken and they take out of their purse a crumpled dollar bill as a donation to send that missionary to India, and they think they shall have thousands of souls in heaven because they gave.

After Adam and Eve were driven out of the garden of Eden, their sons Cain and Abel were taught to bring God offerings. The first one who brought an offering was Cain. He brought of the fruit of the land. Genesis 4:2, "Cain was a tiller of the ground." Abel brought of the flock the gift of a lamb. Both were worshipping God, both were bringing a sacrifice. One gift was received and the other was rejected. What was the difference between Cain's and Abel's offerings?

Cain's did not have the value that Abel's did. It doesn't hurt to pull the vegetables out of the garden. They don't feel pain. They don't even know what is happening. That is an offering that does not greatly cost the giver or his gift. But when Abel worshipped, he brought a living thing, perhaps a little lamb that had followed him, that had known his call. Jesus said the sheep know the voice of the shepherd and follow him. And this little lamb had known the voice of Abel. It would eat out of his hand; he had carried it on his shoulder. It was a living creature with the stream of living blood in it. It had a heartbeat and it had feeling. It was something that could love. Not only did Abel love it, the lamb also loved Abel; and when Abel brought it as an offering to God it cost not only Abel something, it cost the lamb the price of its own life. That is why God received the one and not the other offering. For He, too, one day would give a great sacrifice that not only would cost Him His LAMB, but would also cost the Lamb His life.

When you give "things" such as houses, money, food, valuables, you do well; but when you give "life," such as your children, your wife or husband, your people or yourself, you are giving like God gave. When you give the first, the price is not very great. You are the only one who feels the sacrifice, for the house and money cannot feel anything. But when you give the latter, then not only you but your children also will feel the sacrifice of your giving.

When Russia's great martyr Peter Vins was imprisoned for the last time for preaching the Gospel, he had a nine-year-old son George. From the prison he wrote back to his son these words in a poem:

TO GEORGE

> My son, my son, my precious son,
> In innocence you suffer shame.
> You're forced involuntarily
> To suffer for the dear Lord's Name.
>
> But I pray, when you're grown and strong,
> You'll choose the thorny path of Christ.
> That willingly you'll suffer wrong
> And pay love's precious, costly price.
>
> When as a youth then brave and strong,
> Whose childhood's golden days have passed,
> With eyes of hope so pure and young
> You face your future dreams at last.

> May you surrender your strong will,
> Your life, your strength, so pure and free,
> The dreams your heart did dream and hope
> To Christ, who is your destiny.
>
> Peter Vins
> 1932 Labour Camp
> Svellaya Bay, U.S.S.R.

George grew up and chose the way of the cross. He has spent many years in prison. And now his son, too, has chosen the way of the cross and is a prisoner in Russia. That makes three generations who have been imprisoned for Christ.

This was a great and costly sacrifice that these fathers made, for it not only cost their own lives but the lives of their children. Not only do they suffer, but their children and their wives have to bear the burden of the heavy cross. But they do it all with joy by God's grace because their love is so much greater than ours is.

We must be careful of our motive for doing and giving. Let our worship of God be in Spirit and in Truth. Let our service for Him be motivated only by pure love. Not everyone who is in the ministry is motivated by this love. They may have started out that way, but there is a dangerous "political game" in religious organizations that can cause the destruction of our soul even while we stand behind the pulpit. A man of God had a vision of heaven. He saw the throne of God, and sitting close beside the Lord were some plain looking men. He asked the angel who was with him, "Who are these here so close to the throne?" The angel said, "Those are the humble pastors. When they were on earth they loved the Lord and served Him with a pure heart. They were not famous, nor did they preach to great crowds. Some of them were very poor and had to work in order to stay in the ministry. But they loved God and were faithful, and the Lord has chosen them to sit by Him in glory." The man of God asked, "But why aren't some of the big preachers up here? I saw them way back there in the great throng. Surely they did greater works than these pastors. They should have a great reward, too." The angel shook his head sadly, "They already had their reward. They have received the praises of men and now they are where they belong, in the vast multitude."

It is possible to give a lifetime in service for God, live and die on a mission field, and still not receive any rewards. It is possible to have your name on the honor roll of church history and be the spiritual leader of tens of thousands, and be lost. There will be more than one pope in hell.

On the other hand, few see the little woman who never testifies because she is so very shy. She has little to give because she has nothing of earthly possessions; but God sees her and the angels have kept the records and some day she will be taken to the treasure room of heaven and adorned in exquisite robes of glory that are far beyond her wildest imagination and she will say, "Why am I honored thus, while endless ages fly?" And He'll answer, "Child, it is because I've chosen you." Her love, her prayers, her heart of mercy and humility will have enabled her to bring the perfect sacrifice.

Why do we give? What is our true motive for giving? Do we give for show? Do we give so that people will see how good and holy we are? Do we do it because we HAVE to keep the laws? Or do we give because we want a reward? How did God tell us to give?

He told us to give cheerfully (2 Corinthians 9:7) and not grudgingly, because if we gave like that we were obviously giving without love. He also told us to not let our left hand know what our right hand does (Matthew 6:3). When you give, do not broadcast it all over. I have a sad feeling about the income tax deductible system that has been incorporated in our giving here in America. We have all fallen in a trap. While I understand that it has become necessary, still I fear for what lies ahead. How sad, that a worldly system can cause us to lose our heavenly reward! Let us be careful that we give out of our heart of love. If we give for the praises of men, we have had our reward. We should give because we love, expecting NOTHING in return. Jesus said that the Pharisee loved those who loved him. We must do better than the Pharisee.

God spreads the tables of the blasphemers just like He does the tables of His own children. He clothes the harlot and the saint; He pours out His love on all. Why? Because He is the Father of Love. Do they love Him back? No, they curse Him and take His name in vain. They mock Him and ridicule Him and break all His laws, but He loves them still and so must we also love—not because they love us back, but because we live on that higher plane, by that higher law, and are of another order. This is the law of the kingdom, and as a child of the kingdom of God you will obey the laws of that kingdom and they will set you free from the laws of the lower kingdom.

The greatest gift that love can give is FORGIVENESS. It is also the most important. If you give it, your soul is free from hates and hurts; but if you do not give it, you can be destroyed by what you keep for yourself. You cannot give forgiveness without love. Love will enable you to rise above your enemy with his hates and give him love, calling him a "friend" in your heart even as Jesus did with Judas. When you love your enemy you will "cover his sins." You won't go around talking about your enemy. You won't tell everyone what he is doing to you. You will be quiet and keep on loving him and blessing him and praying for him. Sometime, somewhere, your enemy will know the truth. Maybe it won't be in this world, maybe it will be in the next, but he will know. Love does not stop with death and neither does hate stop with death. So do not keep hate in your heart, because five minutes after you are dead you will still have the same thing in your heart that is there right now. You must purify yourself NOW. The Word of God says, "He who hath this hope, purifieth himself, even as He is pure" (1 John 3:3).

I want to share a strange incident which my father seldom spoke about, but which I know must be truthful, as he was a very honest man who never told a falsehood or exaggerated in any way.

When I was about seven years old, one night my father

was awakened by a violent slap on his back. He thought perhaps Mother had hit him in her sleep because she was the only one in the house who could have done it.

"What is the matter?" he asked her. "Why did you hit me like that?"

She replied that she had not done anything. My father knew then that he had been hit by someone other than a living being. He lay awake thinking about it for hours. The next morning he heard that in the same hour as he had been struck in the night a neighbor who lived about six miles away, who hated him and held a grudge against him, had died. My father always believed that this man, with his unforgiving heart, had passed his way and struck him before leaving the land of the living forever.

Many await the hour of death to purify their hearts and purge themselves of all iniquity and others hope that their loved ones will say prayers for them after they are dead and pay for the masses so that they may escape purgatory. But, my friend, NOW is the day to be cleansed of hate and evil. Now is the time to give forgiveness. It is only as we forgive that we can receive forgiveness. I hate to think of the destiny of the soul of that man who struck my father in the night as his spirit was going to its eternal abode. He went out without forgiveness, therefore he could receive none on the other side when he stood at the river of death, where two eternities meet.

Love can conquer. Love succeeds when all else has failed. Love is the perfume of the flower that kisses the heel of the one that crushes it. If we are like the lily of the valley or the rose of Sharon, when we are crushed and broken we will only leave a fragrance. We will not curse that which crushes us. We will not do anything to harm it. We will leave a blessing on the hand that has hurt us.

Chapter 19
LOVE SEPARATES

"And the leper in whom the plague is, his clothes shall be rent, and his head bare, and he shall put a covering upon his upper lip and shall cry, Unclean, unclean. All the days wherein the plague shall be in him he shall be defiled; he is unclean: he shall dwell alone; without the camp shall his habitation be" (Leviticus 13:45, 46).

Many times as we have read God's laws about the leper, we have felt that God was hard and cruel. It was hard for us to accept the fact that He said people would have to be shut off from their family and friends as long as the plague was upon them. They had to have a mark on them that identified them for what they were. They had to wear covering over their upper lip like the Moslem women in the eastern lands. It was like a mask that covered up their mouths. Their garment must be torn and ragged and they had to live alone without the camp with other lepers. They had to cry out, "Unclean, unclean," wherever they went.

The awful, hard part of it was that never again could they live with their loved ones. The husband could never hold his wife in his arms anymore. The mother could not cuddle her baby at her breast. It seemed so cruel, but there was a reason that God separated the clean from the unclean. The reason was that leprosy was a very contagious disease for which there was no cure, except by a miracle. It ate away at the flesh and the muscles, causing deformities and mutilations that made the poor victim not only ugly but gave intense pain and suffering. I have seen many lepers on the mission field. It is not hard to spot them, even though they do not have the signs that God gave them in the Bible. There is a smell of decaying flesh that is not easily forgotten. You would never take one of these poor creatures into your home to play with your little children unless you were ignorant of the consequences. The horror of leprosy and the curse that came with it have caused it to be a type of sin to all teachers of the Bible. The rules for the leper were hard ones and yet we see God's love in them, for God in His love was protecting the clean from the unclean. He knew that the same deadly disease would soon spread throughout the camp if there were no laws of separation.

Many times we have wondered what to do in a similar case amongst the brothers and sisters in the family of God. We have been taught through the Word of God to love one another. This means welcoming the stranger, being a good Samaritan and reaching out the hand of help to someone in need. Love means forgiving your brother who has fallen. Love is reconciliation. Love is kind and beautiful. But HERE is also love. Here is somebody who belongs to the family but can never again come into the fellowship of the family, not because there is no love—the love is there (they longed greatly for their loved one's return)—but there had to be a separation because of the uncleanness and the danger of that deadly disease.

There may come a time in your spiritual growth when you are going to be tried and tested in this same thing. You will have to know who you can welcome into your arms and extend the right hand of fellowship to and who, on the other hand, you will still love but because of the Love of God in your heart will have to close the door and say to them, "We are sorry, but we are not permitted by God to have you in our home or have any kind of fellowship with you." We will have to clearly tell them, "Your dwelling is without the camp. You cannot again be in our fellowship." This is not because we do not love that one, but because we must protect that which is holy from that which is unholy, and we must guard the flock which the Lord has put in our care.

Many people think that because God told us we should love, that we must love the "snake" to our bosom. It was when Eve was having fellowship with the serpent that she fell victim to his wiles. You cannot let the pervert sleep with your children, nor can you let the mad dog loose in your house. If you sit at the feet of the prophetess Jezebel who commits fornication while she attempts to teach the Bible, you will be led into uncleanness and permissiveness. If you attend the synagogue of Satan, you will soon be his disciple. You cannot press the scorpion to your heart and not be stung by him. This is not love, this is foolishness. We must discern between truth and error, between the Holy Spirit and a religious spirit, between our liberty in God and lasciviousness.

Many previous lives have already been destroyed because they made that mistake. The tragedy of Jonestown and the followers of James Jones is an example of this. They meant well. They wanted to stick by their leader. Everything they did, they did for love. They gave up their homes, families and friends, and finally their lives. God does not want us to be fools who will destroy ourselves.

When should we send the "leper" out of the camp? John, the disciple of love, says, "If there come any unto you, and bring not this *doctrine*, receive him NOT into your house, neither bid him Godspeed: for he that biddeth him Godspeed is partaker of his evil deeds" (2 John 1:10, 11). These seem like harsh words for an apostle of love like John. But he was trying to protect the flock from "wolves." Paul said to the church of Ephesus, "I know this, that after my departing grievous wolves shall enter in among you, not sparing the flock. Also of your own selves shall men arise, speaking perverse things to draw away disciples after them" (Acts 20:29, 30). These men of God knew that the church had false brethren who were living unclean lives, walking in unrighteousness, who seduced the unwise and unlearned. Paul said, "They creep into houses, and lead captive silly women laden with sins, led by divers lusts, ever learning and never able to come to the knowledge of the truth" (2 Timothy 3:6, 7). He said a form of godliness is not enough. We have to live in the power of it.

When God called out the children of Israel, He commanded them to live a life that was separated from the nations around about them. "Take heed to thyself, lest thou make a covenant with the inhabitants of the land whither thou goest, lest it be for a snare in the midst of thee" (Exodus 34:12). Paul said, "But now I have written unto you not to keep company, if any man that is called a brother be a fornicator or covetous, or an idolater, or a railer, or a drunkard, or an extortioner: with such a one DO NOT EAT" (1 Corinthians 5:11).

This law of love comes right into the depths of our lives. Paul warns, "Be not unequally yoked together with unbelievers, for what fellowship hath righteousness with unrighteousness? What communion hath light with darkness?" (2 Corinthians 6:14). Young woman, think wisely before you marry that sinner. Do you want your children to be raised by a man who does not love your Jesus? Maybe you think you can change him. If you cannot change him now, you never can! For the sake of your unborn children do not make a terrible mistake that will not be eradicated in your lifetime or even in theirs.

When I was a child I read a story that I feel I should remind you of. Mother goat had many little goats. One day she said to her kids, "Children, I have to go out for a while. Be very careful and do not open the door for anyone. The wolf is about, and he will try to eat you." They all said, "Don't worry, mother, we won't open the door."

After the mother goat was gone, the wolf came and knocked on the door. In a high voice he said, "Let me in. I am your mother."

But the wise little kids looked under the door and saw the black feet of the wolf. They said, "Your voice sounds like our mother, but your feet are not the same. Our mother has white feet and you have black feet. You are not our mother. You cannot come in."

I warn you that not everything that comes to your door speaking swelling words is sent from God. The devil quotes Scripture very skillfully. He also shows signs and wonders in his attempt to deceive the elect. He sometimes goes to church, too. How will you know the difference? Look at the feet! Are they walking in cleanness and holiness, abstaining from the very appearance of evil? Or is the sign of the wolf in their pathway. They may come and even pretend to repent. They may speak sweet, honey-like words that will sound genuine. But if you open your heart to those who are not sent from God, you will be destroyed.

The trouble today is that many "little kids" think they know more than "mother goat." She knows the danger and warns them, but they think they can let the wolf in the door and play with him a little bit and that it will not hurt them. But this is impossible. The wolf will leave his teeth-marks on them. They will be fortunate if they come away with their lives. We must not rebel against those whom the Lord himself has placed over us as our spiritual mothers and fathers. They may not be perfect, but they are appointed by God. If you will receive their admonition in love you will be protected by their wisdom.

A time was given in which the leprosy was checked again. The mercy of God can give another chance. We must be wise to know when that time comes. Do not confuse true repentance with sham. Nor can you cast out the truly repentant soul. It was the duty of the priest to go without the camp to the leper on the day of his cleansing and to look to see if the leprosy had been healed. We are all priests unto God. It is our responsibility to know the clean from the unclean. What God hath cleansed let no man call unclean. But if you see the evil leprosy is still there, then the separation must continue. But do not stop loving the leper.

Chapter 20
LOVE IS IN THE LIGHT

Part 1

The greatest book of mystery is the Holy Bible. It is the mystery of God's love for mankind. The greatest book of mystery in the Bible is the book of Revelation. But the greatest chapter of mysteries in the Bible is the first chapter of Genesis. Chapter 2 and chapter 3 are also filled with the secrets of God. Out of chapter 1, I have chosen verses 1-5 as the greatest verses of God's mysteries in all literature on the face of the earth. Let us look at verses 1-4: "In the beginning God created the heaven and the earth. And the earth was without form, and void; and darkness was upon the face of the deep, and the Spirit of God moved upon the face of the waters. And God said, Let there be light: and there was light And God saw the light, that it was good: and God divided the light from the darkness."

For your interest I would like to quote these four verses as they are written in The Holy Bible in Modern English, which has been translated directly from the Hebrew by Ferar Fenton: "By Periods God created that which produced the Solar Systems; then that which produced the earth. But the Earth was unorganized and empty; and darkness covered its convulsed surface; while the breath of God rocked the surface of its waters. God then said, 'Let there be light'; and God divided the light from the darkness."

This creation of LIGHT was not the creation of the sun, moon and stars. It is later, in verse 14, on the "fourth day" that these heavenly bodies were created. This was a different "light." It had nothing to do with the latter lights of heaven. What then is this mysterious light that overcame darkness, triumphed over it, and stole time from its power of rulership?

This is none other than God's divine presence and His glory being beamed onto a scene of chaos, such as was the condition of this earth before God set His divine love upon it. Somewhere in the secret antiquity of yesterday God blasted this planet Earth into existence. To scientists, this is no marvel; they know that new planets are being created constantly in outer space. In this way our planet was also created. It is a part of that great expansive handiwork of God Almighty. Our former condition was without form and void. Darkness was upon the face of our waters as the murky depths convulsed in millions of degrees of heat and molten lava. Just what made God choose this particular planet as the object of His redeeming love and grace, I do not know. I know that Satan also chose it and since that time both light and darkness have struggled to rule over it. Was this the abode of Lucifer when he was cast out of the presence of God? Is that why Jesus calls him the prince of this earth? Did he bring the darkness of his own presence upon the face of this planet? Is hell in the bowels of this planet? Was Satan speaking with authority when he said to Jesus, "All the kingdoms of the world, and the glory of them will I give thee, if thou wilt fall down and worship me?" Notice, Jesus did not tell him that these kingdoms did *not* belong to him! He answered him, "It is written, Thou shalt worship the Lord thy God, and him only shalt thou serve" (Matthew 4:8-10).

Another question I would like you to ponder over is: Was Lucifer there when God created this planet, and did he have a part in its original construction? Was he the ruling prince of this part of God's universe before he fell and was cast down from his position of authority? It is written of him, "Thou hast been in Eden, the garden of God; every precious stone was thy covering. . . . Thou art the anointed cherub that covereth and I HAVE SET THEE SO: Thou wast upon the holy mountain of God; thou hast walked up and down in the midst of the stones of fire. Thou wast perfect in thy ways from the day that thou wast created, until iniquity was found in thee. . . . thou hast sinned, therefore I will cast thee as profane out of the mountain of God: and I will destroy thee, O covering cherub, from the midst of the stones of fire. Thine heart was lifted up because of thy beauty, thou hast corrupted thy wisdom by reason of thy brightness: I will cast thee to the ground. . . . Thou hast defiled my sanctuary by the multitude of thine iniquities . . ." (Ezekiel 28:13-18).

What catastrophic drama really did take place back there? Were the stones that are on this earth at one time gems of sardius, diamond, sapphire, topaz and emerald? Read it again in verse 13. Where does one find these gems; are they not in the bowels of this earth? Did Lucifer in retaliation toward God, because of his damning judgment, destroy this planet in one last act of revenge? Is the earth we see today the original one, or is it a recreation of another planet that has known a holocaust unwritten in history, but evident in its geological construction? What really happened between verses 1 and 2 of Genesis, chapter 1?

And if Lucifer did try to destroy the handiwork of God's creation, would God let him succeed in completing his work of destruction? Would God not intervene? I believe that THAT is when God, seeing the darkness that was more than the natural darkness but was a demonic, spiritual darkness manifested by satanic interference, moved on the scene and declared, "LET THERE BE LIGHT!" Yes, and this is the LIGHT that LIGHTETH every man that cometh into the world (John 1:9). This is not the light that one sees with the eyes. Even a blind man can see this LIGHT. It is the light of enlightenment, the one that the darkness of evil cannot hinder or absorb.

What was this "Day" that resulted from the Light conquering the darkness? Was it only the period of time between sundown of one day and sundown of the following day? Or was it the period of time between sunrise and sunset? I believe that this "day" can be more easily understood when we think of the words of Jesus, "I must work the works of him that sent me, while it is day: the night cometh, when no man can work" (John 9:4). Webster defines *day* as *a time specified for work.* The "day" spoken of in Genesis 1:5 was not a period of twenty-four hours, but a time for God to do His mighty works.

The word "night" in Hebrew comes from the word *laylah* which means "a twist away from the light," i.e., *to turn away from the light,* and it also means *adversity.*

Why did God permit darkness to exist? Notice, I am NOT speaking about natural darkness. When He spread the mantle of His glory over this planet, could He not have banished the darkness of evil forever? Surely He could have, but He had some apparent reason for allowing the "night" to exist. In Ephesians 6:12 Satan is called the "ruler of darkness." God came down to take the planet earth away from Lucifer by shedding His light and glory over it. He split the ruling darkness in half and in that instant the glory of God's light began to drive back the powers of darkness that were in control and that had created chaos. And when God saw this light He said, "IT'S A NEW DAY!" And it was the beginning of a wonderful new period of time for God to do His mighty works.

It was the origin of all God's known creational works. It was the demonstration of His greatness. The glory of God was thrown out over space. You and I were there that day to see it, but we don't remember. However, God tried to remind Job when He said, "Where were you when I laid the foundation of the earth? . . . When the morning stars sang together, and all the *Sons of God* shouted for joy?" (Job 38:4, 7). Some day we will remember what we saw on that glorious day of splendor and beauty when the Glory of God was spread out, not only over this little planet, but over all the universe. For we, too, are called sons of God (1 John 3:2, "Beloved, now are we the sons of God, and it doth not yet appear what we shall be: but we know that, when he shall appear, we shall be like him; for we shall see him as he is." This glory of God is the Light of God and it was through this demonstration of LIGHT that all life began to exist.

The word LIGHT in Hebrew is *owr* which means *illumination, lightning, happiness,* etc. He is our Happiness because He is our Light.

Without light there could be no life. John, speaking by God-given revelation says, "... the life was the light of men" (John 1:4). Jesus said, "I am the light of the world: he that followeth me shall not walk in darkness, but shall have the light of life" (John 8:12).

What IS that light that gives enlightenment and life? It is the very essence, the ultimate nature of God himself. He IS the Light of the world. That is why Jesus could say, "I am the light of the world." Jesus was God.

There can be no darkness in God's presence. That is why, in speaking of the Holy City in Revelation 21:23, it says, "And the city had no need of the sun, neither of the moon, to shine in it: for the glory of God did lighten it, and the Lamb is the light thereof." THE GLORY OF GOD IS LIGHT—whether it be in the Holy City or here on earth. John the revelator says, "There shall be NO NIGHT there" (21:25). Hallelujah! There shall be no prince of darkness there! The terrific struggle between good and evil will have come to its final end. Not only is this planet earth a battleground between good and evil, Satan and God, but also you and I who were created out of the dust of this earth are a battleground for the conquest of all ages. As long as we live in the flesh we will fall victim to the kingdom of darkness because we are allowing the cursed earth to rule. But when we live in the Spirit, we are living as Jesus lived and we are conquering the powers of darkness. Jesus died to translate us out of the kingdom of darkness into the kingdom of His dear Son. Oh, may God help us to possess our God-given rights as sons of light and love!

Today there are two kinds of people in the world. They are the sons of light and the sons of darkness. The Essenes, whose writings have been discovered in the Qumran caves at the Dead Sea, have always believed that the final battle of all ages will be the battle between these sons of light and the sons of darkness. Don't you think for one minute that God is going to permit you to go A.W.O.L. while the battle of all ages is going to be taking place on the final battlefield of this planet! You better make up your mind you are going to be there—on one side or the other! You say, "But what about those who have died?" They will be there, too. I see them coming with the armies of heaven just like Jude saw them: "Behold the Lord cometh with ten thousands [myriads] of His saints to execute judgment upon all, and to convict [original Greek] all that are ungodly among them of all their ungodly deeds" (Jude 1:14, 15).

Either we are children of light or children of darkness, and all our multitude of words and niceties which we portray to deceive people will not be able to protect us on that day. Our protection will be the LIGHT that is shining through us. John clearly tells us that that LIGHT is none other than LOVE. "He that LOVETH his brother abideth in the LIGHT" (1 John 2:10). Here we clearly see that love is in the light. God wants His light to shine through us by the love that is in our hearts.

What was creation? It was an act of love. Without love, God could not have created a single thing. It was the light that divided the darkness. Love conquers hate. The greatest miracle that we, as children of God, can do is to banish the powers of darkness by the love of God in us. If we are to represent God we must be like Him. The Bible says GOD IS LOVE! It does not say GOD IS POWER! It was through love that He had His power. Any power without love is a terrible thing. It can be very evil. Satan has a certain amount of power. This is the darkness that God has permitted to exist for a time. This is the "night" of our time. The thing that the church of God needs is not power, but rather it is LOVE. When we start seeking for the right things we will have the results that our life is supposed to have in our time on earth.

In Exodus 28:30 we read, "And thou shalt put in the breastplate of judgment the Urim and the Thummim: and they shall be upon Aaron's heart, when he goeth in before the Lord. . . . and Aaron shall bear the judgment of the children of Israel upon his heart before the Lord continually."

We have already mentioned how that Aaron the high priest had to wear the breastplate at all times. We also said that the Lord wants us to wear the breastplate of love and faith over our hearts. In that breastplate there were to be two things: the Urim and the Thummim. These are two objects of mystery. No one living today has ever seen them. To understand a little about them, we must try to understand their meaning in the Hebrew language. Urim means *the plural of flame, the oracular brilliancy of the figures in the high priest's breastplate.* Thummim means *one of the epithets of the objects in the high priest's breastplate as an emblem of complete Truth.*

So the Urim and Thummim spoke of two great attributes of God—LIGHT and TRUTH. Aaron was commanded to carry Light and Truth over his heart. He could not approach God's presence without them. They must also be our attributes. We, too, cannot approach God unless we come in the same way. That light of love must be in our hearts at ALL times. Do not think for a minute that you can come into His presence with hate and unforgiveness in your heart. Nor can you come without perfect truth. If you play the hypocrite, your soul is in danger.

Aaron was told he must bear the judgment of the children of Israel continually upon his heart. Judgment means to be able to discern a situation and to judge it rightly. In Numbers 27:21 it says, "And he [Joshua] shall stand before Eleazar the priest, who shall ask counsel for him after the judgment of Urim before the Lord: at his word shall they go out, and at his word they shall come in, both he, and all the children of Israel with him, even all the congregation." We find here that in the Urim there was counsel and light. Why was there counsel? Why was there guidance? Because there was light in it and light guides. It was close to the heart, the source of love's emotion. From here it streamed out light and guidance, not only for one man Joshua, but for all the children of Israel. Joshua needed guidance because he was their leader. They would know when to go to battle and when not, and they would find God's perfect will for them from the Light.

That shows us that there is Truth in the Light. Remember the light is love. Light is the demonstration of love that will give us correct guidance so we will do the will of God.

Love is "the beaming out of God's personality" and in that love is a light to show you where to go. It is that "lovinglight" that told Joseph to take Mary and the baby Jesus and go to Egypt to escape Herod's executors. It also told him when to come back. It was in that light that Jesus did all His earthly ministry. That is why He could say that He was the Light of the World. He told US to walk in that Light also. And John said that if we have that Light in us we will love our brethren. We must be careful we do not mistake the advice of men for the guidance of the Light.

There was a prophet whose name was never given, who was told by God to go to Jeroboam, the king of Israel, and give him a prophecy of judgment. When he did that, the king was so angry that he stretched out his hand and cried, "Arrest him!" Immediately the king's hand was crippled and he couldn't use it. When he cried for the prophet to heal him, he was restored. God had told this prophet who could do these mighty deeds that he must not stop to eat or drink with anyone on the way. He was to return straight home. This was not a hard thing to do. To speak God's word before all the enemies was a hard thing—they could have killed him—but he did it. Then came the test in small things. On the way home the son of another prophet met him and said, "Please come and visit my father. He is also a prophet like yourself, and an angel has told him to invite you to our house to eat." The prophet was hungry and he no doubt thought, "I did a great work for God. I got a revival started. Now I can let down on the standard. I don't think God will mind if I stop and have a dinner with this famous prophet. After all, an angel told him to invite me. Now I am getting so great that angels have to do all these fine things for me." So he went. It was as they were eating that the words of judgment came out of the false prophet's mouth. NOW he had to speak the truth. "WHY did you disobey God and stop to eat when God told you not to stop on the way to eat? You will never reach home!" And he never did. He got on his ass and started for home but a lion met him on the way and killed him (1 Kings 13:1-32).

What was the matter with that prophet? As long as he went by God's guidance he was safe, but when he went by man's advice it was his doom. He went even by a religious man's advice. But it was wrong. He did not go by the guiding-light. And that is why so many of God's people are DEAD today. They are not only dead physically, but also spiritually. They have been listening too long to the wrong voice because they have no light within them.

Saul hated David for so long that finally he could not get any guidance from God any more. Hate will put the light out in our soul. Love will enlighten us and show us the way to God. In the end, Saul destroyed himself. Many will destroy themselves as they lose the light of God because of hate, bitterness, grudges and listening to the wrong voice.

Where does the light speak? It speaks where it is—right within us. God breathed within us the breath of life. We became a LIVING soul. That light is in the life that God breathed into us when He lighted up our soul with His light. When God created you, He put something of His own eternal life into you. The spark of God is in you. The Quakers were right. This spark of light is none other than God's own life in mankind. And it is there in your soul that God speaks from. Right from inside you. When we deaden this voice by constantly disobeying it, we diminish our ability to hear God speak to us. Then we can no longer hear with the spirit-ears, and so we start to rely on the natural ears. That is how we can get the wrong guidance.

The priest was ordered to carry the light over his heart because the light must be united with love. We will lose our guidance if we lose our love. When we are guided by our ears, we are not guided by love. We are guided by senses.

There are three ways in which God's children are being led:

1. They are guided by the love of God ruling in every decision they make.
2. They are guided by circumstances.
3. They are guided by their senses.

Let us strive to get our guidance by the first of these, for it is the highest order. As His love enlightens us, we have that URIM within our hearts.

You say, "Where is that Urim and Thummim today? Why did we lose it? Where did it go?" It was lost when the children of Israel, because of their great wickedness, were led into Babylonian captivity. It was never found after that. Nobody knows what has happened to it. We know that when they returned from Babylon they did not have it (Nehemiah 7:65). They hoped then that a priest would be found who might have it. But no one "stood up with it." That was 2,500 years ago and no one has ever found it since. But there is a wonderful promise that we are not hoping and waiting in vain for the Urim and Thummim.

In Deuteronomy 33:8 Moses was giving an end-time prophecy to the tribe of Levi and he said, "Let thy Thummim and thy Urim be with thy Holy one..." This prophecy was given almost one thousand years before the Urim and Thummim were lost in the captivity. Moses said that the Urim and Thummim would be given to those who would stand with God at the waters of Meribah. Meribah means "the place of proving and testing." It is the place where the children of Israel were tried to see if they would be faithful to God. I believe that if we come through the trials and testings of life where our faithfulness is tested and proven, God will give His priestly people the Urim and Thummim again. We are living in the end-time when all of God's children are going to be tried and proven; and out of that proven company God will choose His priests whom He can trust to give guidance to others.

In Revelation 2:26-28 it says, "He that overcometh, and keepeth my works unto the end, to him will I give power over the nations: And he shall rule them with a rod of iron . . . and I will give him the morning star."

What is the morning star? It is the same star as the evening star. It is the first star out at night, way off in the western horizon, close to the new moon. And it is also the last star you will see in the morning, just as the sun is breaking through the darkness of the night. There in the east is that beautiful, big morning star. It is coming around on the other side of this planet.

The Lord said, "When you overcome every temptation with a heart full of gratitude and praise to God in the hour of testing, then He will give you the MORNING STAR." As the darkness of a long night begins to fade and the lesser stars grow dim, your morning star will still shine in its splendor even more beautifully, because it is the only one left. That is the glory of God in the early hours of the morning after the darkness of a long night of adversity. Hang on a little longer, children of God; when there is only ONE star left, the sun will soon usher in a new day. The name of that morning star is Venus. It is named after the goddess of love and beauty in Roman mythology. It is the star of love and beauty. God says, "I'll give you the star of love and beauty. After the long night of trial and testing you will be shining out with such a beautiful love that you will look like an angel because you will *be* like an angel. The glory of God will translate you into that glory which you desire." This is the promise of God.

Moses promised us way back there, that the sons of trial and testing would have the Urim and Thummim. "Oh, Moses, we have waited a long time since you prophesied those words. Already 3,500 years have gone by. It is time that this prophecy should be fulfilled. Without it, we do not have the guidance we need." Oh, may God give us that morning star—

that millenium star of love and beauty!

What is a star? It is a sun. Venus, however, is not a real star; it is a planet, the second in order from the sun. So the morning star is actually a planet! What do you see when you look at a planet? Without the sun being reflected from it, it is nothing but a ball of stone, rock, dust, etc. But when the sun shines on it, then it mirrors that beautiful reflection of the sun. So what you actually see on Venus is the sun shining on it and reflecting back to us on earth. And you and I are nothing but dust. Out of dust we were created and there is no light in us, except for that little soul which God put right inside of us. When we let that light of God in us get bigger and bigger and allow that love of God in us to develop, we shall begin to reflect His splendor, His beauty and His love out into the darkness of the night. This treasure have we in earthen vessels (2 Corinthians 4:7).

When God created man and breathed the breath of life in him, He breathed love into him. That love is the light and the life of all the human race. Jesus said, "Ye are the light of the world" (Matthew 5:14). He also said, "The light of the body is the eye: if therefore thine eye be single, thy whole body shall be full of light. But if thine eye be evil, thy whole body shall be full of darkness. If therefore the light that is in thee be darkness, how great is that darkness" (Matthew 6:22, 23).

You are a little "planet." If you are able to reflect the glory of God's Son, you will become the light that you reflect. But if the light of God's love cannot penetrate into your innermost being, you will be filled with great darkness.

It is not our own self-made love that we reflect. We do not have any. It is HIS eternal, glorious, beautiful, perfect love which He placed into us from the beginning when He created us and breathed in us and we became a living soul. As long as it radiates from us we will have His guidance.

Part 2

The light that God spoke into being at the beginning of His creative work, and which filled the entire space with the radiating glory of God's presence, is not only the light that creates, it is also the light that sustains. If that light of God ever forsakes this creation then all will be destroyed in a moment of time. This light and this glory of God is NOT visible to the natural eye of man because man has been blinded since the fall. We are partially blind. There is a "veil" between our eyes and the spirit world. Scales are on our eyes. We need to have our eyes anointed with eye salve in order to let us see again what we shall one day see. The only things that are visible to us are the natural, material things. We live in the realm of the senses, except for now and then when God lifts that ban and we are able to see what we call visions. It is then that we can see angels, demons, the saints, our heavenly home, the agony of hell and Jesus our Lord. There is a very real spiritual world that is around us all the time, but it is only made visible to the spiritual eye and not to the natural eye.

This is also true about our ability to hear. There are sounds which our natural ears cannot pick up. There are notes so high in the scale, with vibrations so fast, that our natural ear is unable to pick up those vibrations and so we cannot hear these sounds. Even the dog can hear sounds which we cannot. The sound of heaven's music is always in the air, and now and then souls have heard that music. The voice of my Lord is speaking at all times, but only now and then is my ear quickened enough to hear that voice.

During a time when I was living alone I remember one afternoon while I was resting, suddenly I was awakened and Jesus was whispering in my ear and telling me that in these last times there would be a glorious manifestation of the Elect, and His mighty power will fill those whom He had chosen to represent His glory on the earth. And then the tenor of His voice changed and He began to whisper. It was the voice of the most beautiful Lover. Full of love, He whispered right into my left ear, "I am coming very, very soon."

I will never forget that. I had heard my Lord speak audibly with these natural ears. But He is speaking ALL the time. If only we could hear! We would be able to listen to the heavenly choir. One evening, as one of our End-Time Handmaidens was walking from one building to another, she heard the heavenly organ being played. The sound of that triumphant, lively, majestic music was so magnificent it filled the whole valley! There wasn't a person in miles who could have done it. Neither is there another house around from which the music might have come. She was hearing the organs of heaven.

God is beginning to visit this world one more time. Strange manifestations are beginning to take place. Not long ago Paul Harvey, the well-known news commentator, said, "Well, it has happened again. Another driver picked up a hitch-hiker, and he said to him, 'Fasten the seat belts.' He put on the seat belt and the shoulder belt, and then he turned to the driver of the car and said, 'Do you know that the Lord Jesus Christ is coming soon?' The driver was shocked. He turned to answer him, and the man was missing! The car was going down the road at about 70 miles an hour, the car door had not been opened, the safety belt was still fastened, and his passenger was missing! Who was he? Either an angel or a glorified saint returned to give a message from God. I must warn you, we are having visitors from another world!" We don't always see them because our vision is only partial, but God is beginning to take away our blindness. He says to the indifferent Laodicean church that did not have perfect love, "Anoint thine eyes with eyesalve, that thou mayest see." (Revelation 3:18) Let the darkness be removed. For almost 6,000 years this world has been in darkness, but there is a light shining from God that is growing brighter and brighter and one of these days it will forever destroy the darkness. Hallelujah! And we are called to be a part of that light.

Isaiah, the great prophet of the Millenium, commands us

"Arise, shine; for thy light is come, and the glory of the Lord is risen upon thee. For behold, the darkness shall cover the earth, and gross darkness the people: but the Lord shall arise upon thee, and His glory shall be seen upon thee. And the heathen shall come to thy light, and kings to the brightness of thy rising" (Isaiah 60:1-3). The glory of God is risen upon YOU. It is on you because it is IN you. Remember, the Lord told us He would give us the morning star. That means that we are going to BECOME that bright and beautiful morning star which comes up to announce, "Behind me the sun is coming." The first thing that will happen before Jesus personally appears is that His sons of glory will begin to shine. His forerunners, like John the Baptist of old, will announce His coming by being the anointed bearers of the light. The Christ-ones. They are already appearing, telling the world that the Sun of Righteousness is coming with healing in His wings. Redemption, salvation and deliverance for the whole of God's creation are within the time of the present generation. God is going to finish the glorious work of creation that He began on this world, and He is going to finish it in US!

There is another thing we lost. We not only lost our eyesight and our hearing, we have also lost much of our memory. We do not even remember our whole lifetime on this planet. Some of us cannot remember what we ate for supper three days ago. None of us remember the time we spent in our mother's womb. And yet most of us were there for nine months. But that does not mean that we did not exist. As infants and little children we developed every day until we could talk and walk and communicate. Our senses were so keen that at the age of three we could have learned three languages perfectly, and yet we can remember practically nothing of those first three years of our life.

God said to Job, "Where were you when I laid the foundations of the earth?" Beloved, I believe that one day when His light shines in and illuminates our minds, we will remember. There are secrets locked in the mind that hypnosis can unlock. I do not believe in hypnosis. I feel that when man uses it, he is using a power to unlock the memory that is not permitted by God. But one day God will, through HIS LIGHT, unlock our memory and we will know as we are known. This is what will give us guidance. Through this light we will be able to rule the earth. Paul said, "Know ye not that ye shall judge angels?" (1 Corinthians 6:3).

Paul also said that we can speak the language of the angels when we speak through the anointing of the Holy Spirit (1 Corinthians 13:1). Where did we get this ability to speak a language we have not heard since we left heaven? Could it be that the quickening we receive through the baptism of the Holy Spirit is a part of that glorious millenium-enlightenment that we are awaiting? I believe it is. This is also the reason why many when they are filled with the Holy Spirit see visions. Here in America we seek tongues, and tongues are good; but we need to seek *God*. When we have the mighty fullness of the Holy Spirit, it will touch more than our tongue; it will touch our eyes and our ears and our memory. It will go into the depths of our being. On the mission field I have seen the mighty outpouring of the Holy Spirit. Children were taken into the heavenlies. They saw angels, talked with Jesus and visited their heavenly mansions. The true visitation from God will be so dynamic that it will shatter our previous reservations and traditions which have blinded, deafened and dulled our spiritual understanding.

It will also touch the heart. As we lost our spiritual sight, hearing and memory, we have also lost our love. We cannot find one another in the spirit and so we judge without mercy or compassion. That is why there is so little love in the church today. The churches are full of criticism, hatred, fighting, division and we all cover it up with a cloak of hypocrisy because we blame it on someone else. We think we ourselves can do NO wrong. We assume that we are pleasing to God and, though we are not as good as we might be, He loves us as we are. We have become blind, leading the blind. And there is no light in us. Because we do not have love, we have become the children of darkness. The hypocrites are many and the LOVERS are few.

The world is without enough witnesses because we do not have enough lovers. It is not more missionaries, preachers and evangelists we need—it is LOVERS. We have not been able to attract the sinner because it is going to take love, and we don't have it. But we ARE going to get it. Isaiah said, ". . . the glory of God shall be seen upon US." And then, that is when the heathen shall come to our light.

Paul said something which seemed to be almost boastful. He said, "The Lord commanded us saying, 'I have set thee to be a light of the Gentiles, that thou shouldest be for salvation unto the ends of the earth' " (Acts 13:47). God is choosing us to be lights for the salvation of the whole earth. That is what light does. It will bring salvation in this end time to the entire world, and if we will not have that light in this end time we are not obeying and fulfilling our call.

In Philippians 2:15 Paul said, "That ye may be blameless and harmless, the sons of God, without rebuke, in the midst of a crooked and perverse generation, among whom ye shine as lights in the world." We see here that the sons of God are the lights of the world. And the only way we can be this is to be blameless. And how can we be blameless if we don't have love? Love is the fulfilling of all laws.

In Ephesians 5:8 Paul says, "For ye were sometimes darkness, but now are ye light in the Lord: Walk as children of light." And then He tells us what our fruits should be if we are children of the light: goodness, righteousness and truth.

Isaiah says in 25:3, "Therefore shall the strong people glorify thee, the city of the terrible nations shall fear thee." When God will glorify His chosen ones, He will put such strength in them that the terrible nations shall fear them. In verse 7 he says, "And He will destroy in this mountain the face of the covering cast over all people, and the veil that is spread over all nations." Hallelujah! the veil over our eyes, the dullness of our ears will be removed in that day of our glorification. And then verse 8 sums it all up in final victory: "He will swallow up death in victory; and the Lord God will wipe away tears from off all faces; and the reproach of His people shall He take away from off all the earth: for the Lord hath spoken!"

Oh, what a glorious day awaits us tomorrow! Oh, how my heart and soul long to enter into that day! Old things shall pass away and ALL things shall become new.

"We have been with child, we have been in pain, we have as it were brought forth wind: We have not wrought any deliverance in the earth; neither have the inhabitants of the world fallen," but something is going to happen. We shall fall in love with our heavenly bridegroom and within the bride a miracle of immaculate conception shall take place. The sons of God, the beautiful people, strong and anointed with love, shall arise. And when they do, "Thy dead men shall live, together with my dead body shall they arise. Awake and sing, ye that dwell in dust: for thy dew is as the dew of herbs and the earth shall cast out the dead" (Isaiah 26:18, 19).

Chapter 21
LOVE WEEPS

"Jesus wept" (John 11:35). How strange that the shortest verse in the Bible speaks one of the most poignant messages! Just two words, and yet it is a complete sentence. It is so small that one can easily overlook it and miss it completely. But for the one who is observant, it is like a streak of lightning on a dark night, or the comet trail of a falling star. "Jesus wept!"

The crowd that followed Jesus was always very large. His critics were many, but of true friends who received Him and took Him into their homes, He had very, very few. Several days before that dramatic scene, He received the message, "Lord, behold, he whom thou lovest is sick." Immediately He knew that this sickness was for the glory of God. He could rest in this knowledge. When you "know" something, you do not have to be encouraged to believe. You are past believing. To "know" is greater than "to believe."

Because He "knew," He finished the work He was doing and then He went to Bethany. As soon as Martha heard that Jesus was coming, she went out to meet Him. Then she came back in after talking to Him, and secretly told Mary that the Master had come and was calling for her. There was a crowd at the home that day and they immediately followed her because they thought she was going to the grave and they wanted to go along with her.

As Jesus looked around about Him and saw those people, He was looking right inside of them. Many of them were members of the family, others were neighbors and friends. There were a few idle, curious ones, inquisitive about what was going on. A few of the critics were also there. You get all kinds of people in a crowd. He could see their sorrow. Here they were, crying about a man who was dead. Jesus was not crying for Lazarus, even though he was dead, because Jesus knew where Lazarus was; right then he was in the presence of the angels. Jesus knew that Lazarus was having a great time singing in the choir of heaven and that he was amongst those who love God. Lazarus was a friend of Jesus and that had made him a friend of God. But Jesus saw the sorrow in the hearts of the ones he loved. He saw the confusion in Martha's heart about the words He had just spoken to her earlier. He remembered her saying to Him, "Master, if you had been here, my brother would not have died." He knew that she was doubting His love.

Yes, Jesus wept; but He didn't weep for Lazarus, He wept for the others. The Jews seeing Him weeping said, "Behold how He loved him!" They did not know that He was crying, not for Lazarus, but for them. He was crying because of the multitudes of people who had lived years and centuries long in unbelief, and how the curse of sin had brought death upon all generations from the time of Adam. This love which was in His heart reached down, not only for Lazarus' sisters, but for the generations who had suffered because the grave had been victorious and death had conquered. He looked back over the past 4,000 years of suffering where men had died and gone to an eternity without God. He saw the widows and orphans who had suffered because the one they loved and needed had been taken from them by the grim reaper of death. He wept for the generations of those who had suffered the sting of death. That is why Jesus wept that day. It was not because of Lazarus. He knew what He was going to do with Lazarus. Lazarus was a picture of the millions of souls who had died through the years of the past. He saw again on the faces of those standing by the terrible look of fear and hopelessness that death brings, and He wept.

He was feeling the hurt that you felt when you laid your beloved one in the grave, and He wept for you. Yes, beloved, He wept for you!

As He stood there, He knew that it was good that He had come. Had He not just said to Martha a few minutes earlier, "I am the resurrection and the life; he that believeth in me, though he were dead, yet shall he live: and whosoever liveth and believeth in me shall never die" (John 11:25, 26). He wept because He knew who He was, that He was the resurrection and the life and that He had come to suffer for a suffering world, and that they were rejecting Him and His life-message. They hated Him and rejected Him, no matter how much He loved them. They refused His help and died in their sins in spite of His love; and so He wept!

He knew that He would raise up Lazarus, even though his body was already rotting in the grave. This was a sign of what He wanted to do for the whole world. But they didn't want him. They didn't love Him; they didn't recognize Him; so He couldn't help them. And still He loved them. So He wept!

Today Jesus looks over the world; He sees us in a way we cannot see ourselves. We are a lost people, a generation in darkness. We are a people who are suffering and who are going to suffer more. Every day and every week brings another toll of death and suffering. In one week alone, some time back, 150 died in a train crash in Paris when two trains crashed into each other in a tunnel. Another plane with over 100 people could not take off from the airport in London, England and crashed with all souls on board. In Hong Kong a terrible typhoon washed down the great tenement buildings where hundreds lost their lives. A great flood swept through three states of the U.S.A., thousands had to flee from the rushing waters, many died. All this in one short week. And it is getting worse. It is not going to get better. While all this is going on, we read about it in our newspaper or hear about it on our newscast and we forget about it, but Jesus weeps. If we had only a little of His love, we would weep also. Perhaps

He weeps because we don't weep. He weeps about our hardness of heart and our indifference to the tragedies of this world. He sees souls perishing and going to hell, and He weeps because we do so little to save them.

As Jesus was coming down from Bethany and looking out over the city of Jerusalem the Bible says, "He beheld the city, and wept over it, saying, if thou hadst known, even thou, at least in this thy day, the things which belong unto thy peace! but now they are hid from thine eyes. For the days shall come upon thee, that thine enemies shall cast a trench about thee, and compass thee round, and keep thee in on every side [lay siege], and shall lay thee even with the ground, and thy children within thee: and they shall not leave in thee one stone upon another; because thou knewest not the time of thy visitation" (Luke 19:41-44).

Jesus wept for Jerusalem because He saw the coming calamity. He saw the tribulation that was at the door. He wept for their children who would be trampled under the feet of the Roman horses. He wept for the young virgins who would be ravaged and murdered. He wept for the mothers who would see their sons slain before their eyes. He wept for the religious Jews who would die in their religion. He wept for the beautiful temple that would lie in a heap of rubble where once it had proudly stood. But most of all, He wept because the whole thing could have been averted, if only they had known that God had visited them!

Sure, God loves America! He loved Jerusalem even more! But if we do not know the hour of God's mercy and do not accept His grace, we will also be visited by another visitor and the next one will be more cruel than the Roman army. Oh, friend, is Jesus weeping today for America? Is He weeping through you? Do you love your nation enough to weep over it? Love must weep!

Paul caught a glimpse of Jesus weeping when he wrote, "Who [Jesus] in the days of his flesh, when he had offered up prayers and supplications with strong crying and tears unto HIM that was able to save him from death, and was heard in that he feared" (Hebrews 5:7). Paul knew that Jesus had cried out to the Father with STRONG CRYING and TEARS. There in that Garden of Gethsemane He agonized for a lost world that was even then preparing to crucify Him. Gethsemane means "oil-press." It is the place where the oil is pressed out of the olives. God has to put us into the hard places so that the oil will flow from our lives to bring blessing to others. But, oh, how the tears flow at our Gethsemane!

It is impossible to love greatly and not feel the pain that comes with love. Paul said, "Love suffers long." A great love will break the hardness around our hearts so that the oil can be poured out.

In Song of Solomon the bride says, "I am sick of love." There is such a thing as being "lovesick." In our modern day we don't want to accept the suffering that comes with a great love. We want only the joy, not the pain. And yet it is out of the pain that our greatness is born. Look at the face of Beethoven and you will see a man who suffered intense agony. He was tortured by a love which could never be fulfilled. Yet, out of that pain have come some of the greatest masterpieces of music this world has ever heard.

Great genius and great love can never be separated; in fact I am not sure but that that they are one and the same thing. When deafness struck Beethoven, the young woman he loved separated herself from him. Music was his only solace. His heart was filled with divine love, and through this gift he sought to express his love. Within the sealed-up casements of his soul Beethoven heard the Heavenly Choir; and as he walked, bareheaded, upon the street, oblivious to all, centered in his own silent world, he would sometimes suddenly burst into song. At other times he would beat time, talk to himself and laugh aloud. He walked the woods and traversed the fields alone and unnoticed, and there, out under the open sky, much of his best work was done. The famous "Moonlight Sonata" was shaped on one of these lonely walks by night across the fields when the master could shake his shaggy head, lift up his face to the sky, and cry aloud, all undisturbed. In the recesses of his imagination he saw the sounds. There are men to whom sounds are invisible symbols of forms and colors. When love spurned him, and misunderstandings with kinsmen came, and lawsuits and poverty added their weight of woe, he fell back upon music, and out under the stars he listened to the sonatas of God.*

Why are we no longer producing great symphonies that cause the soul to be reborn? Why is our art becoming increasingly more vague and meaningless? Is it because we have come to a new generation that is afraid to "give themselves?" Are there no geniuses because there are no great lovers? Are we so fearful of suffering and pain that we cannot release the eternal quality of the soul that lies cramped and sealed within us? Do we cover our true self with a cloak of lightness that borders on giddiness? Has our empty-heartedness evidenced itself by the music we appreciate? Why does this generation prefer the thunder of "rock" to the sweet call of the lovebird? And is Jesus weeping because we are afraid to weep? Do we really think that anything precious can be attained without great cost? We cry to be used by God, but are not willing to pay the price, and so the cross stands empty because we will not permit the pain that it will cost us to be His disciple.

THE PAIN

> The Pain . . . like a dagger it pierces my heart
> And twists its sharp edge round and round
> Until I cry out, and teardrops start,
> And I wonder, how long can I still cry's sound.

**Great Musicians* by Elbert Hubbard.

The Pain . . . it comes and goes alway
I never know when it will strike again
Just when I think I'm free and gay,
Suddenly it's there . . . the same old pain.

The Pain . . . which sometimes dies, when joys
Which flow with it, seem to overbound,
And then, when it joy's flame destroys
Reign supreme, while I suffer its return.

The Pain . . . how much longer will you last?
I suffer so, that I fear I can no longer bear
This everlasting torment that lives only in the past
Of memories of happiness now gone, and only care.

The Pain . . . this price so costly, must I always pay
And must I always live with aching in the depth of me?
Oh God, will there never come a happy day
When pain will cease in rapturous sight of THEE?

Chapter 22
LOVE WASHES FEET

"Now before the feast of the passover, when Jesus *knew* that his hour was come that he should depart out of this world unto the Father, having *loved* his own which were in the world, he loved them unto the end. . . . Jesus knowing that the Father had *given all things into his hands,* and that he *was come from God,* and *went to God,* He riseth from supper, and laid aside his garments and took a towel, and girded himself. And after that he poureth water into a basin and began to wash the disciples' feet, and to wipe them with the towel wherewith he was girded" (John 13:1, 3-5).

One of the greatest secrets of humility is hidden in these verses. I want to draw your attention to them. Jesus could afford to be humble because He was not battling with any inferiority complex like so many of us do. We are so afraid to do any humble task because we don't want to lose our dignity. We are trying to attain a higher station in life. This is always the result of trying to prove who we are. But the true sons of God do not need to prove anything to anybody. Jesus knew who He was, and because He knew, He could do the work of a slave, which is what foot-washing really was.

First of all, Jesus knew that His hour had come. Oh, if only we would be able to recognize the times and the seasons! If we would have this enlightenment of time in this end-time! We have come to a time when there is no more time to live a life of pretenses. It was His hour of THE CROSS and THE CROWN. A little further in this chapter, verses 31 and 32,

Jesus referred to His hour of crowning glory. Listen to what He says, "Now is the Son of man glorified, and God is glorified in him. If God be glorified in him, God shall also glorify him in himself, and shall straightway glorify him." How wonderful to realize that our Crown is in the Cross. It is impossible to have one without the other.

Governor John Bowring (1792-1872), who was at one time the governor of the British Colony of Hong Kong, was so deeply impressed by the towering ruins of the old St. Paul's cathedral in Macao which had been destroyed with fire, that he wrote the great and well-loved hymn:

> In the Cross of Christ I glory,
> Towering o'er the wrecks of time;
> All the light of sacred story,
> Gathers round its head sublime.
>
> When the woes of life o'er take me,
> Hopes deceive, and fears annoy,
> Never shall the cross forsake me:
> Lo! it glows with peace and joy.
>
> When the sun of bliss is beaming
> Light and love upon my way,
> From the cross the radiance streaming
> Adds more luster to the day.
>
> Bane and blessing, pain and pleasure,
> By the cross are sanctified
> Peace is there that knows no measure,
> Joys that through all time abide.

I, too, have often been moved deeply by this same sight. It is plainly visible as one comes into the harbor. All of the cathedral is in ruins, except for the front wall. There on the top is that beautiful cross standing like it stood on the first morning it was put there over one hundred years ago.

We will be glorified only as we accept the cross that the Lord has given us. Jesus knew that the hour to accept His cross had come. If we can know when our time has come to take up our cross, then we will be ready to do the humble things that pride would never have permitted us to do.

The SECOND thing that enabled Jesus to wash the feet of His disciples was that He LOVED them, and that He had loved them all the way through to the end. Love will make an idiot out of you. For the love of a child you will do silly things like making faces, acting like a clown, jumping around, etc. You can humble yourself and come down to the level of a child to reach them in their own capacity of humor and entertainment. There will be times when love will humble us down to people of a lower spiritual plane than ourselves, so that we can teach them a lesson which they would never be able to learn otherwise. Proverbs says, "Answer a fool according to his folly, lest he be wise in his own conceit" (Proverbs 26:5). Proverbs 24:7 says, "Wisdom is too high for a fool." The Love of God will enable you to "wash the feet" even of those who would betray you. Jesus washed the feet of all His disciples, even the feet of Judas. If you know who you are in God, that your hour has come and that you have enough of God's love in your heart, there will be no task too lowly or humble for you to perform. You can dig ditches, plow a field, scrub floors, carry out garbage and clean toilets with the same grace as you can pray and preach, if you are a son of God. But if you are not a son of God, then these tasks will be a thorn in your flesh and an embarassment to your "reputation" which you are seeking so hard to build up.

One of the greatest men of God who ever lived in Canada was J. H. Blair. He was the district superintendent of the Pentecostal Assemblies of Canada. He was also in charge of their great annual Braeside Camp Meeting. In those days they did not have the bathroom facilities that we have today. They had outside back-houses which soon began to smell atrociously when 5,000 people gathered together and all used them. Every morning early this high servant of God would himself, personally, clean out those toilets. No one dreamed, when he stood on the platform several hours later and swayed the multitudes with his anointed preaching, that, instead of praying in the early hours of the morning to get the mighty anointing that was his, he had been cleaning out their own toilet. Beloved, the anointing does not always come on our knees; sometimes it comes when we roll a stone from a well (Jacob), dig a well (Israel), grind the millstone (Sampson), flee from our enemies (David), or slave in the salt mines of Patmos like John.

The THIRD thing Jesus knew was that God had given all things into his hands. It is time that we are reminded of who we really are in the kingdom. We can stop hanging our head in shame, put back our shoulders and adjust the queenly (or kingly) crown, take our scepters and begin our place of leadership and rulership right now. Our hour has come for our glorification! Jesus has given us power against unclean spirits, to cast them out and to heal all manner of sickness and all manner of disease (Matthew 10:1). He has said, "Behold, I give unto you power to tread on serpents and scorpions, and over all the power of the enemy: and nothing shall by any means hurt you" (Luke 10:19). Paul said, "In all these things we are MORE than conquerors" (Romans 8:37). In 2 Corinthians 2:14 he said, "Now thanks be unto God, which always causeth us to triumph in Christ, and maketh manifest the savour of His knowledge in every place." John said, "Greater is he that is in you than he that is in the world" (1 John 4:4). The psalmist said, "Through thee will we push down our enemies: through thy name will we tread them under that rise up against us" (Psalm 44:5). "For whatsoever is born of God overcometh the world" (1 John 5:4).

Oh, hallelujah! Jesus knew He was "born of God." It is time that we who are truly born again know that we also have been "born of God." And in knowing this truth, let us take our place as overcomers, conquerors and spiritual victors in the name of our Lord Jesus Christ. The world is waiting for the manifestation of these "sons" of God who have been born of God for this hour. Let us begin by washing feet.

The FOURTH thing that enabled the Lord Jesus to wash feet was that He knew where He had come from. Beloved, some of us have forgotten where we have come from. We "lord it over" the sinner and backslider and feel superior to them because we have forgotten that there was a time when we ourselves were sinners. Paul always remembered that he was the "chiefest of sinners." The Word of God says, Look to the rock from which you have been hewn and the hole of the pit whence ye are digged (Isaiah 51:1). God had to constantly remind Israel that their father was an Amorite and their mother a Hittite, and that He had found them naked, unpitied, cast out in the open field, filthy in the blood of their birthing, and He had, in compassion, spoken unto them, "LIVE!" and had breathed life into them, covered them with His skirt, washed them, anointed them, adorned them and given them the finest of flour, honey and oil. He had made them to prosper into a great kingdom with renown and beauty that was praised among the heathen and perfect in the comeliness which God had put upon her (Ezekiel 16:14).

Israel had to be reminded that she had not acquired these things by her own righteousness, but by the mercy and goodness of God toward her. We need to be reminded of this same truth many times in our lives.

I often think how we are like the unmerciful servant who owed the king ten thousand talents, but because he had no way of paying it back, and the king was going to sell his wife and children as a payment, he fell down and begged, "Lord, have mercy on me, and I will pay thee all." The king was moved with compassion and freed him from the debt. But this same servant went out and found one of his fellow-servants which owed him a hundred pence, and he laid hands on him, took him by the throat and demanded of him, "Pay me that what you owe me!" When this poor man could not pay him back, he threw him into prison till he should pay the debt. The report of what had happened went back to the king. The king became angry and called him in. He said, "O thou wicked servant, I forgave thee all that debt, because thou desiredst me: Shouldest not thou also have had compassion on thy fellowservant, even as I had pity on thee?" In anger he threw him to the tormentors till he could pay all that was due him (Matthew 18:23-35).

Jesus knew by revelation where He had come from. Some of us know by the memory of our past deeds where we have come from. But before our birth there are secrets of eternity which have not been revealed to us. This goes back into the predestination of God's elect. God said to Jeremiah, "Before I formed thee in the belly I knew thee; and before thou camest forth out of the womb I sanctified thee, and I ordained thee a prophet unto the nations" (Jeremiah 1:5). Jeremiah could stand before his persecutors and mockers because he knew what he was. God had revealed to him his birth was predestined and his calling was that of a prophet.

Solomon knew who he was, for God had told his father David, ". . . I will set up thy seed after thee, which shall proceed out of thy bowels, and I will establish his kingdom. He shall build an house for my name, and I will stablish the throne of his kingdom for ever" (2 Samuel 7:12, 13). Solomon knew he was king by divine appointment and he knew that he was to build the temple for God.

Sampson knew that he was born to be a deliverer in Israel, for the angel of the Lord had visited his mother while she was still barren and said to her, ". . . Thou shalt conceive, and bear a son. . . . and he shall be a Nazarite unto God from the womb: and he shall begin to deliver Israel out of the hand of the Philistines" (Judges 13:3, 5). Sampson knew what he was born to be and how he must observe certain laws to attain unto the high calling of God that was on his life.

Joseph knew who and what he was. God had spoken to him in dreams. Even though he was sold into slavery and landed in prison, he knew that one day his brothers would bow before him.

Abraham knew who he was. David knew who he was.

Saul knew who he wasn't and that is why he shook and trembled.

Christ knew who He was; Mary knew who she was, and so did Elizabeth, her cousin. Paul knew who he was (a light to lighten the Gentiles), and John the Baptist knew who he was (a voice crying in the wilderness). He said, "I am not the Christ!" When you know who you are, you will not try to be somebody else. You will be content in your order.

The FIFTH key to Christ's greatness was that He knew that He was going to God. Oh, hallelujah! He knew His future. It is so wonderful, in these dark times that we are approaching, to know that we have read the last chapter of God's book of destiny and we know where we are going. We know it will be better than today. The future is as bright as the promises of God. The future is the presence of God. It is the loosening of every earthly bondage, the deliverance from every physical weakness and pain, the winning of every battle and conflict, the forgetting of every heartache, the laying down of every cross, the freeing of every burden and the forgiveness of every unpaid debt. It is to return to our God and our heaven, to fly as the clouds, unlimited by physical strength and set free from all force of gravity. It is singing with angel choirs, playing heavenly instruments in the orchestras and symphonies above. It is walking into a paid-for mansion—tax-free, sitting and dining with saints. It is seeing Jesus and having Him say, "Well done, thou good and faithful servant, enter into the joys of the Lord." It is being able to say with Paul, "I have fought a good fight, I have finished my course, I have kept the faith" (2 Timothy 4:7). No wonder Paul could say, "I am now ready to be offered."

Some years ago the doctors discovered I had cancer. I was tired and weary with life and more ready to go than to stay. I did not want to live any longer. I had served God with the best of my strength and with the utmost of sacrifice that I was possible to give Him. It was during that time that I wrote a poem I would like to share with you here.

GOODBYE!

I'm ready to go, my bags are all packed,
And the last goodbyes I have said;
I've taken a last look at all I once loved;
The last of my tears have been shed.

I stand at the door with my bag in my hand,
I've travelled with it many a mile;
But now it's not filled with trinkets or clothes,
But with souls I have found this last while.

I'm anxious to leave, it pains not to go,
For I reckoned the price long ago.
And said goodbye then to the world and its charms
For I long but for Jesus' dear arms.

My ears have long waited Thy dear call of love,
My eyes have gazed, longing for Thee
And now when You call, I will run with a bound
And no more will be parted from Thee.

The ones that I love, I will meet over there,
The others, I guess I won't miss.
'Cause if now we're distant in heart on this earth
Then up there they'll no longer be missed.

The road has been long, and I'm tired and worn,
The pain of my heart gets more strong
But soon 'twill be over, once You come for me
And together we climb that last hill.

I know I'm not worthy to open heaven's door,
And walk on those pure streets of gold
But the door has been opened by Your Precious Blood
And Your love for me never grew cold.

'Tis true, I have failed You, I bear it with shame
The thoughts of my weakness and sin,
But soon I'll pass over and be changed in Thy Name,
Then I'll never remember again.

My faults, sins and failures You said were forgiven,
Oh, Jesus, my heart's filled with praise.
Goodbye then, my neighbors, my friends and my foes,
You are free at last of my stay.

The sound of the wheels I hear from afar,
He's coming! —He's coming for me!
My fairest Lord Jesus, the One I adore,
I'll follow this last mile with Thee.

It is when you know that every day you live is an added day of grace, that you can wash the feet of others.

Chapter 23
LOVE IS IN THE GLORY

The glory of the Lord has always been of greatest importance to the children of Israel. The Shekinah was the supernatural light that appeared on the mercy seat in the Holy of Holies. The abstract noun SH'KINAH means literally "indwelling." It does not appear in the Bible, but the related verb does: MISHKAN (the dwelling). It was one of the names for Moses' desert tabernacle. God's presence was manifested in the burning bush, in the cloud of glory that was seen on Mount Sinai, then in the tabernacle, and later in the temple. In the first few centuries A.D., Aramaic versions of the Old Testament introduced the word "Shekinah" as a reverent circumlocution for God. In Exodus 25:8 an ancient translation reads, "I will let my Shekinah dwell among the children of Israel."

It is interesting to notice that the Shekinah is referred to as feminine in more than a grammatical sense from the third century on. The Shekinah is called "she." "She" is spoken of as being omnipresent in the world, but more often "she" is physically localized. The Jerusalem temple was built to be "her" permanent home. When this temple was desecrated and destroyed, Ezekiel saw "her" move out from the Holy of Holies and stand over the threshhold of the house (Ezekiel 10:4). Jewish history tells us that the Shekinah wandered to the Mt. of Olives or into the desert and waited vainly a few months for Israel to repent, then for a while withdrew to heaven. After decades of exile, partial return and the building of a second temple, some say "she" visited it intermittently. When the temple was destroyed for the last time in 70 A.D., "she" moved on to the principal synagogues of Babylon, where "she" not only appeared from time to time but made "herself" audible in the sound of a bell. "She" is believed to be a comforter of the sick, a helper of those in need, and especially tender toward repentant sinners. "She" would descend and rest upon any who performed good deeds, even if they were pagan idolaters, and would also "rest" between worthy husbands and wives. "She" accompanied her people through the centuries of exile and mourned with them ("she" was seen by one mystic in widow's garb by the Wailing Wall), "she" came to be identified with the Ideal Israel, the faithful Community which awaited redemption.*

This feminine aspect of the eternal God is the "El-Shaddai," the mother-nature of God. It is in this realm that the Shekinah is revealed and does its high office-work. You will remember us mentioning in chapter 13 that God had created Adam male and female. If God created man male and female, it was because bisexuality somehow belongs to His own nature. The fact has been recognized by early rabbinic commentators that this is true. One even concluded that God had made Adam androgynous, and later separated him into Adam and Eve. Lantero states that "it is recognized that while individuals belong to one sex or the other, we are all androgynous in the sense of having both male and female hormones, as well as potential character traits traditionally associated with both sexes."

Feminine Aspects of Divinity (a Quaker publication) by Erminie Huntress Lantero.

This beautiful aspect of the mother-nature of God is one which we need to meditate more upon. Why is it that the Glory of God, His Shekinah, seems to be resting in greater magnitude on the daughters of Eve in this generation? This is very evident, not only in one country but in all of the nations where I have worked for God, and especially where the women have been permitted by their male elders to let God's glory be borne witness of through their freedom to speak. The women are the great intercessors, the fasters, the praisers, prophetesses, missionaries, healers, and they are fast becoming the deepest of the teachers. Men have not been quick to ordain them to the ministry, but God has been doing it since the beginning of time. Judaism itself is on the threshhold of ordaining women into rabbinical ministry. They have already been granted the privilege of an *Aliya* at Torah-reading services and women have been given the permission to be counted as a part of the *minyan* for services. Sally Priesand has already been ordained by Hebrew Union College, the Reform seminary. Many other young Jewish women are seriously interested in the rabbinate as a career. The seminary's rabbinical school has 126 male students; but more than half of its 200 graduate students are women. One congregation in Indianapolis is already served by a husband-and-wife rabbinical team, both graduates of a reconstructionist seminary. It seems the daughters of Zion are preparing to be "the tabernacle wherein the Shekinah can once more take residence."

And without this Shekinah, this Glory of God, none of us are anything—be we male or female. It was the Shekinah that Moses saw in the burning bush. It appeared on the top of Mount Sinai and then descended into the Holy of Holies. It spoke with Aaron and gave guidance to Moses. It is none other than the very presence of God. And because God is love, the Shekinah is the manifested glory of God's loving nature—both mother-love and father-love. I want to give you some Scripture references for your study on this subject:

Exodus 40:34-38   "The GLORY OF THE LORD

	filled the tabernacle..."
Leviticus 16:2	"... I will appear in the CLOUD upon the mercy seat."
1 Kings 8:11	"So the priests could not stand to minister because of the cloud, for the GLORY OF THE LORD filled the house of the Lord."
Ezekiel 10:3, 4	"And the CLOUD filled the inner court, then the GLORY OF THE LORD went up from the cherub, and stood over the threshhold of the house..."
Luke 2:9	"And lo, the angel of the Lord came upon them, and the GLORY OF THE LORD shone round about them; and they were sore afraid."

Let us look again at John 13:31, 32, "Therefore, when he was gone out, Jesus said, 'Now is the Son of Man glorified, and God is glorified in him. If God be glorified in him, God shall also glorify him in himself, and shall straightway glorify him.'" In John 12:23 Jesus said, "The hour is come, that the Son of man should be glorified." Jesus was referring, not only to the cross that lay before Him, but to His glorious entrance into His full place of power which He was returning to with the Father.

In John 17:1 He said, "Father, the hour is come: glorify thy Son that thy Son also may glorify thee." He is saying that as God glorified Him, He would be enabled to glorify God. We cannot begin to glorify God without first receiving glory from Him. The spirit of glory rested upon Jesus right after this. It was manifested as Jesus began to suffer. The Glory of the Lord is accompanied with suffering. Do not forget this fact. It is impossible to receive Glory without the price of suffering. We know that, of all beings on earth, there never has been one who has been so glorified as Jesus was. Originally He had shared the glory of the Father in heaven, and now He could only return to it through the gateway of suffering. It is significant that He had to suffer to receive back the Glory which was His rightful inheritance. If Jesus who is the Prince of Glory and, as it tells us in Psalm 24:10 the King of Glory, had to suffer to be restored to His original glory, there must be a purpose for it. I believe that He is showing us, this fallen race, the way to Glory.

John 17:4, 5 says, "I have glorified thee on the earth: . . . And now, O Father, glorify thou me with thine own self with the glory which I had with thee before the world was." Jesus is taking us way back to the same place with Him before we ever were born. The day when He together with the Father created all the universe and all that is in it, Jesus was there in the full glory of His kingly rights—and yet he had to suffer to receive back His glory.

John 17:10 says, "And all mine are thine, and thine are mine; and I am glorified in them." Do you realize how important we are? We are the jewels of Glory! Jesus said that He was glorified in us. Just before that He said the Father was glorified through Him. And now He says that Jesus is glorified through us. Can you see the pattern? The Holy Father, God, is glorified through the life and suffering of Jesus and Jesus is glorified through our life and suffering.

What was the most significant thing about the life of Jesus? It was His love for mankind. Through His love, the Father was glorified. And what is it in our lives that will glorify Jesus? Will it not be the same thing? As we pour out love, we will bring glory to Jesus and the Father.

John 17:22 says, "And the Glory which thou gavest me I have given them that they may be one, even as we are one." The glory is already our inheritance right. It has been written out in Jesus' last will and testimony and it has been signed with His blood.

Paul said the same thing in Colossians 3:4, "When Christ, who is our life, shall appear, then shall ye also appear with him in glory." We have never yet seen the full manifestation of the glory of Christ. We see it in part in some of the miracles which He did. We saw it in part during the scene of transfiguration on the mount. We saw a glimpse of it at the garden tomb when the soldiers fell down like dead men and we saw some of it when He ascended into heaven. But the magnitude and the splendor of our glorified Jesus is waiting until the time when we will be able to bear it to be revealed to us. Our Adamic nature could not look into such magnificence. And then, when we think that the Lord said through Paul, "Then shall we also appear with HIM in Glory." Do you realize what glorious future awaits the glorified children of God?

In John 17:24 we read, "Father, I will that they also, whom thou hast given me, be with me where I am; that they may behold my Glory, which thou hast given me: for thou lovedst me before the foundation of the world." Jesus linked together the Love that His Father had for Him and the Glory that His Father had given Him.

John 16:14, "He shall glorify me: for he shall receive of mine, and shall show it unto you." Jesus said here that the Father was going to show His disciples His glory. Of all the New Testament writers, none wrote so much about Glory as Peter did. John was the one whose subject was Love, and Paul was the one to emphasize Grace, but Peter was the one who wrote about the Glory. When you study 1 and 2 Peter you will find that he mentions the Glory at least twelve times.

The Glory is very important to us. It is a part of our inheritance. It was so important that Jesus prayed for it to come back into His life and also that it would be given to us. If Jesus wanted it again and desired it for us, then it must be of great significance. I want what Jesus wants, and I am not asking for something that is not my right. He said that He had given us this grace, and if it's mine I want to know what I am receiving. It is like receiving a beautiful present for Christmas, which is all wrapped in a pretty paper and ribbon, from someone you know loves you very much. You would not think of leaving it untouched. You would hardly be able to wait until you opened it to see what is inside. If the Glory was Peter's message, then let us see what Peter has to say about it.

1 Peter 1:8, "Whom having not seen, ye love; in whom, though now ye see him not, yet believing ye rejoice with joy unspeakable and full of glory." This was written to a people who had never seen Jesus. Peter is saying, "You haven't seen Him, and yet you love Him. And as you love Him, you rejoice with unspeakable Glory. He said, "Because you believe, you are rejoicing with great joy, which is full of glory." There is glory therefore in our rejoicing and in our joy. There is no glory if we go around with a long face and look mournful. A joyful people are a glorious people. Have you ever noticed how the one who is always fault-finding, grumbling, complaining, worrying and fussing about everything has not got any glory in his life. All these negative habits rob us of the Glory of God. Let us be careful that we do not fall into that rut, lest we displease our God.

1 Peter 1:11, ". . . The Spirit of Christ testified beforehand the sufferings of Christ, and the glory that should follow." As Jesus anticipated the cross that was before Him, He did not complain, "Oh, Father, I am so worried about all I have to go through!" No, He asked for suffering. He knew it was the gateway to His Glory.

1 Peter 1:21, ". . . God, that raised him up from the dead, and gave him glory; that your faith and hope might be in God." As Jesus was raised up from the dead, He took back His Glory.

1 Peter 2:12, ". . . that . . . they [the heathen] may by your good works, which they shall behold, glorify God in the day of visitation." The heathen shall see the Glory of God in you, by your good works, on the day of visitation. They may not be able to see the Glory of God now, they may even think you are an idiot. They call you a fanatic, mock you and ridicule you, but on the day of visitation they shall have to acknowledge the truth, and then they will see the Glory of God on you as the Father rewards you for your obedience to Him. On that day of your glorification you will have the full

vindication. Let us wait until that day comes.

1 Peter 4:13, 14, "But rejoice, inasmuch as ye are partakers of Christ's sufferings; that, when his glory shall be revealed, ye may be glad also with exceeding joy. If ye be reproached for the name of Christ, happy are ye; for the spirit of glory and of God resteth upon you: on their part he is evil spoken of, but on your part he is glorified." What do you feel resting on you today? If you do not feel any spirit of Glory, one of the reasons could be that you are not getting any persecution. We have so many cowardly Christians who are afraid of taking their stand for anything they believe in, for fear that they will be persecuted. We ought to be ashamed of ourselves. It is no wonder we do not have any Glory in our lives. Sometimes I fear that the Shekinah has lifted off America and moved over to Russia, where the saints are indeed suffering for the name of Jesus. Do not be afraid of having evil spoken against you. Rejoice! And pity those who speak evil against you, for there is no spirit of Glory resting on them. God is put to shame through their lives. The Glory of God is what changes us into His image and prepares us for translation.

1 Peter 4:16, "Yet if any man suffer as a Christian, let him not be ashamed; but let him glorify God on this behalf." It is in suffering that we glorify God.

1 Peter 5:1, "The elders which are among you I exhort, who am also an elder, and a witness of the sufferings of Christ, and also a partaker of the glory that shall be revealed." Peter is saying that as he was suffering for Christ he was partaking of Christ's coming Glory. Peter was looking into the future when the great rewards would be given to those who suffer for Jesus.

1 Peter 5:4, "And when the Chief Shepherd shall appear, ye shall receive a crown of glory that fadeth not away." Special awards of honor and distinguished service beyond the call of duty shall be given by the Lord to those who have suffered. One of these rewards will be the Crown of Glory.

1 Peter 5:10, "But the God of all grace, who hath called

us unto his eternal Glory by Christ Jesus, after that ye have suffered a while, make you perfect, stablish, strengthen, settle you." Our calling is unto His Eternal Glory and we will arrive there only after we have suffered a while. The suffering will perfect us, stablish us, strengthen us and settle us.

2 Peter 1:17-19, "For he received from God the Father honor and glory, when there came such a voice to him from the excellent glory, This is my beloved Son, in whom I am well pleased. And this voice which came from heaven we heard, when we were with him in the holy mount. We have also a more sure word of prophecy; whereunto ye do well that ye take heed, as unto a light that shineth in a dark place, until the day dawn, and the day star arise in your hearts." Peter says that the day star shall arise out of the dark night and shine in our hearts. As it breaks out upon our own heart and soul, we will be translated into the Glory of the morning star that we read about in Revelation 2:28. The morning star and the day star are the same star. This Glory has been promised to those who overcome. Every man who has lived has wanted to see the Glory of God. Moses said, "Show me Thy glory!" And the Lord showed him His Glory. That was the difference between Moses and the other prophets. God said, "If there be a prophet among you, I the Lord will make myself known unto him in a vision, and will speak unto him in a dream. My servant Moses is not so, who is faithful in all mine house. With him will I speak mouth to mouth, even apparently, and not in dark speeches: and the similitude of the Lord shall he behold" (Numbers 12:8). "And there arose not a prophet since in Israel like unto Moses, whom the Lord knew face to face" (Deuteronomy 34:10). Moses had a relationship with God like Enoch did. He was greater than a prophet. The day of prophecies is soon going to close. The Bible says, "Prophecies shall fail"—they shall be phased out. I do not mean that we will no longer accept them, but we will come into a new dimension where we will know God and talk face to face with Him like Moses did. No prophet ever had to prophesy to Moses; he was greater than the prophets.

May the Lord bring us into that high relationship. Moses got there because he prayed, "Lord, show me thy glory" (Exodus 33:18).

Paul says in Romans 3:23, "We have all sinned and come short of the glory of God." Ever since man lost his first estate of Glory through the fall, man has striven to regain that lost Glory. Through the centuries, man substituted earthly glory for the heavenly Glory. Now, man is no more content with the earthly glory. He is reaching out to receive back again that which was once his—the perfection, the beauty and the powerful adornment of his first, original creation. As we clothe ourselves in love, we begin to again be adorned in our earlier garments of creation and prepare ourselves to stand detached from the earthly and thus enter into our glorious inheritance of Glory. Man will never be satisfied until he has again regained that which he has lost, the Glory of God. The re-entering into our Glory will be the full and final manifestation of the sons of God and their literal return to paradise, the Garden of Love.

In 1 Corinthians 15:40 Paul says, "There are also celestial bodies, and bodies terrestrial; but the glory of the celestial is one, and the glory of the terrestrial is another." I have a terrestrial body because I belong to the earth and it is made out of the dust of the earth. But the Bible says that there is also a celestial body. The celestial body is completely different from the terrestrial. It is as different as heaven is different from the earth. The terrestrial body has glory, but the celestial body has greater glory.

In verses 41 and 42 Paul says, "There is one glory of the sun, and another glory of the moon, and another glory of the stars: for one star differeth from another star in glory, so also is the resurrection of the dead." Paul is telling us that there are different degrees of glory which will be manifested on the resurrection day.

Verse 42: "So also is the resurrection of the dead. It is sown in corruption; it is raised in incorruption:"

Verse 43: "It is sown in dishonour; it is raised in glory;

it is sown in weakness; it is raised in power:"

Verse 44: "It is sown a natural body: it is raised a spiritual body." This "it" that Paul is speaking about is your body and my body. He is saying that it is "sown in dishonour." This sowing refers to the laying of the body in the grave. There is nothing very glorious about a funeral service, no matter how we decorate it with flowers, or how many pretty songs we sing, or eulogies we bring. Every funeral means that somebody died, that death is victorious. It tells us, "The body is sown in dishonour." As long as we continue to die, we have not attained unto our full Glory. Enoch entered in and he escaped death. Elijah entered in and he escaped death. But, thank God, even though we don't attain now, we have the hope that on the morning of resurrection we shall be raised incorruptible, in strength, power and glory. On that day death is swallowed up in victory, and this corruptible shall put on incorruption and this mortality shall be transformed into immortality. All shall be raised in different degrees of Glory, according to the degrees of love and righteousness that we lived in while still in our mortal body. We shall shine as the stars in many different degrees of Glory.

Chapter 24
LOVE OBEYS

Jesus said to His disciples, "If ye love me, keep my commandments" (John 14:15). In verse 21 of the same chapter He said, "He that hath my commandments and keepeth them, he it is that loveth me: and he that loveth me shall be loved of my Father, and I will love him, and will manifest myself to him." In verse 23 He says, "If a man love me, he will keep my words: and my father will love him, and we will come unto him and make our abode with him."

We are living in a time of rebellion. Everyone seeks to "do his own thing." There is great danger in this spirit of rebellion. Isaiah 1:20 says, "... if ye refuse [to be obedient] and rebel, ye shall be devoured with the sword: for the mouth of the Lord hath spoken it." Our very spirit of rebellion is what enables us to invent weapons of destruction, some of which are so terrible that they are kept in utmost secrecy. I have heard that there is a secret weapon which, if interrupted or released, could destroy the entire surface of the earth in two or three seconds. It would burn everything that has oxygen in it. It makes the hydrogen bomb look like a matchstick beside it. Rebellion has destroyed Iran, Afghanistan, Cambodia, and is making a good job out of destroying Great Britain and America. No one wants to be led. No one wants to obey or come under authority, and so we destroy ourselves by our defiance and rebellion because we do not have the love it takes to obey.

There are many wonderful promises given by God to

those who will obey. Let us look at just a few of them:

Isaiah 1:19. God says, "If ye be willing and obedient, YE SHALL EAT THE GOOD OF THE LAND." God has promised prosperity and good health to the obedient.

Exodus 20:6. God says He will, "SHOW MERCY unto thousands of them that love me, and keep my commandments." We have never had a time when we needed God's mercy and love more than now.

In Exodus 23:22, 23 God promises, "But if thou shalt indeed obey his voice, and do all that I speak; then I will BE AN ENEMY UNTO THINE ENEMIES, and an adversary unto thine adversaries for my angel shall go before thee into the land of the Amorites . . . and I will cut them off." God said that He would fight on the side of those who would be obedient to Him and He himself would cut off their enemies.

Deuteronomy 4:40, "Thou shalt keep therefore his statutes, and his commandments, which I command thee this day, that it may go well with thee, and with thy children after thee, and that thou MAYEST PROLONG THY DAYS UPON THE EARTH, which the Lord thy God giveth thee, forever." Obedience to God is the key to long life right here on the earth which He has given us forever.

Deuteronomy 11:26, 27, "Behold, I set before you this day a BLESSING and a curse; a blessing if ye obey the commandments of the Lord your God, which I command you this day." These blessings are very numerous. We can find them in Deuteronomy 28:1-14.

Deuteronomy 11:14, 15, "I will give you the RAIN of your land in his due season, the first rain and the latter rain, that thou mayest gather in thy corn and thy wine and thine oil, and I will send grass in thy fields for thy cattle, that thou mayest eat and be full." God will control the weather of the nation that obeys Him.

Mark 3:35, "For whosoever shall do the will of God, the same is my brother, and my sister and mother." Jesus promises us FAMILY RELATIONSHIP with Him if we will do the will of God.

John 7:17, "If any man will do his will, he shall know of the doctrine, whether it be of God, or whether I speak for myself." Special discernment is given to those who do God's will so that they can know what is a false doctrine and so that they will be able to accept that which is the truth. This is something we need greatly in these days when there are so many false cults and over-emphasis on one Scripture which are bringing imbalance to the church.

Yes, Jesus said if we would love Him we would keep His commandment. What was His commandment? That we have love. John 13:34 says, "A new commandment I give unto you, That ye love one another; as I have loved you, that ye also love one another." This is THE commandment that Jesus gave us, besides that He gave us no other commandment. All the laws of God are hidden in the commandment TO LOVE.

Satan can imitate many things, but he cannot imitate love. Jesus said, "By this shall all men know you are my disciples, if ye have love one to another." Satan cannot imitate this love. He can imitate miracles and signs and wonders but he is a failure when it comes to LOVE. This is the one sign that we Christians should have. This is the true sign of discipleship. Everyone who pays this price and follows Jesus is a disciple. It means obedience. It is impossible to be a disciple and be disobedient. God knew that we were born with a will. Most of us have a very strong will. It can be our greatest enemy. There is only one thing that gives us victory over our will ruling us and destroying us, and that is the will of God. When God's will rules our will and the two are locked together with one purpose, it is a great team— one that God can use to the tearing down of the strongholds of Satan. It is only as we take up our cross and submit our will that we come into the place where God can use us to bring great victories on this earth.

The story is often told how Constantine, the great Roman emperor whose heart was leaning towards the Christians, saw a great cross in the sky on the day before he was to go to battle against mighty enemy forces. The words were given to him, "In This Sign Conquer," in the Latin tongue. He knew this was the sign of the Christians. It is with this sign that he went into battle and God gave him a glorious victory. From that time on he was a Christian.

Today the cross is still the sign of victory. Paul said, "God forbid that I should glory, save in the cross of our Lord Jesus Christ, by whom the world is crucified unto me, and I unto the world" (Galatians 6:14). It is in this great act of obedience, the taking of our cross, that we are crucified unto the world. Only love will enable us to be crucified. Only love will enable us to obey His command, "Deny yourself, take up your cross, and follow Me."

In the wilderness God wrote His commandments upon tablets of stone. These were placed in the Ark of the Covenant which was inside the Holy of Holies. But this is a new day. In 2 Corinthians 3:3 it says, "Forasmuch as ye are manifestly declared to be the epistle of Christ ministered by us, written not with ink, but with the Spirit of the living God; not in tables of stone, but in fleshly tables of the heart." Today, the law of God is written on our hearts of flesh. It is only as our hearts are tender and sensitive toward God that He can write His laws on our hearts.

Hebrews 8:10 says, "I will put my laws into their mind, and write them in their hearts: and I will be to them a God, and they shall be to me a people." When Jesus told us to love, He was not asking us to do something that is impossible. He asks of us something that is absolutely natural for the child of God, with the mind of Christ and the heart of flesh. The Law of God has been written on our hearts, and out of the heart flows the issues of life. Jesus said that it was out of our hearts that both evil and good came (Matthew 15:18, 19). We prove by our life what is written on our heart. It is no use pretending to be something when you are another. Your very facial expression will reveal who you are. And if you should put a veil over your face to cover it, then the vibrations will flow out of you to reveal what you are. But most people reveal what they are just by opening their mouths. Others are a little more clever. They know how to talk the right things at the right time. But if you wait long enough, the truth will bear witness of itself, whether it be good or evil.

The Law of God rested in the Ark of the Covenant. That is also where the Shekinah rested. When our hearts become the Ark of the Covenant because we house the law of God in our hearts, then the Shekinah of Glory will rest over us also.

Chapter 25
LOVE SAVES

One night I had a small tragedy. It was past midnight when I had finished listening to Beethoven's Fifth Symphony and went up to my bedroom. I had taken the pins out of my hair and it was hanging loose when I picked up my toothbrush, put the toothpaste on it and started to brush my teeth. My hair fell forward into the basin and I pushed it out of the way. In that instant I felt a slight pain in my right ear. I finished what I was doing and took a look. My right earring was missing. I immediately started looking for it. It was very precious, made with blue sapphires and diamonds, a gift my husband had given me for Christmas. It was from Australia. I anxiously searched all over and then knelt down and searched the carpet by the sink. It was nowhere to be found. I was afraid that it had gone down the drain. Just then my husband Jim came in the room. I told him what happened and he, too, got down on his knees and searched with the aid of a flashlight. When he, too, couldn't find it he said, "Gwen, it must have gone down the drain." He said, "Don't worry, I'll get it out." He went out to the shed and brought in his tool box. It was then around one o'clock in the morning. I knew he was tired, but he was not complaining over the fact that he had to go back out to get his tools.

He first tried to pull out the plug and "fish" it out with a long, magnetic tool. But when we tried the tool on the remaining earring, we found that there was no magnetic attraction because it was made out of white gold. So that meant pulling the plumbing apart below the sink. He began to work at that while I waited. After what seemed like hours, but was only minutes, he got it loose and brought the curved part of the pipe (trap) out and started dumping its contents into a little basin. Out came hair and muck and, finally, the precious blue sapphire earring. Oh, hallelujah! I gave him a big hug and loved him more than ever for his loving ways. He had saved my earring from Australia!

It is this same kind of grace and patience that God has in His heart every time He stoops to save one of His precious jewels. Most of us can never know the anxiety that He feels when we are lost. Nor do we realize what muck and filth we have fallen into when finally, after years of love and patience, He has detached us from the pit we have fallen into and has brought us safely back into His loving fold.

Jesus tried to explain it to us in the kind of language we could understand when He told the parable about the Good Shepherd who lost that one precious sheep and left the ninety-nine to search for it, or the one about the woman who had ten pieces of silver and when she lost one piece, she lit a candle and swept the house and sought diligently till she found it.

Love will make you go "out of your way" to help someone in need. It will give you the strength and the grace to take time to search for that lost soul and bring that one to God before it's too late. Love cares when the prodigal comes wandering home, back to Father's house, and love will make a feast of welcome for that lost, repentant soul.

Love will cause you to do what you would never do under normal circumstances. I want us to look at a beautiful story of saving love in the Old Testament. The story of beautiful Abigail.

If we could just behold the mighty power there is in love, we would begin to learn to understand His saving power. Abigail, this housewife in the hills, had this wonderful revelation of love. She had never seen David. She had only heard about him. But the story of his great victories had touched her heart; and when ten thousand maidens of Israel sang the praises of David and danced on the streets of the cities of Israel as he came back the captain of the hosts of Israel from the battlefields, this woman would join with them up there in her tent, praising the God of Israel for sending a deliverer to save them out of the hands of the Philistines. She thanked God that there was a man who dared to stand against the dreadful and evil Goliath. She never realized for one moment that one day the opportunity would come for her to meet this hero. Nor did she dream that she would one day be his wife and live in the palace of the king of Israel. This David was the captain of the hosts of Israel, praised by the multitudes and married to the daughter of Saul; and who was she, this little woman of the desert? He wouldn't even look at her. She was a "nobody."

But one day a new rumor drifted through the hills, a rumor that Saul had turned to hate David and David had fled to the hills of Judea. Later she heard how his life was hunted by Saul. Many times she must have prayed, "O God, protect that man who has been anointed to be our king."

And then one day the whole thing began to involve her own life. One of her servants came to her and said, "Mistress, I have bad news for you. David and his men are out in the hills near us. As we were keeping our master's sheep in the wilderness, David and his men were near there also. We got to know each other and they were friendly to us and protected us also from dangers in the open field. Now David has sent one of the men to ask your husband to give them something because these men are very hungry. But our master was very angry. He was full of hate and he mocked David's men and said that he didn't even know who David was. He must know about him, but he does not want to recognize him. He sent the men away without giving them anything. I am afraid now, because your husband has been acting like a fool and he will bring great trouble upon us all. You must do something."

The responsibility of many lives was suddenly upon her

shoulders. If you can love, the Lord will lay the responsibility of saving other lives upon you. In that hour, the decision that she would make would affect the lives of not only her family and her servants, but many in Israel for centuries to come. It would not be an easy decision to make. She would have to go against her husband in order to save lives. In fact, she did not dare to even let him know what she was going to do, or he would stop her. His name was Nabal, which means a fool. How can a fool have the wisdom to save souls? Maybe that is the reason that he was given that name. Maybe he had never had enough love to keep him from being a fool.

Love gave Abigail wisdom, because Love has wisdom. She gathered some things together: bread, meat, wine, corn, figs and raisins, and started out on her way to David. When she met him, he was already on his way, his heart full of anger and revenge, to kill her husband and every member of that household.

She fell at David's feet and said, "I accept all blame in this matter, my lord. Please listen to what I want to say. Nabal is a bad-tempered boor, but please don't pay any attention to what he said. He is a fool—just like his name means. But I didn't see the messengers you sent. Sir, since the Lord has kept you from murdering and taking vengeance into your own hands, I pray by the life of God and by your own life, too, that all your enemies shall be as cursed as Nabal is. And now, here is a present I have brought to you and your young men. Forgive me for my boldness in coming out here. The Lord will surely reward you with eternal royalty for your descendents, for you are fighting his battles; and you will never do wrong throughout your entire life. Even when you are chased by those who seek your life, you are safe in the care of the Lord your God, just as though you were safe inside his purse! But the lives of your enemies shall disappear like stones from a sling! When the Lord has done all the good things he promised you and has made you king of Israel, you won't want the conscience of a murderer who took the law into his own hands! And when the Lord has done these great things for you, please remember me!"*

This is one of the most beautiful prophecies in the Bible. The wonderful thing is that it was not given by a prophet at all. It was given by a little housewife whom no one had ever heard prophesy before. But it came out of a heart that was full of love; and it proves to us that when a heart is full of love it has the authority to speak God's word. It is not how much learning we have that authorizes us with God. We are not given authority because of a certain position we have with men. The thing that authorizes us with God is that our hearts are full of His love. Love must be the inspiration of every task we try to perform. We should never ever seek to do anything to prove how good we are, or how right we are. Everything that we do should be searched out to be sure it is truly motivated by one thing alone, and that is love. Love is very powerful. Love is so mighty that it protects those who have it. And it protects those whom we love also.

Abigail took the whole blame on herself. She said, "I accept all the blame in this matter." We know that she was not to blame, but the truth is that you cannot get mercy for someone until you take the blame on yourself. You must identify yourself with somebody else's failure. Her husband was a wicked and cruel man. She did not mention how cruel he was, only that he was a fool. And as a fool, he should be excused. Because she took the blame, she showed the love and beauty of her soul to David and this touched his heart, so that his sword was put again into its sheath. It was under the anointing that she said David's life was without sin before God. Only perfect love finds a mortal faultless.

As I read the psalms of David, I have been touched to see how many deadly enemies David had. And yet we see such perfect love in his life. He was always protected in a supernatural way because of the love that filled his heart.

In the King James version we read, "A man is risen to pursue thee, and to seek thy soul: but the soul of my lord

---

The Living Bible.

shall be bound in the bundle of life with the Lord thy God; and the souls of thy enemies, them shall he sling out, as out of the middle of a sling." If you can love like David loved; if you can love with that perfect love, then your life will be bound up in a bundle of life with the Lord your God. Isn't that the most wonderful protection there is! I pray that nothing but love will control us, for if anything else than love controls us, we become a knife in the hands of the devil and we are the ones who will suffer, even if the other person is wrong and we are right.

Through Abigail's love she saved the lives of her family and her servants' families. She even saved her husband Nabal's life. But it was God's time to take him and God did that. He smote him and he died ten days later.

When David heard about this, he sent for Abigail to come to him and she became his wife. So she began to share his safety and blessing. The prophecy she had given him became her own. You never know when you give someone a prophecy, maybe that one will share your life one day.

In my life story, *Unconditional Surrender*,* I tell how, in a meeting in Santa Barbara, California, God gave me a prophecy for a man I had never seen before in my life. I tell how I struggled to give it to him because I had been told he was a Baptist and I was sure he would not accept the prophecy. But I feared to disobey the Holy Spirit and so I gave it, thinking he would never see me again anyway. That prophecy changed that man's life. It also changed mine, because that man later became my beloved husband, Lt. Col. James von Doornum Shaw. Like Abigail, God let me share in his honor and his rewards and every good thing that God said about him became mine.

It is love in the heart of a man that will drive him to go to the hell of the front lines to save his country from destruction when the enemy comes against it. Love will send a mother into a burning house to bring out her baby. Love will

---

*See order form in the back of the book.

cause you to go to the uttermost parts of the world to rescue the perishing and care for the dying. Love will give us again a compassion for those who are lost. It is time for the church to

> Throw out the life-line across the dark wave,
> There is a brother, who someone should save;
> Somebody's brother! Oh, who then will dare
> To throw out the life-line, his peril to share?
>
> Soon will the season of rescue be o'er,
> Soon will they drift to eternity's shore;
> Haste then, my brother, no time for delay,
> But throw out the life-line and save them today.

I have a feeling that our burden is not so much to save souls as to add members to our church roll, to enlarge our crowds and to become famous. We need a fresh baptism of love that will enable us to have the burden for souls that will give us the kind of love we need to save a sinner from hell.

Chapter 26
LOVE QUALIFIES

John 13:23, "Now there was leaning on Jesus' bosom one of his disciples, whom Jesus loved." This is the story of one of the greatest disciples of love that Jesus had. John wrote the Gospel according to St. John, but the wonderful thing was that he was so humble he hid himself in this book. He also did that in the epistles of John. It was only in the book of Revelation that he revealed himself as the writer. John was promoting Someone greater than himself. He was promoting the One he loved, Jesus Christ in His wonderful beauty, to the world. John mentions himself in the Gospel of John, but his name is not told. He speaks about himself in the third person and calls himself "that other disciple," or "the disciple whom Jesus loved." I believe that this shows the character of a beautiful person. There is so much showmanship in the world today that sometimes I am sick of it. I often wish I could leave the ministry because I hate advertising and publicizing and sounding a trumpet before myself. But when we see the life of one of the greatest men of God and his ability to hide himself in the Love of God and still be one of God's greatest servants, then we take courage that it is possible to remain hidden in the Lord.

Not everyone who is great is seen before the people. Many of God's greatest ones, who are the closest to the Lord, are hidden from all. If you want to be great in God, you must learn the secret of being hidden in Him. Anyone can be great in the world if he has talents, and a little pull with the right people! But not everybody can be great in God.

Look at the life of John. He began very humble and lowly. He was only known as the son of Zebedee. He was a fisherman and the son of a fisherman. He was a young man who did not have much education. Most of his training had been in how to catch fish on the sea of Galilee. God chooses in His own way. And God had chosen John before he was born.

God had His eye on you and He knew you and chose you before you came to earth. David said in Psalm 139: 15, 16, "You were there while I was being formed in utter seclusion! You saw me before I was born and scheduled each day of my life before I began to breathe. Every day was recorded in your Book!" (The Living Bible). Hallelujah! My diary has already been written in heaven. It is now my responsibility to so live in the Spirit that I will fulfill it to the last detail.

I believe that God predestined John to be born in Capernaum. And Jesus went there to find him and the other disciples, James, his brother, and Peter and Andrew. He went to Capernaum to find the men who had been placed by God upon the earth for that time and that generation. And when He found them, they were ready to follow Him because they were born to be followers of Jesus Christ.

John was a young man. His mother's name was Salome. We don't read much about her except that she was one of Jesus' followers. Many people have the idea that because he leaned on Jesus' bosom he was one of these gentle, meek, effeminate types. But the description given of him in Mark 3:17 shows that he was not. Jesus gave him and his brother a new name—Boanerges—which means "Sons of Thunder." So you can see they were men with strong temperament, men with zeal and energy. They were men who believed in calling down fire when they thought fire was needed to punish the opposers of Jesus. This is what happened in the beginning of their ministry. The reason they wanted to call down fire was because this certain village had rejected Jesus and they were so angry with those men that they wanted to send them to the same place as Sodom and Gomorrah. John had a lot to learn and he learned his lessons well. One of them was that "thunder" does not win. He learned that "fire" is not the answer. Before John closed his ministry on earth, he learned one beautiful secret and that was that LOVE is the answer. It was then that he wrote that glorious letter of Love, the First Epistle of John.

John was given special privileges because of his ability to understand Jesus. If I am going to do something, I will not go around and tell it to people who do not understand my heart. I will only reveal it to those who have a heart of understanding toward me. If I open my heart and share it with a friend, it is because I feel that my friend will understand. Unfortunately, sometimes I have made mistakes and revealed my heart to people who have not understood. This is because I am not perfect in knowledge. But Jesus was not imperfect in knowledge and so He told the deep things of His heart to the ones He knew He could trust. And He did not make any mistakes like we do. One of the places where John was privileged to share the secret of Jesus was in the home of Jairus, when Jesus raised Jairus' daughter from the dead.

Another place where he was privileged to be with Jesus was on the Mount of Transfiguration. It was here that the glory of God was revealed to the three chosen disciples, Peter, James and John. They saw the translation of Christ before their very eyes. They didn't see Him as the Son of Man but as He was indeed, the Son of God. Jesus forbade them to tell what they had seen to anyone else. Jesus knew that they loved Him enough to keep His secrets. Love keeps secrets (Matthew 17:1-9).

In this end time, the most glorious things will be done in secret. When God is whispering these secrets in our hearts, our hearts will be filled with joy and glory. And already He has started to do it. It is wonderful to find here and there a "John" or a "Peter" who has heard the same secrets of God that we have. They have seen the same glory we have seen. They dare not share it with the public or they will be destroyed.

If Peter and John had told the people that they had just seen Moses and Elijah, they would have been destroyed by the religious Pharisees. No one would have believed them any more than they would believe you if you came out of your room and said to your family, "I was just talking to Elijah!" They would think you had gone completely crazy. Love qualifies you to keep God's secrets.

Mark 13:3, 4 says, "And as he sat upon the mount of Olives over against the temple, Peter and James and John and Andrew asked him privately, tell us, when shall these things be? and what shall be the sign when all these things shall be fulfilled." Jesus begins His glorious discourse on the end time and tells these four what He could not tell the multitudes. If you want to know the end-time secrets, you must read this chapter. They were permitted later to tell it just as He had told it to them. But for a time they could not talk about these things to anyone. Sometimes, that which must be kept secret today can be revealed later. We must know the timing of the Holy Spirit.

In John 18:15 we read how Jesus took Peter and James and John into the garden on the night of His betrayal. They saw the agony of Jesus as He wept beneath the old olive trees of the garden. They saw the officers come to arrest Him. They saw Judas give Him the kiss of betrayal. The intimates of Jesus will see many things that the crowd knows nothing about. And they will bear witness of it at the right time to the glory of God.

When Jesus was taken under armed guard to the house of the high priest, these men were with Him, following from a distance. John, in referring to himself, calls himself "another disciple." When they got to the house, only John was permitted to go inside. Peter had to stay outside in the courtyard. The writer of John says that this disciple was known unto the high priest. I do not know how the high priest knew John, for John in his modesty never ever revealed this secret. Not only did he get inside, but he spoke to the woman who kept the door and brought in Peter also. Love will not only enable you to gain entrance, but to bring others in as well. John watched as they falsely accused Jesus, slapped Him in the face, spit on Him and called Him a devil, blasphemer and hypocrite. John was permitted by the grace of God to stand and see with his own eyes what no other of the disciples was permitted to see. Love is the key that will take you to the innermost secret of martyrdom. Love alone will make you worthy to stand with your Lord in His hour of suffering.

John 19:26, 27, "When Jesus therefore saw his mother, and the disciple standing by, whom he loved, he saith unto his mother, 'Woman, behold thy son!' Then saith he to the disciple, 'Behold thy mother!' And from that hour that disciple took her unto his own home." This disciple is John; again he does not tell his name. Jesus, in the midst of His pain and suffering and rejection, did not forget the mother He loved. Where could He find a better heart than John's. He chose John because John qualified through love. He did not choose a rich man who had a fine home with many servants to take care of His mother. He could have chosen Martha and Mary and Lazarus; He loved them, too, and they loved Him. He could have chosen Joseph of Arimathea, but He chose the one who had leaned on His bosom. The one whom He could trust to keep secrets. He was the closest to Jesus. There was no one whom Jesus loved more than His mother, so He gave her into John's care. As He gazed on her standing there weeping at the foot of the cross, her heart broken, He knew that His own brothers could not understand Him or accept Him. They would not be able to comfort this broken-hearted mother. She was more than His mother at this time. She was a woman with a broken heart, without a home, a widow whose husband had died; and because her other sons and daughters had not accepted Jesus she, too, would be an outcast from the family, even as He had been.

There are not many disciples like John. There are many Christians, but few who have the capacity to love like John loved. We have many Christians who will entertain you if you are rich or well-known or important; but the outcasts and the rejects and the stranger, the one whose life has been full of mistakes, the sinner they don't want. We don't want the over-emotional woman, the fanatical man who shouts, "Praise the Lord," at the wrong time. They will embarrass us. We don't want the one who has no tithes and offerings to bring. We don't need him. We like people who are respected, people with positions of responsibility and dignity. We want the titled and the educated. But the one who is standing and weeping, we do not want. And because the church has not the spirit of Jesus, we choose the wrong ones to do the things that only a John should do.

Again, John mentions himself in a hidden way. John 20:2, "Then she [Mary Magdalene] runneth, and cometh to Simon Peter and to the other disciple, whom Jesus loved, and saith unto them, 'They have taken away the Lord out of the sepulchre, and we know not where they have laid him.' " Mary Magdalene had just been at the tomb. She had seen that it was empty. She runs to tell Peter and John, and again John calls himself, "the other disciple whom Jesus loved." Immediately, they both ran to the tomb. The "other disciple" ran faster than Peter. John does not brag about what a good runner he was at that time. Many of us would like to put our name in right there. This was a greater race than any Olympic race. This was a race to the grave of our Lord. When John arrived, the awesomeness was so great that he was overwhelmed. He could feel the presence of the glory of God. He stopped and stood still for a moment. Peter came running behind him and went right in ahead of him.

One more time John mentions himself in a hidden way. John 21:7, "Therefore that disciple whom Jesus loved saith unto Peter, It is the Lord!" The disciples had just been fishing all night when the resurrected Jesus suddenly appeared. John was the first of them to recognize the Lord. I can just hear the excitement of his voice as he realizes that Jesus is standing there on the shore, "It is the Lord!" When we see someone we love, we get excited, too. His heart just turned right over. Love gave him clearer vision and perception.

It was the preparation for something that lay ahead, even greater, when on the Isle of Patmos he would be visited by Jesus on the Lord's Day and be given the great revelation of the end time which we are now seeing fulfilled before our very eyes.

The closing ministry of John is shrouded in mystery. Tertullion reports that John was plunged into boiling oil from which he miraculously escaped unscathed. It is still annually commemorated on May 6. John's Feast Day, however, is December 27. The belief that John did not die is very old (Mark 9:1-2, John 21:23). In some of the apocryphal writings it is assumed he was translated to heaven like Enoch and Elijah. Only the future will reveal the final secrets of this saint's life. We know that he loved greatly. Did he love so greatly that one day as he walked with God, he was no more because God took him?

Chapter 27
LOVE MAKES GREAT SOLDIERS AND KINGS

Gideon

As we looked into the life of John we realized that he was the most intimate of all of the Lord's disciples. God always follows the same pattern. He cuts down, cleans out and separates. He is always putting His people through the sieve so that He can have the most precious wheat close to Him. These are the ones He wants, and to whom He wants to reveal Himself. Anybody can be an outer-court Christian, but it takes those who really break through to know their God who will be in intimate relationship with the Father. These are the ones who will fight the great battles of the Lord.

There never was a greater battle of the Lord than in the days of Gideon when the Midianites came up against Israel. There were hundreds of thousands of enemy soldiers who were arrayed against God's people. When the final victory was won, those of the enemy who died in battle numbered 120,000. So you must realize what a great army that was. The children of Israel had nothing to fight with. They didn't even have sharp knives. Their files had been taken away from them, too, by the nations that had oppressed them. They were the most helpless soldiers the world has ever seen. But they had a great God, a God who was determined to keep the glory for himself in the battle which He was going to win for His people. When the people of Israel cried out to God, God heard their cry. God sent an angel down there to choose a man. He was a man in a home where they were worshippers of idols. God chose him because he was born for the task. The night of his call, Gideon tore down the idols of his family. He had had a meeting with God. God gave him the strength to clean out everything that would hinder him. When you have a meeting with God you'll clean out everything in your life that will hinder you from being used of God. Gideon gave the call for Israel to prepare for battle. The children of Israel gathered themselves together. The Lord said to them, "There are too many." By that time Gideon was shaking and trembling because he didn't feel that there were enough of them. He only had about one tenth of the men that the enemy had. God said, "There are too many! I don't want to fight with many. I want to fight with few. Because I want them to know it is I who won the victory!"

God always did things that way and He is going to do things that way now. He is going to choose out the few of His end-time soldiers, those who have fallen in love with Jesus, those who are determined to go all the way and pay the whole price. So God said, "Let those who are tired and afraid go back home." And 22,000 went home. That left 10,000. Gideon must have shaken his head in consternation. "God, how do You expect me to win the war with so few? I had a hard enough time getting them together, Lord. I worked all this time gathering them here, and now You are telling me to send them home?"

There are a lot of things we don't understand. God has a way of cleaning out His church or his "bridal company." And He is going to clean it out. We must be careful to LET Him do it.

One day the disciples went to Jesus and said, "Lord, look at all of those people who have left us. How do You feel about that, Jesus?" He answered, "They went out from us because they were not of us. If they had been of us, they would have stayed with us." God is going to do the same today. He is going to let people come and He is going to let them go, and we must not grieve when the fellowship which we once had with precious friends suddenly breaks off and they leave us. If they were of us, they would have stayed and battled the battle with us. They would have stood with us in the storm and fought hand to hand. So Gideon had to say, "Goodbye!" and 22,000 went home, leaving him with 10,000 men to fight against over 200,000 well-armed soldiers.

And then God said to him, "My dear boy, there are still too many! I can't win the battle with so many." I am sure that about that time Gideon thought he was listening to false doctrine.

The Lord said, "Take them to the waters, and there I will try them FOR you." It was too hard for Gideon to do any trying himself. The thing was too difficult for him. He loved them all. He wanted them all. He wasn't going to send ONE of those precious ones away. There were the sons of Naphtali, Asher, Manasseh, Zebulun and Ephraim . . . he loved them all. He wanted them all. And the Lord said, "*I* will do the trying. *I* will do the testing."

Today God is still doing the testing. Everyone of you is going to be tested. If you haven't been tested yet, you will be tested to the extremity of your capacity to endure. And many times you are going to say, "Oh, what is the use of it! I am just going to give it all up!" But this is the hour when you are going to prove if you are made of gold or tin. We all must go through the testing. I have to go through it often. Don't think it is easy to be a woman in the ministry. It is hard enough to be in the ministry, but to be a woman in the ministry is much harder. That is why you don't see many women in the ministry. It is because you have to really be dedicated to God. The enemy works very strongly against women's ministries. Many times women come to me and say, "Sister Gwen, I would like to be in the ministry. Some day I am going to be an evangelist like you. I will be very great. I will preach all over the world." I know they don't even know what they are talking about. There is no great honor in being a lady preacher. There is not any glamor in preaching the Gospel. But there are a lot of tears, misunderstandings and criticism. A woman in the ministry has to stand up against a lot of evil powers, false judgment and prejudices through years of misinterpretation of the Scriptures. But God works through feeble vessels to show us His glory. God said, "I will try them!"

God will try you. We are at the day now where the Midianites will come against the church of God and God is choosing out Gideon's army. You are going to see them turn back by the thousands. And if they will not go back, God himself will send them back. God is going to have a very holy company in the end time. He is going to have a people who are pure and spotless before Him in Love, a people who are ready to fight the battles of their God. There were 300 left when God was finished trying them.

If you look at 300 against 200,000, you would say, "Madmen!" That is just the kind God is going to use . . . madmen for God! Oh, Lord, give us some like that right in the End-Time Handmaidens who are crazy enough to believe everything that God says, and then we will see God do great things.

As they went into the battle in the name of the Lord, God gave them a great victory. They were that little "barley loaf" that rolled into the Midianite camp and knocked all the tents over. On the night before the battle when Gideon got scared, the Lord said to him, "Go down into the enemy's camp and I will show you something." They were all sleeping. God said, "You spy around down there. If you are afraid, take your servant with you." As Gideon and his man came into the camp, they heard two men talking together. One of them said, "I had a funny dream. All of our tents were standing here, and suddenly there came this small barley loaf rolling into our camp and it knocked all of our tents over. What do you think that means?" The other one answered, "Oh, brother! I can tell you the meaning of that dream. It's not a good one. That barley loaf you dreamed about is Gideon and his army. I am afraid we are in for a bad time. God is going to give him the victory."

Gideon was so blessed through that dream and its interpretation that he said, "Arise, for the Lord has delivered into your hand the host of Midian!" They began their battle in the middle of the night with a light in a pitcher and a trumpet in their mouth. What a way to go to battle! See what God is trying to show us! You are not going to win by sword or bow and arrow. For 2,000 years the church has tried to win the battle with "sword and arrow." Lay down thy sword Jesus said, "He who takes the sword shall perish by the sword."

You will only win through the light. The light was hidden in the pitcher, but when the pitcher was broken the light shone around the camp. Through the Light of Love you will win the victory. The Love of the Lord is our only true Light. Let us break our pitchers. Let God take you and break you so that the light of His Glory can shine through you. When you go through a trial, it breaks you. That hour when you are broken, it will reveal if there is light in you. Some people when they are broken reveal only darkness. Others when they are broken will reveal only the light in them. And that light will put terror in the hearts of the enemy. There is nothing that the world is more scared of than light. There is nothing that the world will fight more than the true light. There is nothing that the devil is more afraid of than Love. Because that is one thing he cannot mimic.

David

In 1 Samuel 16 we see how Samuel was brought to the house of Jesse to choose out a king for Israel. The seven sons of Jesse were brought before Samuel, one by one. The first one, Eliab, was tall of stature and handsome. Samuel was human, even though he was a prophet. As he looked at the fine-looking, young man smiling confidently before him he said, "Surely the Lord's anointed is before me." But the Lord said unto Samuel, "Look not on his countenance, or on the height of his stature; because I have refused him: for the

Lord seeth not as man seeth; for the man looketh on the outward appearance, but the Lord looketh on the heart." Later on we found out why the Lord had rejected him. He was the one who mocked David as David went out to fight against Goliath. He did not have a clean heart. God knew this and had rejected him already.

Then came the next one, Abinadab. And God said, "Neither have I chosen this one." Then came Shammah and God said, "Neither have I chosen this one." After six of Jesse's sons had passed before Samuel and God had said repeatedly, "I have not chosen this one," Samuel was beginning to wonder if he had heard right.

Finally Samuel asked Jesse, "Are all your children here?" Father Jesse said, "There is the youngest, he is keeping the sheep. We never see much of him. He is always out there in the hills playing his harp. I am afraid my boy David won't amount to much 'cause he is such a dreamer. He is always singing out there in the fields, that little dreamer-boy of mine."

"Bring him in," commanded Samuel. So David was hurriedly brought in from the fields. I can see David coming, rushing into the house. His face flushed with hurrying, sweat on his forehead, dusty and dirty, and stinking just like a sheep. I can imagine how his little old heart was beating excitedly. He had just heard that the mighty prophet Samuel had come to their home and was calling for him. As he came inside and looked at all of his brothers standing around, and saw Samuel with his long, white hair and eyes that could look right through you, it was like seeing God. He trembled inside and thought, "It is one thing to fight a lion or a bear, but to stand before a prophet like him, that is something else." Samuel heard a voice saying, "Arise and anoint him, for this is he." God had chosen His man. Samuel took the horn of oil and anointed him in the midst of his brethren and the Spirit of the Lord came upon David from that day on. The anointing makes the difference.

It can be the same with you. This can be that day in

your life when God will give you the anointing you need which will change your life. There is SOMEONE standing beside you with the anointing horn in His hand. The Father has sent the Holy Spirit and He is searching out a chosen people for Himself, a people who are small and insignificant in their own eyes, a people who have been meek and humble before their God. What was David's qualification? He had a shepherd's heart. He loved those four-legged creatures. He loved them with such a love that he had risked his life for them. When a bear came into the flock one day, he fought that bear for his little lambs. When a lion came into the flock and grabbed one of his sheep, David fought with him and took the sheep right out of his mouth. He didn't even stop to think how dangerous it would be for himself. Take a bone away from your own pet dog, and it is dangerous; how much more when you take it away from a hungry lion. But David only thought of one thing, and that was to get that sheep out of the lion's mouth. He fought with that wild beast and delivered it from the fierce beast. Why? Because he loved that little sheep. David had passed the test of Love.

Jesus said, "Greater love hath no man, than that he lay down his life for his friends" (John 15:13). This was David's law. He loved those sheep. He was willing to give his life for those sheep and that is why God could give him the nation of Israel as the sheep of his pasture. God knew that he would love them with a love that was like madness. He loved Israel like that, and that is why he fought the battles of his God for Israel. That is why he so quickly became the captain of the hosts of Israel. The Bible says that when David went out to battle, God went with him. And every battle he was in, he won. No soldier fought more battles in the Bible than David. There is not a record of one defeat. The secret of his victory was LOVE. This is what made him king.

God is choosing His kings today. Do you want to be a king some day? Do you want to sit on the throne with the Lord? Do you want to rule and reign with Him? You can, if you have love . . . for the sheep.

Chapter 28
LOVE DISCIPLINES

A Scripture that used to grate on me as a child when my father read it is, "He that spareth his rod hateth his son: but he that loveth him chasteneth him betimes" (Proverbs 13:24). The Living Bible quotes it, "If you refuse to discipline your son, it proves you don't love him; for if you love him you will be prompt to punish him." Since I have become an adult and had three sons of my own I have learned a new appreciation for what God says about correcting our children.

We are living in a generation of lawlessness. It is a time when man is doing that which is right in his own eyes. Not only are our families undisciplined, but our nation is also. This lack of discipline has crept into our families, our government, our military and our churches. It is like a cancer in the bloodstream of humanity. Our law enforcers are throwing up their hands in hopelessness because even our prisons are undisciplined. Justice itself is undisciplined. And it all began back there when, for lack of love, we let little "Johnny" do what he wanted to do. If we are not careful, the Year of The Children will turn out to be the Year of Anarchy and Rebellion. Our children do not know that we love them, because we do not discipline them.

It takes effort, time and concern to discipline your child. That is why God said that if we don't punish them when they need it, it is a sign that we don't love them. It is a sign of indifference to the child's need when we do not stop to correct that little one in its childish mischief. Proverbs 19:18 says,

"Discipline your son in his early years while there is hope. If you don't, you will ruin his life." King James Version says, "Chasten thy son while there is hope, and let not thy soul spare for his crying." It is healthy for a child to cry. It is normal. It is the thing that will bring the music and art into expression as it develops.

I do not believe in constant nagging and scolding and picking on a child. The discipline should have as much loving care in it when administered as the food we prepare for the child or the clothes we purchase for it. It is not in a spirit of anger or display of rage that we should correct our children. It should be in perfect love.

My father was always very strict with me. I was his firstborn. I believe that parents have a tendency to be more strict with the first child than any of the others. I can remember very clearly my father "spanking" me. I remember one time when he took a leather strap and spanked me with it. He said to me, "Daughter, I hate to do this. I love you so much and it hurts me more than it does you. But you have been disobedient and I must punish you." As I saw the tears running down his cheeks while he was hitting me, I felt like the worst criminal in the world. Those tears made me feel worse than the pain of the leather strap. My father never had to rebuke me more than once. All he had to do was look at me—and that melted me already. And I loved my father.

My father was fighting the rebellion in his daughter. It is not an easy thing with which to deal. Proverbs 22:15 says, "A youngster's heart is filled with rebellion, but punishment will drive it out of him." The King James Version says, "A rod of correction will drive it FAR from him." That old-fashioned paddling board that hung on the wall, or that strap in the teacher's desk was as necessary as our daily bread. It did not make "wrecks of society" out of us. I fear that since we have taken the rod of correction out of our schools, we have done our children more harm than good. We have also taken authority away from our teachers. I have spoken to many teachers who said they would never want to again be in the teaching profession because of the fact that they have no power to be disciplinarians of their students. Our old teachers loved their pupils in a special way. There was a code of honour and respect between teacher and pupil which is not found in our schools today.

The greatest "rod" of correction, the Bible, has been taken out of our schools. When that Book of Moral Ethics was removed from our classrooms, it made way for a spirit of lawlessness and rebellion to come in. Discipline is defined by Webster as "training that corrects, molds, or perfects the mental facilities or moral character. Control gained by forcing obedience or order." As you read this definition you realize that this is just what our nation needs today.

Why are parents rebelling against their children receiving training in mental and moral aspects? Why do they agree to allow their children to be disorderly? In some cities little children run wild in packs like dogs and molest old people, steal, break into houses and damage property. The law can do nothing about it because they are minors. And the parents do not care. If the law tries to step in, the parents turn the law on the law enforcers.

When we were children, we were threatened by our parents that if we would be punished at school for any misdeeds we had done, we would be punished again when we got home. The parents stood behind the teachers for the sake of raising their children in a way that would bring respect to home and community. Why are we afraid of correcting our children? Has Satan deceived us into thinking that by spoiling a child it will love us more? Or do we think that a spanking will kill it? Proverbs 23:13 says, "Don't fail to correct your children, discipline won't hurt them! They won't die if you use a stick on them! Punishment will keep them out of hell." Those are strong words. But they are God-inspired words and they need to be heeded.

God is not only our Father, He is our Teacher and He is also our Law-giver and Judge. As such, He has full authority to discipline us when we need it. He said in Deuteronomy 8:5,

"Thou shalt also consider in thine heart, that, as a man chasteneth his son, so the Lord thy God chasteneth thee." That is a sign of family relationship when our Heavenly Father chastens us. It is a sign of His fatherly love and care for us.

Psalm 94:12 says, "Blessed is the man whom thou chastenest, O Lord, and teachest him out of thy law." It is a great blessing for us when God takes time to chasten us.

Proverbs 3:11, 12 says, "My son, despise not the chastening of the Lord; neither be weary of His correction: For whom the Lord loveth he correcteth; even as a father, the son in whom he delighteth." I believe that the Lord especially loves those whom He takes time to train and to chasten.

The word "chasten" in Webster is defined as, "to correct by punishment or suffering, to prune of excess, pretense or falsity." It is a great work of Grace which God does in our lives when He prunes us of our excess, our pretense and the falseness in our lives. Jesus said, "Every branch in me that beareth not fruit he taketh away: and every branch that beareth fruit, he purgeth it, that it may bring forth more fruit" (John 15:2). That word "purge" means "prune." Jesus was saying that if the branch is dead, God throws it out; but if there is life in it, it will be pruned so that good fruit will come from its life. This is what correction does in our lives. It brings the best out of us.

Hebrews 12:5-8 says, ". . . My son, despise not thou the chastening of the Lord, nor faint when thou art rebuked of him: for whom the Lord loveth he chasteneth and scourgeth every son whom he receiveth. If ye endure chastening, God dealeth with you as with sons; for what son is he whom the father chasteneth not? But if ye be not chastened . . . then are ye bastards." I like the way Living Word puts it, "My son, don't be angry when the Lord punishes you. Don't be discouraged when he has to show you where you are wrong. For when he punishes you, it proves that he loves you. When he whips you it proves you are really his child."

We do not care about correcting the child on the street. We will not bother with the one who is not our own. When

God takes time to correct us and help us to come under the control of His divine government, it is one of the greatest signs of His love that we have.

God disciplined His great saints. David knew the rod of God, and he humbly cried out, "Let me fall into the hands of God." If you need correcting, fall into the hands of Someone who loves you. You will find that the same One who lays the stripes across your back in punishment will also heal the wounds when you repent of your mistakes.

Chapter 29
LOVE COMMUNICATES

Love has a way of communicating that is all its own. Because love lifts us above the natural and usual level of feelings we are able, when we love deeply, to communicate on another level. It is much more sensitive in its ability to transmit and receive messages between two individuals. Two people who love each other deeply can speak volumes with the glance of an eye, the motion of a hand, the movement of a shoulder or even the invisible vibrations that proceed from a person's body. It is almost impossible to deceive someone who loves deeply, unless they want to be deceived because they are afraid to pick up the truth for fear that it will hurt them.

Love is much more than a human emotion; while it is that, it is something still more. It has the stamp of divinity upon it. One might be able to compare love with Jesus Christ. Christ was all human and all divine. This is true about pure love also. It is human and it is divine. Because it has the human element in it, it is possible for love to become perverted in a way that it will lose its balance. People who love in an unnatural way bind the one they love to them with that unnatural love. A mother can destroy her daughter by being overly protective. A wife can destroy her husband by hanging on to him too tightly and a husband can destroy his wife by a possessive love. Of course, this can work in the opposite way also. A wife can be jealous or possessive and a husband can be too restricting with his wife. This is often the result of insecurity. The one who is secure in his or her love does not need to hang on or feel jealous.

While it is true that love can be twisted because of its human characteristic, it is also true that love can be the most perfect, beautiful, eternal, heavenly treasure that humanity has ever inherited from God Almighty. It is the very God-nature implanted into the human race. It is much higher than friendship, liking, attraction or affinity. Love is devotion, loyalty, concern, tenderness and attachment of the heart, mind and soul of one person for another. It is feeling in one's being the vibrations of the Holy Trinity, for it comes from the Holy Trinity. "The love of God is shed abroad [poured] in our hearts by the Holy Ghost which is given unto us" (Romans 5:5).

We see then that pure love is inspired by the third member of the trinity, the Holy Spirit. Oh, how we should praise and thank God that we have this blessing, that the Holy Spirit is loving through our being. Not only is this true of the Christian, but every good-living non-Christian who has the capacity to love and does the works of the righteous man because he has a good heart, is also loving through this touch of God's Spirit on his life.

If the Holy Spirit, who knows all things (is omniscient), loves through us, then He also sees through us and understands through us and there should not be misunderstanding between two people who claim they have the Holy Spirit in their lives. If there are misunderstandings, then something is wrong. One or both of them are not allowing the Spirit of God to show them the root of the matter which causes the friction. Sometimes we do not want to accept the blame because we are proud, stubborn and unteachable. If the Holy Spirit cannot show us what is wrong with us, then certainly we will not receive admonition or correction or reproof when it comes through a human channel, even if that human is speaking to us in a spirit of love and wise counsel.

I believe that when one is deeply spiritual and can hear God's voice, that one is not easily deceived even by seemingly religious people or false "friends." I remember an elderly, saintly woman of God in Germany who was instrumental in inviting people to come and minister in different churches and city halls of South Germany. She did not regard what people said about anyone. She went to God personally and asked God what He had to say about each person that contacted her. And God spoke to her. He would tell her clearly, "He is a good man. He will bless your people. People speak against him, but I love him." Or God would say, "He is evil, have nothing to do with him." She could look at a picture and find that person in the Spirit, and other times she didn't even need to see a picture. I remember telling her once that I had heard that a certain man was coming to Germany. She answered me, "Yes, I know, but I am not inviting him to speak in our church. I want to have nothing to do with him." When I asked her why, she answered me, "Because he is evil." I did not dare ask her any more. I knew the man, and I knew that she had heard from God. Sad to say, later he did go to Germany, but she had already gone to heaven and another, not so wise as she, invited him to speak and he did much harm to the kingdom of God.

As we come into the fullness of the Spirit, we shall be able to judge after the Spirit and not after the flesh; 2 Corinthians 5:16 says, "Henceforth know we no man after the flesh." We misjudge people because we look at them and judge them after the seeing of the eye and the hearing of the ear. This is why God's church is failing in its ability to reach fallen man. Jesus, because His love was perfect, judged in righteousness. Isaiah said in 11:3, 4, ". . . He shall not judge after the sight of his eyes, neither reprove after the hearing of his ears: But with righteousness shall he judge." This was because Jesus was able to see mankind through the Holy Spirit's perception. Deuteronomy 29:29 says, "The secret things belong unto the Lord our God." And God has the prerogative to show them to any one of His children any time He sees we are able to cope with these secrets or desire them for the good of mankind.

Our communication will be perfect when our love for

each other is perfect. I believe that in heaven much of our communication will be without words, and yet it will be perfect. We will not have to talk to each other, or explain things to each other; we will know all things without the encumbrance of words, words, words. Oh, how tired I sometimes get of words! I thank God for the relationships in life that God has given me where the sensitivity is so keen, that when I speak only half a sentence, the one I am with already knows exactly what I am referring to, or what I am thinking. Often I don't even need to say a word. But this is only where love is great, not only for me, but also for God.

Words belong to the flesh realm. That is why the world is filled with them. Babel belongs to Babylon. Webster defines babel as "confusion of sounds or voice, a scene of noise or confusion." God wants to bring us out of this flesh realm and into the Spirit realm. And yet we base so much of our entire opinion about places and people by the "flesh reports" we receive about them.

However, I believe that for the elect of God, the day of the flesh realm is over. We want the genuine. Philippians 1:10 says, "That ye may approve things that are excellent; that ye may be sincere and without offence till the day of Christ." The day of Christ is at the threshhold and we must be very careful to be sure that we are without offence, and that we are truly a sincere and genuine people in whom God sees no flaws. When the Holy Spirit has done His work of purifying me, then I can see others more clearly also. But first the work must begin in me. It is only as I look out through a clean windshield that I can see what is in front of me when I am driving down the road. As the eyes of my spirit are cleaned through the work of the Spirit of God in my life, I am able to see with a vision that is more than 20/20. In that hour I can do more, with God doing it through me, than if I do it in my own strength. God can do more in five minutes than I can do in five years. There are no limits when we move by the Spirit of God.

In Genesis 6:12, 13 we read, "And God said unto Noah,

'The end of all flesh is come before me; for all flesh has corrupted his way upon the earth.' " The flesh rule is over. The Spirit within us is crying out to be recognized. We must know each other after the Spirit. We must *see* each other in a new way. We must *see* the potential of God in others, even though in the natural we only see "the devil."

I believe we will be able to help our sons and daughters if we can find them in the Spirit. We cannot help them unless we find them in the Spirit. Sometimes the more we try to bridge the gap, the wider the chasm grows because they resent our efforts. We are working at it in the flesh way. Maybe the Holy Spirit is saying, "Leave them alone!" or "Give them time!" And we have no patience, so we destroy the good that absence, silence and time alone can do to bring healing. It is no use to try to reason with them; God says, "The natural man receiveth NOT the things of the Spirit of God: for they are foolishness unto him: neither can he know them, because they are spiritually discerned" (1 Corinthians 2:14). Then he goes on to say, "But he that is spiritual judgeth all things." If we are spiritual we will be able to judge or "find" our children and others in the Spirit. While it is true that we can and must discipline them when they are young, there comes a time when we do not have the same jurisdiction over them, either because of age or distance. Then we cannot control them by the flesh any longer. We can only reach them through the Spirit of God. And in order to minister to them, or anyone in the Spirit, we must ourselves LIVE in the Spirit. It is no use to think we can live in the flesh and control others in the Spirit. We are only deceiving ourselves.

This is the trouble with the church. We are trying to reach people through program and emotion. The emotion is in the soulish realm. It is beautiful and meaningful and very important, but it is not the zenith of perfection in attaining unto high spiritual dimensions of godliness and holiness. Therefore our experiences with God are very shallow. We go to a certain church because we like the way the choir sings, or the Tiffany stained-glass window which inspires us when the minister's sermon gets monotonous, or the pipe organ is the finest in the city, or the minister is dynamic with a vibrant personality. And then we wonder why we do not go deep in God. We are in the soulish realm. Surely it's beautiful, but it's all flesh.

Many are reaching out to God, but they don't know how to get free. Their heart's cry is, "Set my spirit free that I may worship Thee. Call, and I will come within Thy sanctuary." In many people there are the attributes of God which have not been released. They are waiting for you to "find them in the Spirit" by the love of God in your heart. Don't point out their faults to them, but see them as God sees them. Many fall away because we don't love them or know them by the Spirit. We are critical until we are able to find others in the Spirit. Only *love* will reach a fallen man or woman. Pointing out his or her faults will turn them off.

I can't help others until I find them in the Spirit, and I often, almost always, when dealing with difficult ones have to go to God and say, "Lord, I don't understand that person; let me find that one in the Spirit. Let me see them as You do." Sometimes what He shows me prepares me for a big disappointment. I am able to accept people's failures more easily when I find them in the Spirit. I cannot minister to them until I find them in the Spirit, because I cannot minister in love until I find them in the Spirit. It is only in the Spirit that I have mercy, kindness and the courage to correct them and exhort them. When you sit in God's presence, His wisdom becomes your wisdom, His mind becomes your mind. Paul said, "Let this mind be in you, which was also in Christ Jesus." This is what "seeing in the Spirit" is all about.

In Galatians 6:1 Paul says, "Brethren, if a man be overtaken in a fault, ye which are SPIRITUAL restore such an one in the spirit of meekness; considering thyself, lest thou also be tempted." It is only if you are in the Spirit that you are spiritual enough to restore someone else who has fallen. It is not if you are religious or good, but if you are SPIRITUAL that you can restore that one, and you must do it with a spirit of meekness that comes as a result of having found *yourself* in the Spirit, which can be a humbling experience.

In Galatians 6:3, 4, Paul says, "For if a man think himself to be something, when he is nothing, he deceiveth himself. But let every man prove his own work." Sometimes the hardest one to "find in the Spirit" is one's own self. We protect our flesh, feed our flesh, dress our flesh, comfort our flesh, massage our flesh, rest our flesh, thrill our flesh, anoint our flesh, wash our flesh and save our flesh. Most of our life is taken up with doing something for our flesh. No wonder it survives so well! Meanwhile we starve our spirit, turn a deaf ear to our spirit, drive our spirit, unclothe our spirit and destroy our spirit in hell. The spirit within us cries out for God and we try to satisfy it with more flesh. That is why this world is in such a mess! The spirit within us wants to fast and the flesh wants to eat steaks, so we eat a steak. The spirit wants to pray but the flesh wants to sleep, so we sleep. The spirit wants to read the Word of God but the flesh wants to relax with a mystery book, so we read a mystery. The spirit wants to be like its Maker but we are trapped by our image, so we stay in our likeness instead of in His. When will we find ourselves in the Spirit and minister to the needs of the man within?

The wonderful part of finding someone in the Spirit is that you will not only know their needs and faults, but WHY they are like that. You can give righteous judgment when you realize why they are like they are. Sometimes God will let you see their hereditary roots or their environment or their physical infirmities. These things will help you to understand them without judgment.

We have come to a new day; let us step into it by the help of the Holy Spirit. God will not permit flesh to boast. We will not be able to say, *"My* sermon brought her to Christ, *my* prayers were answered, *my* hands laid on that body brought healing." We will have to give the glory to the Lord God instead of to ourselves and our program and our organization. Perilous times are coming and also glorious times.

There will be danger, persecution, betrayal and false prophets in our midst. Spies will come into the camp. Let us find *them* in the Spirit also.

Jesus found Nathanael in the Spirit. He said, "Behold an Israelite indeed in whom is no guile." When Nathanael, in amazement, asked, "Whence knowest thou me?" Jesus answered him, "Before that Philip called thee, when thou wast under the fig tree, I saw thee" (John 1:47, 48). Yes, Jesus had found Nathanael in the Spirit long before He ever saw him with His eyes.

Jesus also found the woman of Samaria in the Spirit. He not only knew her sin, her past, but also her thirst for God and her ability to receive the truth that He was the Messiah. If Jesus had listened to the gossip or seen her only as a man sees a sinful woman, He would have avoided her; but He saw her need and heard her heart's cry that was hidden behind her spoken words. We will hear the heart's cry of people when we find them in the Spirit.

Barnabas found Paul in the Spirit when the whole church was against Paul because they feared him, and he went to Tarsus to look for him and brought him to Antioch and introduced him to the church there. Later, Barnabas and Paul parted. Their split was because of John Mark. John Mark had failed them once before and gone back home to Jerusalem. Later Barnabas wanted to take him along the second time, but Paul didn't want to be bothered with him because of his past mistake. So there was a sharp contention that came between them which resulted in their going separate ways. In the end Paul said to Timothy, "Bring John Mark to me, he is profitable to me for the ministry" (2 Timothy 4:11). It took Paul many years to find John Mark in the Spirit, but Barnabas had done it all along, for Barnabas had the same grace for John Mark as he had had for Saul of Tarsus. Even as he had found Saul in the Spirit, he had found John Mark in the Spirit and had known that John Mark was sorry he had failed the Lord and run off from his missionary field, and was wanting to get back into the will of God. Paul was not infallible. He had made a mistake but, thank God, when writing his last letter to Timothy we see that he acknowledged that John Mark was valuable for the ministry, even though there was a time when he was so much against him that he broke his friendship with his dearest friend Barnabas because of his antipathy against this young man. At last, in his closing and final letter that the church possesses, he finds John Mark in the Spirit. Time had softened Paul and made him more tender. It is also in this last book and last chapter, and almost the last verse, that he mentions one last name as being one of those who are with him in his final hour of trial and martyrdom, and it is the name of a woman, Claudia. Maybe in the end Paul found his sisters in Christ in the Spirit, too!

Chapter 30
LOVE FORGIVES

The ability to forgive is one of the greatest gifts that God has imputed to man. Except for the grace of God in our lives, no one has the capacity to truly forgive. Webster defines forgive "to cease to feel resentment against an offender: to give up resentment of or claim to requittal for . . . an insult: to grant relief from payment of some debt." Only God can forgive, and that is why we are unable to forgive unless God, by the Holy Spirit, works this grace in our lives.

The Christian faith is the highest of all religions, when we live out its rules. But if we only talk it and preach it but do not live it, then it becomes a mockery to its Founder. The difference between Christianity and other religions such as the Moslem is that we are commanded by our Prophet and Saviour to forgive. Yesterday's newspaper had a small article in it which I would like to quote for you:

> Chaudhry Zahur Elahi, the Pakistani Political Affairs Minister reported at Rawalpindi, Pakistan that former Premier Zulfikar Ali Bhutto will not escape hanging because Islamic law does not empower the head of state "to commute the death verdict of a murderer."

This was in the Arkansas Gazette, February 18, 1979.

Bhutto was Premier in West Pakistan when that nation went to war with East Pakistan and India, and he was filled with hate toward them. The spirit of the man was almost demonic. Thousands lived in fear of him. Later he was ousted by the military and subsequently sentenced to a death verdict for which there is no clemency under Moslem law. Islam, which is his religion, does not permit mercy. The law of the Moslem religion is a life for a life. We may be shocked by this, but this was also the law of Judaism and Moses. The Word of God is full of it. Read Leviticus 24:19, 20. "And if a man cause a blemish in his neighbor; as he hath done, so shall it be done to him; Breach for breach, eye for eye, tooth for tooth; as he hath caused a blemish in a man, so shall it be done to him again." Deuteronomy 19:21 says, "And thine eye shall not pity; but life shall go for life, eye for eye, tooth for tooth, hand for hand, foot for foot."

Only Jesus had the power to lift that law and commute the death verdict that was on mankind. As we look into the Old Testament, we see very few who had the power to forgive. Among the list of those who had this grace we will see some of the great heroes of heaven's Hall of Fame. There was *Isaac,* who not only forgave but made a feast for Abimelech whose servants constantly fought against Isaac's men for every well that they dug and thereby forced Isaac either to fight or move on.

Joseph was able to forgive his brothers who had sold him into slavery and caused great grief, not only to himself but to his beloved father. But Joseph knew that "All things work together for good to them that love God." He said to his brothers, "Now therefore be not grieved, nor angry with yourselves, that ye sold me hither: for God did send me before you to preserve life." (Genesis 45:5)

There was *Hosea* the prophet who forgave his wife Gomer when she went back to her life of prostitution and bought her from white slavery to become his wife again. And he did this at the command of God (Hosea 3:1, 2). Is this not strange when God told Moses that such a woman should be stoned to death for this same sin (Deuteronomy 22:24 and John 8:7)?

So strong was this law that in the days of Jesus when

the woman was caught in adultery and brought to Jesus they said to Him, "Master, this woman was taken in adultery, in the very act. Now Moses in the law commanded us, that such should be stoned: but what sayest thou?" Jesus knew that if He agreed with them He would go against Roman law and they could accuse Him of being a lawbreaker. If He said they should not stone her, then they would accuse Him of breaking the laws of Judaism. So in wisdom He answered, "He that is without sin among you, let him first cast a stone at her." This took care of the matter. When they had all stealthily crept away from there because they were condemned of their own sins, Jesus said to the woman, "Neither do I condemn thee: go and sin no more" (John 8:3-11). The Lawgiver had found the sinner-woman in the Spirit and had given her another chance. How many times has God said to you, "Neither do I condemn thee; go and sin no more?"

In the same way as He has forgiven us, we should forgive others also. Jesus taught us to forgive. This law of forgiveness is very strongly imprinted on the heart of every true follower of Jesus Christ. It is a part of our Lord's Prayer, "Forgive us our trespasses, as we forgive those who trespass against us." Jesus said in Matthew 6:14, 15, "For if ye forgive men their trespasses, your heavenly Father will also forgive you; But if ye forgive not men their trespasses, neither will your Father forgive your trespasses." You can see that He introduced a new law of love, a law of forgiveness because Love must forgive. He said to His followers, "Ye have heard that it hath been said, An eye for an eye, and a tooth for a tooth; But I say unto you, That ye resist not evil [don't pay back the evil you receive]: but whosoever shall smite thee on thy right cheek, turn to him the other also." This was not the law of Moses, this was the law of the angels (Matthew 5:38, 39).

Jesus taught us that if we are bringing our gifts or standing before the altar of God and suddenly remember that a friend has something against us, we should leave our sacrifice there beside the altar and go and apologize and be reconciled to him, and then come and offer our sacrifice to God (Matthew 5:23, 24). Even if we are not to blame, God expects us to live by this higher law of taking the blame upon ourselves like Jesus did when He was crucified and died in our stead. How can we be a "Jesus" to the world if we do not do what He did?

The warning is very strong in Mark 11:26 where Jesus says, "But if ye do not forgive, neither will your Father which is in heaven forgive your trespasses." It seems that the extent of our forgiveness from God is dependent on the extent of our ability to forgive others. We are all going to need mercy some day; let us therefore give mercy so that mercy will be given to us when we need it. Jesus said, "As ye would that men should do to you, do ye also to them likewise. . . . Judge not and ye shall not be judged: condemn not, and ye shall not be condemned: forgive, and ye shall be forgiven" (Luke 6:31, 37).

Jesus also said, "Take heed to yourself; if thy brother trespass against thee, rebuke him, and if he repent, forgive him. And if he trespass against thee seven times a day, and seven times a day turn again to thee, saying, I repent; thou shalt forgive him" (Luke 17:3, 4). This is the law of Grace. This is what God does every time we come to Him seeking mercy and forgiveness; and if He can do it then, by His grace, we too can do it.

Jesus does say, however, that we should rebuke our brother. There is a time when love rebukes. "Faithful are the wounds of a friend" (Proverbs 27:6). Paul told the church at Corinth to rebuke sin. He was dealing with a sin of adultery and he called the church to deal with it very strongly (1 Corinthians 5:1-5). He later wrote the church and told them that that man had suffered enough and that they were to forgive him and comfort him, lest perhaps he would be overcome with sorrow (2 Corinthians 2:7). The command to forgive does not obliterate the need of a healthy and loving rebuke when a rebuke is necessary.

I have seen the lives of some of God's greatest and most

valuable servants destroyed because the church has not been able to forgive. It seems that we are living under the law of the Moslem religion or Judaism. Jesus came, bringing us grace; and in that grace is the TRUTH of God's mercy and love, a love so great that it can forgive us all of our sins and reckon us clean and pure through the Blood of Jesus Christ. We must be careful when we condemn someone that we are not standing on the side of the Accuser of the Brethren. Remember that Jesus said, "I stand with the accused and not the accuser." These are the exact words He told a friend of mine when He appeared to her visibly and told her to take a sick person to a certain minister for prayer. This friend of mine had heard bad reports about that preacher, so she was very surprised when Jesus told her to take her friend there for prayer. She ask, "But, Lord, I have heard bad things about him!" Jesus answered her, "That is why I want to honor him." She asked, "But, Lord, are these things true that they say about him? Is he guilty?" Jesus answered her, "Guilty or not guilty, I stand with the accused and not the accusers."

Jesus stands at the side of the accused like He hung on the side of the thief on the cross who cried, "Remember me when thou comest into thy kingdom." Jesus could answer him, "Today thou shalt be with me in paradise." Forgiveness is paradise.

It was as they crucified Jesus that He was given the grace to pray for the men who nailed Him to the cross. He prayed, "Father, forgive them; for they know not what they do." They had just stripped Him naked (Luke 23:34).

Jesus showed His followers the law of forgiveness. Not long after that, Stephen cried out the same kind of beautiful prayer as he was being stoned to death, "Lord, lay not this sin to their charge" (Acts 7:60).

Behind the Iron Curtain many of God's faithful children are giving their lives as martyrs in these days. Pastor Richard Wurmbrand, one of God's modern-day saints, tells the story of a man who failed God:

    The leader of the Orthodox Underground in

Romania, a priest by the name of Gheorghe Calciu, has warm brother relations with the persecuted Baptists. He was formerly a fellow-prisoner of mine. Arrested at the age of 21, he spent 16 years in prison for belonging to a patriotic organization. There he suffered the worst tortures, such as being compelled to eat his own excrement and drink urine. One could escape these atrocities only by claiming to be "reeducated in the Communist spirit" and proving it by torturing one's friends. Calciu cracked under this pressure, and became a torturer in his turn, compelling others to eat their outfall and brainwashing them. But after his release, he received grace from God, was converted, and became a priest. From great depths of sin he rebounded toward heights of holiness. Seminarians and other youth flocked to his sermons. When the Communists locked the doors of the seminary to prevent students from going to hear him, the students jumped through the window. The Communists locked the church, so Calciu preached on its steps. He protested against the tearing down of Orthodox churches in Bucharest and Focshani, althought he was advised that priests must be on the side of the atheists who are in power. He continues to stand, although threatened with being locked in a psychiatric asylum.

This is the story of forgiveness. Jesus said that those who were forgiven much, loved much. It is the great love that this man has which gives him the grace and strength to be faithful to the Lord in spite of all the threats and persecution that he is going through.

"And when ye stand praying, forgive!" (Mark 11:25).

Chapter 31
LOVE, THE KEY TO KNOWING GOD

One of the dearest and most precious treasures that God has ever put into my hands is the little book *Intra Muros** by Rebecca Ruter Springer. The edition I have was published by David C. Cook, Elgin, Illinois and even though it was a very old book, that was its 25th printing. *Intra Muros* is the story of a woman's visit to heaven. It is wonderfully written and is one of the most deeply moving records of the Land Beyond The River that has ever been left to mortals. As I read of her encounter with Jesus during her visit in heaven, I received such a longing to know Jesus better. I was inspired to write a little song which I have recorded on my long-playing record, *Sunrise In The Morning,*** and have also included it in our book of songs called *Treasures in Song.*** The words of this lovely song are:

> Let me know You, Let me feel You,
> Let me touch You, Let me see You,
> As I shall know You, As I shall feel You,
> As I shall touch You, As I shall see You,
> Let it not be long, Lord, I cannot wait, Lord,
> All my being longs for You.

---

*Published in an unabridged edition by Engeltal Press. See order form in the back of the book.

**See order form in the back of the book.

There are times in life when the soul of man has such an intense longing to return to God, its Maker, that it would leap out of the body, if that were possible. And yet, one can know God while still in flesh on this planet which is so distant from heaven. I want to dedicate this chapter to this great theme of knowing God.

When I lived in Hong Kong as a missionary, there came to our colony a man by the name of Walter Beuttler. He was one of God's greatest saints of this generation. He journeyed around the world, going from nation to nation, teaching one subject, HOW TO KNOW GOD. He was one of the most satisfying teachers of Holy Writ under whom I have ever had the privilege of sitting. As I listened to him teach night after night, I knew that he was speaking from first-hand experience. This was a man who walked with God like Enoch and who had seen His glory, like Moses, and who had been His friend, like Abraham. I took notes of all he taught, but unfortunately I lost them during the journey of life, so I must resort to my own limited understanding of this great subject and the inspiration which the Holy Spirit gives me as I write.

In John 5:20 we read, "For the Father loveth the Son and sheweth him all things that himself doeth: and he will shew him greater works than these, that ye may marvel." Here is one of the glorious results of love. The Father loves His Son, and as a result of that Love, He shows Him ALL things that He himself is doing. When Jesus was on earth He showed mankind so many wonderful new revelations of the almighty God which man had never before had. We know that John 3:16 tells us that God gave the world Jesus because He loved us. Love is the key of God introducing and revealing the Son to this world. Love is the key of God giving any revelation of Himself to us. We cannot gain knowledge of God by any righteous works which we do, nor by our much activity, but only as our heart responds to His love. When Jesus was on earth, not everyone knew who He was. It was only those who received Him and loved Him who were able to learn from Him. Love makes us receptive to the deeper truths of God. Love makes us teachable and pliable.

A Jewish follower of Jesus Christ has told that he was already a graduate of a university before he ever read the New Testament. He has said that as he read about Jesus, he was compelled to realize that Jesus was no ordinary man. As a Jew, he had been taught about a jealous and angry God. Suddenly he had to realize that Jesus was teaching us about a God who was full of Love. This is true about Jesus. He was the world's greatest revelation of God. And it is no wonder that the Pharisees and religious leaders of His time could not accept Him, because He was completely different from the concept they had of God. He taught us what the love of the Father really was. We had not known until then. We only knew God as a roaring Fire on Mount Sinai who spoke with mighty thunder and lightnings. A God who STRUCK DEAD anyone who would come near His presence, who DROWNED the world because of its sin, who sent PLAGUES on Egypt and destroyed their land, and KILLED their firstborn man and beast. We knew Him as the God who accepted the BLOOD SACRIFICE of tens of thousands of animals at one time alone, who RAINED DOWN FIRE and brimstone on Sodom and Gomorrah because of their perverted spirit of sodomy, and who CONFUSED people with many languages when they attempted to build a tower that would help them ascend to heaven. This was the God they knew.

Then suddenly came a Man, who claimed He was sent from God and that God was His Father. A Man who was teaching a law altogether different, because it was a LAW OF LOVE. Is it any wonder they couldn't understand a man who said He had come from God and yet did not keep the laws which they had received from their former teachers of God's law?

It is evident that we have to know God by the Spirit and not after the letter of the law. As we study the life of Jesus, we learn what love is; and we know what God's love is. Through this revelation, our own hearts are awakened to love.

He loved the Father and the Father loved Him, and revealed the deep secrets to Him.

Have you ever wondered where Jesus was for eighteen years of His life? That was between the ages of twelve and thirty. Have you ever thought about it? What was He doing? What was He learning? Where did He go? There are secrets in the life of Jesus hidden from our knowledge that God never permitted the writers of the Gospels to reveal to us. The American Indians have a legend that He appeared to them. The Hindus of India tell how He visited them also. Certain things must remain a secret until we see Him in Glory.

Even Jesus could not reveal all He knew, nor could Paul, nor Daniel. Daniel, in writing his prophecy concerning the end time, was commanded by God, "Shut up the words, and seal the book, even to the time of the end" (Daniel 12:4). We are in the end time now when the seals will be opened and the righteousness of God will be revealed, a time when even some of understanding shall fall, to try them, and to purge, and to make them white, even to the time of the end. Hearts are hungry for truth. Those who have accepted the redemption through the Blood of Jesus are standing today at the great gates of Paradise, and the angel that stands with the sword of fire will draw back the sword and permit the pure ones to come back into the garden of Eden to eat from the most blessed thing that man has ever lost, the tree of life. We shall partake of His infinite knowledge and revelation. The hungry shall be filled and satisfied. Oh, may God stir up our hearts and make us to see that what we need to do now is to repent of ALL sins and make diligent self-examination so that we will be counted worthy to be restored to His glory and eternal blessings. May God make you hunger for the taste of this fruit from the tree of life. We cannot stop now. We are too close to the end. Let us come into perfection and purity through His Love and we will then be permitted to taste of His fruit and we will then no more be taught by mortal man, but by Him alone.

Samuel

Do you realize that man's natural intellect has nothing to do with knowing the secrets of God? A child can know greater secrets than a great scholar. Samuel was but a little lad when God revealed to him the secret of what He was going to do in Israel. Samuel was able to hear the voice of God more clearly than the glorious high priest, Eli, because he was willing to listen. God chooses to reveal himself to innocent hearts. I am convinced that the time has come when we must put aside our man-taught knowledge and open up our minds to the Holy Spirit, for the hour of our full redemption is come when God will touch our minds and the light of God's glory will shine in us and we shall know by divine revelation what no book has yet revealed. God cannot tell all His secrets in the Bible. Over and over again He says, "I cannot tell you everything." So there must be secrets of God between those two black covers which have not yet been revealed. I believe that when our hearts are open and we love the Father, He will reveal the secrets to us, even as He revealed them to His Son, Jesus. But we will have to lay aside a lot of our man-taught ideas, for men are always learning and never able to come to the knowledge of truth. Jesus gave us a promise. He said that when the Holy Spirit is come, He will teach us all things. None of us have become that advanced in spiritual knowledge that we know all things. Don't you want to know God better?

Daniel

The wisdom of Daniel has been praised by the prophets through the ages. Ezekiel says about the Prince of Tyre, who also was Lucifer, "Thou art wiser than Daniel; there is no secret that they can hide from thee." In other words, Daniel's wisdom was commented upon as being rivaled only by Lucifer himself.

In the book of Daniel we read about the wisdom of

Daniel. It says, "God gave them (him and his companions) knowledge and skill in all learning and wisdom: and Daniel had understanding in all vision and dreams" (1:17). There were no mystical secrets that Daniel could not understand. God spoke to him in the hours of the night through visions and dreams.

What was the secret of Daniel's ability to know God, and in knowing God, to know the plans and purposes of God? In chapter 10:19 we read, "O man greatly beloved..." It is evident that when the Heavenly Being visited Daniel and conveyed to him the secrets of eternity, that he was very much loved, for the visiting Personage called him a man who was greatly beloved.

Daniel's love for God was so great that he defied the order of the king and continued to pray with his window open three times a day, facing the Holy City of Jerusalem. For his love he was thrown into the den of lions. But that same love that gave him divine knowledge also prevented the lions from devouring him. The spirit of love that was on Daniel came upon the lions and they loved Daniel with a supernatural love so that they could not make Daniel-burgers out of him. Later when Daniel's enemies were thrown into the den, they became mincemeat in a few minutes. Even their bones were devoured. Love will lock the jaws of your enemy. And love will give you the key to knowing the secrets of God. The queen said of him, "There is a man in thy kingdom, in whom is the spirit of the holy gods; and in the days of thy father, light and understanding and wisdom, like the wisdom of the gods, was found in him; whom the king Nebuchadnezzar thy father, the king, I say, thy father, made master of the magicians, astrologers, Chaldeans and soothsayers" (Daniel 5:11).

"Daniel was preferred above the presidents and princes, because an excellent spirit was in him; and the king thought to set him over the whole realm" (Daniel 6:3). What was this excellent spirit? It was the same thing that Paul spoke about when he said, "I show unto you a more excellent way" (1 Corinthians 12:31), even the way of LOVE.

In Jeremiah 6:10 we read, "To whom shall I speak, and give warning, that they may hear? behold, their ear is uncircumcised, and they cannot hearken: behold, the word of the Lord is unto them a reproach; they have no delight in it." Here we see why God cannot teach us the secret things. He said the ear is not circumcised. What does circumcision mean? It means "cutting away the flesh, or earthliness." All these earthly things that fill our consciousness hinder us from hearing the eternal, spiritual things. Our ears are so cluttered up with the noice and confusion of our own makings, that they cannot hear that still, small voice of the Lord God as He speaks. It says in this Scripture, "They have no delight to hear what God has to say."

Friend, let us ask God to clean out our ears! When you have a haircut in China, they always finish up by cleaning out your ears. This is very important to the Chinese. Sometimes when you get your ears cleaned out a lot of old wax is removed. Some hear much better after getting that old wax out. Spiritually, the ears of our spirit can hear a voice that is not audible. But why are we not allowing that inaudible voice to register on our consciousness? It seems like our spiritual ears are clogged up with "old wax." We are so filled with the debris of yesterday and self, that God cannot speak to many of us. Until He can speak to us, we will stay in our ignorance. Remember Jesus said, "Their ears are dull of hearing" (Matthew 13:15). Their ears were deaf because their hearts were closed.

John 6:45 says, "It is written in the prophets, And they shall be all taught of God. Every man therefore that hath heard, and hath learned of the Father, cometh unto me." This Scripture does not say that they will be taught by the prophets. They are going to be taught by God himself. And then it says that "everyone that has heard, and has learned of the Father cometh to Me." When Jesus spoke these words, the publicans and sinners, the common and the poor and uneducated had already come to Him. Ninety percent or more of the people who came to Jesus had probably never learned to read. Most of them had never gone to school. And yet, it says they heard the Father and, as a result of hearing His voice, they followed the ONE whom the Father had sent to them. On the other hand, there were the scribes with many years of intensive study, who had spent their whole lives studying Scriptures, yet in spite of their much learning did not find the Christ in their Scriptures portrayed in the One whom the Father sent, even though as we understand it now, He fulfilled all the Scriptures concerning Himself. Of all the nations on earth, none loved the Bible and studied it so extensively as the Jews. Their highest treasure was the scrolls of the prophets, the holy writings of Moses. Their scribes were trained from boyhood to preserve the Word of God. They knew the prophecies and they knew where the Messiah would come from. Still they failed to recognize him when He came, in spite of their knowledge, because they couldn't "hear." They failed to hear because they failed in their love for the Father. Their motive for studying the Scriptures was more out of love for themselves, personal pride in their accomplishment and the ability to debate in long religious discussions. It was a great virtue for them to be recognized as scholars of the Scriptures. They wanted to have a "big name." To have a doctorate in religion does not mean that you know God. It is only in walking in His footsteps that we know Him, and we cannot walk in His footsteps unless we love Him. The Word of God says, "Then shall we know, if we follow on to know the Lord" (Hosea 6:3).

Paul

In Hebrews 5:11, 12 we read, ". . . we have many things to say, and hard to be uttered, seeing ye are dull of hearing. For when for the time ye ought to be teachers, ye have need that one teach you again, which be the first principles of the oracles of God; . . ." Paul is not able to write about some of the greatest mysteries, even the secrets concerning Melchisedec the high priest, because the people were not able to receive these truths. Where did Paul get these secrets? He said that when he became a believer in Jesus Christ he immediately "conferred not with flesh and blood, neither went I up to Jerusalem to them which were apostles before me: but I went into Arabia, and returned again to Damascus. Then after three years I went up to Jerusalem to see Peter, and abode with him fifteen days" (Galatians 1:16-18). Instead of being taught by the great apostles of Jesus, he went into the desert where he stayed for three years. It was here that God taught Paul the secrets concerning the Scriptures. Paul knew things that even Peter and James and John did not know.

Sometimes the love of God will drive you to come apart from others. Paul, no doubt because of the great forgiveness he had received from God for his murder of the Christians, became a great lover of Jesus Christ and lived to suffer for Him like few have ever suffered, finally to die as a martyr in Rome. Paul was unique in his ministry, and sometimes it is hard to see Paul's love which is hidden under his firm and strong ways of dealing with situations, but we can know his love when we study the "more excellent way" which he left for us.

Mark 4:33, 34 says, "And with many such parables spake he the word unto them, as they were able to bear it. And without a parable spake he not unto them: and when they were alone, he expounded all things to his disciples." This is the reason the Lord spoke in parables. He was teaching truths, and yet He covered them up. Why? Have you ever had an intimate secret with somebody? Have you ever noticed when there is a secret between you and another, that when a word is spoken both of you immediately think the same thing? You have a contact through knowledge. Jesus knew that they would know what He meant, even though He told them the Gospel in parables, because the Father had already revealed much truth to them. What they did not understand, He taught them when they were alone.

When I teach the Word of God, I can see things in people's faces. I can see that some of those who are listening already know what I am trying to tell them because they have already heard the secrets of God. When I preach, it is only a confirmation to them. The light beams out from them and their faces shine.

When Jesus taught, He taught in such a way that the mockers could not trample His truths under their feet. He said, "Do not give your pearls to the swine, lest they trample them under their feet, and turn again and rend you" (Matthew 7:6). Jesus had only three years to teach the mighty truths of God. He was always followed by all kinds of people. The true, sincere ones who were ordained by God to know truth were there, and the curious, the mockers, the enemies of Christ who were looking for an opportunity to trip Him up with His words and teaching were also there. Jesus had to have a language to teach them so that those who had ears to hear could hear and the others could not.

When we have the right relationship with the Father, we will see things in the Scriptures which are hidden from the average eyes. When the disciples were alone with Him, He expounded the truths to them. That is the secret: ALONE WITH HIM! It is there He will teach you secrets that He cannot tell others. If He sees that you love earthly things more, He will give you the desire of your heart, but will send leanness to your soul.

Many have asked God to give them the gift of discernment. But if the Lord did give them this gift, the first thing they would see would cause them to sin. They would see such sins in the lives of some people who are Christians that it would give them such a shock they would not be able to live with it. So God in His wisdom limits our knowledge. But He does this only because we are immature and not spiritually capable of handling discernment. But when we have become spiritually mature in God, the doubts which hinder us today will be removed and the veil of unbelief will be torn down. The light of God, revelation, understanding and compassion of Jesus shall be ours. It is then that full knowledge will be revealed to us because we will be able to handle it without it destroying us.

With knowledge must come compassion and understanding. Some of the best-living people have absolutely no compassion or understanding in their brother's or sister's problem. Perhaps it is because they themselves have not had the same experience. So God is permitting many of His children to go through terrible experiences in order that they will not be so critical. Some who have criticized divorced people the most have had to suffer this same trial, either in the lives of their children or even their own lives. It has softened them and taken the sting of criticism out of them, making them much more compassionate and beautiful.

If you are praying for understanding, know that God will take you through a very strange way. God is going to permit you to go through experiences which will be even an embarrassment to yourself. But He will allow it for one reason—that you may be able to understand others when they fail God.

In John 8:26 Jesus said, "I have many things to say and to judge of you: but He that sent me is true; and I speak to the world those things which I have heard of him." Jesus is telling us that He has so much He wants to tell us. I am convinced that Jesus has many secrets He wants to reveal to His own. How long has it been since you heard a secret from the Lord? The Lord is still revealing hidden truths and He says, "There is much I want to tell you." Have you ever been alone with Him with an open heart full of love for Him, so that He CAN reveal these things to you?

Have you ever been absent from a loved one for a long time and when you get together again you have so many secrets to share that you can hardly wait to start talking? You talk for hours into the night and are not even sleepy! That is the way Jesus wants to share His secrets with us, but most of us "fall asleep on Him." No wonder He has to give some of us insomnia! He has to keep us awake so we will listen to Him. We are too active in the daylight hours, so He catches us when we are on our beds.

When Jesus came from heaven, He saw how we little dumb creatures thought we knew so much about God, and we didn't really know anything. We thought we were so intelligent. He wanted to take us into His arms and we said, "Oh, I know more than you do! Who do you think YOU are? Your father is a carpenter. In fact, there is something questionable about your birth! It seems the report has come to us from Nazareth that your parents weren't even married nine months before you were born! Who do you think you are, trying to tell us that God is *your* Father?" Do you remember how they accused Jesus of having an unclean demon and casting demons out through the power of Satan (Mark 3:22, Luke 11:15)? That is the reason they would not listen to Jesus, even though He came bringing them the Father's message of LOVE. He came directly from the presence of God, and they rejected Him because they themselves did not spend time in the presence of God. It is possible to go to temples, synagogues, churches, cathedrals, mosques and kingdom halls and still not be in the presence of God. It is possible to visit all these places every day of your life and still not know God when He is speaking to your heart.

John 16:12 says, "I have many things to say unto you, but ye cannot bear them now." These words were not spoken at the beginning of the Lord's ministry when His followers were new and ignorant of the things which He was teaching them. Nor was it when their heads were still full of fishing and the buying and selling of their fish. No! It was at the end of His ministry, after they had been in His presence for over three years. It was after some of them had even seen His glorification on the Mount of Transfiguration. It was after the miracles and signs and wonders had all been performed.

I could weep when I read these words of our Lord. Think of that beautiful treasure of knowledge which He could not give us because we did not have the ability to accept it! He was not speaking to the crowd or the Pharisees who would destroy Him with the truths that He wanted to share, but to His own intimate followers, the apostles of the

Christian faith, the greatest men and founders of the church of the Living God. "I have many things to say unto you, but ye cannot bear them now." If He could not tell these truths to them because they could not "bear the burden of truth," then I wonder how much He can tell us! He knows that we are just the same as they were. Our simple minds could not accept some of the greatest truths of God. Why could He not tell these truths to them? Was it because they were STILL lacking in love?

We know that when Jesus met His disciples later at the Sea of Galilee He tested Peter: "Peter, LOVEST THOU ME?" Three times He asked Peter that question. Could Jesus not reveal the deeper truths to Peter because Peter did not love Him enough? This seems to be the case, because within hours of Jesus speaking these words to them, Peter denied the Lord. So we know his love was not perfect.

Thank God for the next words of Jesus, "Howbeit when he, the Spirit of Truth, is come, he will guide you into all truth: for he shall not speak of himself; but whatsoever he shall hear, that shall he speak: and he will show you things to come" (John 16:13). Isn't that a wonderful promise! He said that the Holy Spirit would show us the secrets of truth. In verses 14, 15 and 25, Jesus repeats this fact to the disciples. He even says that the Holy Spirit will show us *plainly* the things about the Father. We are now come to that day. Open your heart and let Him teach you!

There is a strange Scripture in Revelation 22:8, 9, "And I John saw these things, and heard them. And when I had heard and seen, I fell down to worship before the feet of the angel which showed me these things. Then saith he unto me, See thou do it not: for I am thy fellowservant, and of thy brethren the prophets, and of them which keep the sayings of this book: worship God."

Who was this glorified saint that John saw? Who was it that was honored to come and teach John the end-time truths which we call the Revelation of Jesus Christ? Either the whole book of Revelation is a lie, or it is possible to be visited by a saint who lived before, one who had been a fellowservant and a prophet. Do you suppose this might have been the one prophet who knew more about the end-time than any other prophets, the one whom God had commanded, "Seal the book, even to the time of the end?" There is a strange parallel between the book of Daniel and Revelation. Both prophets saw nations in the forms of beasts.

On the Mount of Transfiguration Peter, James and John saw Elijah and Moses visit the Lord as He was glorified, and they talked about His death which He was shortly going to accomplish in Jerusalem. If Elijah and Moses could visit on earth, could Daniel? I am not saying it was Daniel, but I am sharing with you some of the secrets of the book of Revelation; and they are still secrets because none of us know the answer to that question.

In Amos 3:7 we read, "Surely the Lord God will do nothing, but he revealeth his secret unto his servants the prophets." The Lord tells us He will reveal secrets. Isn't that wonderful how the Lord can share His secrets with His prophets! Before God sends the final judgment on this earth, the prophets and the heavenly messengers, the angels, will join with us to speak ONE MORE TIME!

The Lord said, "Shall I hide from Abraham the thing which I am about to do!" (Genesis 18:17). God was able to share His secret of the coming destruction of Sodom and Gomorrah because He knew that Abraham was His friend. He said that the nations of the earth would be blessed through Abraham. When we are a friend to God, then He will share His secrets with us because He wants to bless the nations through us. We have a message for the end time, a message of such magnitude and importance that there is not one soul on the face of this earth who will not be touched by it. Let us take this message to the uttermost parts of the earth. Tell it to whomever has ears to hear. Tell it as often as you can, to as many as you can and as much as you can, and leave the results with God. He said, "Is it not yet a very little while, and Lebanon shall be turned into a fruitful field, and the fruitful field shall be esteemed as a forest? And in that day shall the deaf hear the words of the book, and the eyes of the blind shall see out of obscurity, and out of darkness. The meek also shall increase their joy in the Lord, and the poor among men shall rejoice in the Holy One of Israel. For the terrible one is brought to nought, and the scorner is consumed, and all that watch for iniquity are cut off. . . . Therefore thus saith the Lord, who redeemed Abraham, concerning the house of Jacob, Jacob shall not now be ashamed, neither shall his face now wax pale. But when he seeth his children, the work of mine hands, in the midst of him, they shall sanctify my name, and sanctify the Holy One of Jacob, and shall fear the God of Israel. They also that erred in spirit SHALL COME TO UNDERSTANDING, and they that murmured [the complainers] shall learn doctrine" (Isaiah 29:17-24).

Chapter 32
LOVE HEALS

THE TOUCH OF THE MASTER'S HAND

'Twas battered and scarred, and the auctioneer
    Thought it scarcely worth his while
To waste much time on the old violin,
    But held it up with a smile.
"What am I bidden, good folks?" he cried;
    "Who will start bidding for me?
A dollar, a dollar . . . now two, only two . . .
    Two dollars, and who'll make it three?"

"Three dollars, once . . . three dollars, twice . . .
    Going for three" . . . but no—
From the room far back a gray-haired man
    Came forward and picked up the bow;
Then wiping the dust from the old violin,
    And tightening up all the strings,
He played a melody, pure and sweet,
    As sweet as an angel sings.

The music ceased, and the auctioneer,
    With a voice that was quiet and low,
Said, "What am I bid for the old violin?"
    And he held it up with the bow.
"A thousand dollars . . . and who'll make it two?
    "Two thousand . . . and who'll make it three?
"Three thousand once, and three thousand twice,
    "And going, and gone," said he.

> The people cheered, but some of them cried,
>   "We do not quite understand . . .
> "What changed its worth?" The man replied,
>   "The touch of the master's hand."
> And many a man with life out of tune,
>   And battered and torn with sin
> Is auctioned cheap to a thoughtless crowd,
>   Much like the old violin.
>
> A mess of pottage, a glass of wine,
>   A game—and he travels on;
> He's going once, and going twice,
>   He's going and almost gone.
> But the Master comes, and the foolish crowd
>   Never can quite understand
> The worth of a soul and the change that's wrought
>   By the touch of the Master's hand.
>
>   —*Myra Brooks Welch*

Many of us are like the battered and scarred violin which the auctioneer held in his hand. We have lost our music; the sorrows and tragedies of our life have taken our ability to sing out of our souls. To those around us, we are worthless. Our life has become so "cheap" not only to others who have stopped loving us, but even to our own selves, and so we have tried to take our lives. So many women have written to me about "overdoses of sleeping pills and other kinds of suicide attempts." When we try to take our life, it is a sign that life has become cheap to us. But God is trying to tell us something. Listen!

The master who owned that violin and watched it being put on the auction block was grieved when people did not know the worth of his precious instrument. He had made beautiful music with it for years, and he knew the pricelessness of his instrument. He took it into his hands and tuned the strings and played a melody pure and sweet, "AS SWEET AS AN ANGEL SINGS."

Immediately the price jumped from two dollars to two thousand and even three thousand. The touch of the master's hand had restored the value of that instrument. He loved that violin and he knew how to tune it. He knew how to make it sing like an angel. It was the touch of love. Love brought healing not only to the battered violin, but also to the people who listened as the master played it for the crowd.

Does your life feel wasted, useless and vain? Have you been cast on the rubbish heap? Do people think you scarcely worth listening to? Has the price on your life gone down until you feel "cheap?"

Beloved, the Master is standing beside you even now! He loves you because He made you. You are more priceless to Him right now than any treasure in the world. He wants to take you into His hands, with all your scars and out-of-tune strings and He wants to show the world the true value of your precious life. Won't you give Him your life? Won't you let Him do with you as He knows best?

The love that He will pour into the bow which He holds in the hand will vibrate the strings of your life and then the strings of your life will vibrate a song of healing to others. And a miracle will happen. Not only will you be healed, but others will be healed through the music that your life produces. Your life will produce a song of love that will bring comfort and healing to many other battered and scarred instruments. This is the time for the healing of the nations. It must begin in our hearts even now.

I can remember reading the story in a German newspaper of a young girl who was dying of a terminal disease. She lay all day long on her hospital bed, alone and forgotten. Then one day a young man came into her ward and found her lying there. He began to talk to her. A beautiful thing happened; he became her friend. Soon they fell in love. The doctors noticed a change in her physical condition. Her spirit was brightened and her eyes began to sparkle. The look of sadness and resignation to death began to leave and a look of hope and anticipation came instead. Every time that young man visited her, she received new strength. She began to fight for her life. Her life became a prayer, "Oh, God, let me live!"

The young man asked her to marry him. She did not know what to do. But as time went on and her body was awakened to love and desire this man who had brought life to her, she knew that a miracle was happening in her body and she promised to become his bride.

Love is a mighty force. Love began to reverse the disease in her body and she began to heal. Soon after that she left the hospital to become the bride of a man who had loved her when she was dying. Love healed her.

So it is in your life and mine. Sin had left its mark of death on us and we were left forsaken and alone. Some of us anticipated death with relief because life had become unbearable. And then HE came and found us. He taught us to love Him. He awakened our hearts to a new love that we had never known before, a love so tremendous and deep that it overwhelmed all of our weakness and destroyed the curse that was upon us. We found out that HE wanted to marry us and we said, "Yes, Lord! I will be Your bride!" And we left the house of pain and suffering to live a continual life of nuptial love with our Heavenly Bridegroom.

Sometimes it is so hard for us to accept the love that will heal us. But God wants us to know that He is not against us. He is FOR us. He is even FOR the worst sinner in this world. That is why He is so long-suffering and patient and is waiting for them to come to repentance. He is not willing for any to perish, but for all to have everlasting life with Him.

Some people do not want love. They have given themselves over to demonic powers. But still we must love them, because Jesus loves them. God loves them. The Holy Spirit has not left them. The angel still is protecting them, and our love can heal them.

I have a dear friend who was married for forty-odd years to a very mean man. He actually despised her. He never spoke a kind word to her. He stole her mail and hid it. Sometimes she did not find it for months. He mocked her and her God.

She told me it was like living with the devil. But when she prayed about it, she felt that God wanted her to wait and hang on. They left the large city where they had lived and moved out to the country where she had no friends and there was no means of transportation for her to go anywhere. So she became a virtual prisoner of circumstances.

And then one day he found out he had cancer. He was a dying man with only a few weeks left to live. It had happened so suddenly that he was totally unprepared for it. He was taken to the hospital where she faithfully visited him. There on his deathbed he gave his heart to Jesus, received forgiveness of sins, was completely and beautifully changed into a new person. He became so loving and kind to his wife that she said it was as if he were another person. You could not have recognized him. He was gentle and tender to her and her Jesus.

What had happened? The demons that had controlled his life since his early youth had seen that he was dying and they didn't want to stay in that body any longer. So they left and he was able to receive the truth and accept Jesus as his Saviour and be delivered from his sins and his evil nature. What a tragedy that she only had about two happy months with that man, and even then it was not as husband and wife but as patient and a friend. Think of the wasted years! Think of the unnecessary suffering! They could have had a beautiful life together. And yet God's mercy is great; love had hung on and in the end love had healed that man, and some day they will meet in heaven because of God's grace in the life of that wife.

When Isaac's mother Sarah died, he was very sad. One evening as he was walking in the fields and meditating, he looked into the distance and saw Eliezar, his father's old servant, returning with the camels and Rebekah, his bride. The Bible says, "And Isaac brought her into his mother Sarah's tent, and took Rebekah, and she became his wife; and he loved her: and Isaac was comforted after his mother's death" (Genesis 24:67).

Isaac's broken heart was healed when God gave him the love of this precious young woman who had been willing to leave her family and friends to come that long journey across the desert to become his wife. Love will heal all the sadness of your life and give you a new reason for living.

When David's son by Bathsheba was very sick, he was in great mourning. He fasted for seven days, calling upon the Lord to heal his son. But it was not God's will. God took the child to himself. Bathsheba was broken-hearted. The Bible says, "And David comforted Bathsheba his wife, and went in unto her, and lay with her: and she bare a son, and he called his name Solomon: and the Lord loved him" (2 Samuel 12: 24).

This is a sad story. It began when David fell in love with Bathsheba, who was another man's wife. It was such a violent, passionate love which overwhelmed David that he lost all sense of reasoning and did a cruel deed which was beneath his character. He tried to cover one sin with another sin. He ordered Uriah, Bathsheba's husband (who was one of his mighty soldiers), to be placed in the front lines of the battle where brave men die. When Uriah was killed in battle, David married his wife; but God had seen his sin. The child that had been conceived out of wedlock was born. It was the son of passion and lust. God could not let it live, for it would have been a lifelong evidence of David's sin. So God, in love and mercy, took the poor child to heaven. But the mother was grieved. Her heart was broken. Like any mother, she loved this child of hers. He was the fruit of love.

When her heart was broken, David went to her and took her into his arms and comforted her. The Bible says, "he went in unto her, and lay with her: . . ." After fasting seven days, David made love with his wife and she conceived. What kind of child was this that was conceived after a seven-day fast? This was none other than the great and beautiful Solomon. He was the product of holiness, the seed of purity and divine love. The mark of God's love was on his life because David had God's love in his heart when he went in unto

Bathsheba. What beautiful children would mankind conceive today if every sex act were committed in the same beautiful holiness and love that was inspired by a life of fasting and penitence! The world would be filled with Solomons. Solomon was a man of peace. He never went to battle and he never had to engage in warfare. He reigned in peace over the glory of Israel. There has never been a king like him in Israel, or the world.

The love that David had for God healed his broken heart and with that love he ministered to Bathsheba his wife and comforted her, healing her broken heart. The result was that she was able to conceive a child of peace and wisdom. Love heals. Love restores.

I was a broken-hearted woman with many scars when I met my husband, Jim Shaw. His beautiful love for me, which God gave him as he was on a 28-day water fast, was a pure and God-given, holy love. It had the power to heal all the wounds in my heart; and the scars that had left an indelible mark were healed and I began to live again. It was such a tremendous experience that there are no words for me to describe it to you. His love gave me courage and strength and new confidence in myself as a woman. After being told for years how ugly I was, I began to glow when Jim told me that I was beautiful. I could put my shoulders back and walk with pride. I was loved! I was loved! I was loved! It was a beautiful thing. Life was beautiful! I wanted to live! I wanted to give others this love! And that is why I have written this book. I want to share with you the truth that God heals. Because I know that it is TRUE.

This poem was written by one of the daughters of the King to her fiancee:

MY LOVE FOR YOU

My love for you is as warm as the summer sun
    Nestled in peaceful trees.
My love for you is as cool as a winter stream
    Gushing forth praise, for such a wonderful love.
My love for you is as high as majestic clouds
    Swirling in rosy, pink glow,
Caressed in tenderness by the setting sun.

My love for you is as deep as eternity's bosom,
    Echoing light, and love through every cell of my
        being.

Chapter 33
THE MORE EXCELLENT WAY

It would be impossible to close a book about love without stopping for a moment to review the greatest poem to love ever written by mortals, the 13th chapter of 1 Corinthians. Let us begin with verse 1:

"THOUGH I SPEAK WITH THE TONGUES OF MEN AND OF ANGELS, AND HAVE NOT LOVE, I AM BECOME AS SOUNDING BRASS, OR A TINKLING CYMBAL."

Love is more than noise or rhythm. Love is harmony. It is the blending together of two spirits in unity, in oneness. It is the celestial song of heaven. The verse says, "If I haven't got love, I haven't got a song; I have cling-clang." You can get all the pots and pans out of the kitchen and you can bang as hard as you want, and you won't have music. You might have rhythm, but you won't have music. You cannot produce harmony with sounding brass and tinkling cymbals, drums and tambourines. It takes a graduation of sound to make music. The Chinese make beautiful music out of only five notes in the scale. It takes the variation of different lives coming together in harmony to make that beautiful song of love. There is nothing so annoying as noise. Psychiatrists tell us that people are going mad because of noise. Sometimes when I am in a room where there is a lot of noise I have the feeling that I am in hell. It is agony. Heaven is a beautiful place because it will be filled with the harmony of love.

Paul said that messages in tongues when given out of self

instead of inspired by love, are nothing more than noise and confusion. We have been speaking in tongues since the outpouring of the Holy Spirit at the turn of the century. I myself have had this wonderful gift since one month after I accepted Christ as my Saviour. I have heard all kinds of tongues. On the mission field I have also heard demon-possessed Buddhist lamas screaming in tongues and demons have cursed me in tongues out of the mouths of the demon possessed. It is important that our spiritual experience with God is more than talking in tongues. If we have no love in our hearts, then it does not matter what language we speak in, it is no more than bang! bang! bang!

Though we speak in the most gifted tones of oratory and have the kind of charisma that makes our audience spellbound, if we do not have love our words are emptiness. And though we may entertain for the time being, our listeners will leave as empty-hearted as they came, having had their heads brainwashed but their hearts unsatisfied. It would be better to be the humble, uneducated preacher whose grammar is imperfect and have love than to sway the multitudes with empty words and an emptier heart. Everyone emanates what they actually are and not what they say. That is why Paul said words without love are empty. Whereas poorly worded and grammatically incorrect sermons preached in the heat of love will strike a chord in the soul of the hearer.

Verse 2: "AND THOUGH I HAVE THE GIFT OF PROPHECY, AND UNDERSTAND ALL MYSTERIES, AND ALL KNOWLEDGE; AND THOUGH I HAVE ALL FAITH, SO THAT I COULD REMOVE MOUNTAINS, AND HAVE NOT LOVE, I AM NOTHING."

Paul at that time was the foremost man in the early church in regard to having the latest and newest mighty revelations of God. If we have thought that it is the gift that makes the man, we have been fooled. "My, can that preacher preach!" "My, can that person play an instrument!" "My, can that person ever lead the people!" we have exclaimed in reverent awe. And we have regarded the individual as a great one, but often we have not judged rightly. We appreciated the wrong thing. The thing we should have appreciated, we have ignored. And in so doing we have slighted God's great ones. It is evident from this Scripture that great gifts are insufficient. Paul said no matter what miracles we can do or what understanding we have in mysteries, if we do not have love, we are NOTHING. In this end-time many people are asking God to give them great gifts of power. But it's a very dangerous thing to possess the great gifts of God, because if we don't use them in love, we will be destroyed by these gifts

You ask, "How can that be? If someone is healing the sick, isn't God getting the glory?" Not always. Many men and women of God whom God has used have become proud over the gifts which God gave them and they have continued to use the gifts even while their lives were not pure and holy They have even "sold" the gift of God for money. I have heard evangelists promise to give a word of prophecy if a certain amount of offering was placed in their hand. They are making merchandise of the Gospel.

Beloved, that is not a ministry of LOVE, and the Bible says it is NOTHING.

Verse 3, "AND THOUGH I BESTOW ALL MY GOODS TO FEED THE POOR AND THOUGH I GIVE MY BODY TO BE BURNED, AND HAVE NOT LOVE IT PROFITETH ME NOTHING."

You can be burned at the stake and go to hell. You can be a millionaire philanthropist, die a pauper after having given away all your wealth and be lost, if you did these great things without love being your true motive. We can work around the clock and break down physically from overwork for our church or mission or ministry, but if we have not love it is all in vain. Even if we slept only four hours a night and took no time out to eat and wore ragged clothes, if we did not do these things with a heart burning with love, it is all ashes. Many at the end of their lives will find nothing but ashes. If I cannot serve Him because I love Him, I do not want to serve Christ at all.

I once had a vision of a beautiful crown. It was ornamented with exquisite, costly diamonds. The diamonds graduated in size from large to small. The brilliancy was so great that it was almost impossible to look upon this beautiful thing. I asked the Lord what it was. He told me that it was the crown which He had prepared for someone, but because their love was not great enough, they had lost it and it would be given to someone else. The Lord already has the rewards prepared and He wants to give them to us, but we have to pass through the fire and all of our works will pass through the fire with us. At that time God himself will try us and we will not be able to hide anything from Him. May God help us now to see as He sees so that we may be worthy of what He has prepared for us in eternity!

Verse 4: "LOVE SUFFERETH LONG: . . ."

Much of the suffering involved with love is because it is too often unrequited. The wonderful thing is that the love we have for God is always returned to us from God. As we pour out our love, He pours His right back into our hearts; God is no man's debtor. He won't leave you with a knife in your heart or bring you to suicide. He does not give you a mental breakdown because you loved Him greatly. He will just wrap you up in His big, warm arms and hold you close to His heart and you will be comforted and warmed and sheltered all the days of your life. This is what the world needs. This is the kind of love we need in the world. Instead, we have so often the kind of love that is full of agony because children forget their parents, parents neglect their children, husbands cheat on their wives and wives betray their husbands and talk against them.

Paul is saying that love is long-suffering. Love isn't all joy and happiness. There is pain and sometimes even torture in love. Even so, a great love will endure many terrible things. Even as you are reading this, know that it is the tremendous love in the hearts of our brothers and sisters in communist lands that gives them the strength to endure the torture, the slavery, the darkness, the separation from loved ones. Many of them could come out of prison if they would deny Jesus Christ and betray their brethren, but the love in their hearts gives them the grace and strength to suffer long and hard for truth.

"LOVE IS KIND: . . ."

We have already written a chapter about this (chapter 9). Let me add that love cannot do anything that would hurt or grieve the beloved. Love is a "gentleman." Love doesn't push its way through a crowd. Love lets others go first, unless it's necessary for it to go ahead to make a way of protection and guidance. Love gives someone the biggest piece of the apple. Love understands and feels the pain and longings of the loved one. Love doesn't NEED to be spoken; nothing has to be said. Love will control your passions so that you will not sin or hurt anyone. A man who says that he loves a woman and then plays with her heart and hurts it and crushes it, either is a liar or has a demon. A cruel demon spirit that makes him do what he really doesn't want to do can take over his whole personality. And there ARE some people like that who do love a person and yet at times they are viciously cruel to the very one they love; and the reason for that is because the evil spirit has power over them and controls them and forces them to do things which they really do not want to do. But this should not be the case. Love should be stronger than the demon and Love should have the power to cast out the demon. If you have that kind of a demon troubling you and destroying your relationship with your family, then I encourage you to ask for counsel and help from a man of God who can help you by casting out that spirit, and then you should work at nourishing the love in your heart. Love will speak things that will make the loved one rejoice. Love is KIND. It never has a harsh word. If it must rebuke, it will do it in a spirit of meekness and love.

Some years ago I had a beautiful rebuke. I really needed it. It has affected my ministry. It changed it because it came from the Lord through a woman who cared enough to speak to me in His name. I have had all kinds of rebukes; I have had all kinds of letters and advice. I have had anonymous letters that would tear me to thousands of pieces, and they didn't do me a bit of good; they probably did more harm than good because they made me want to find out who the writer was so I could give that one "a piece of my mind!" But this rebuke was beautiful and it was a blessing to me because it came to me in true love.

"LOVE ENVIETH NOT: ...."

Love seeks the good and the happiness of the beloved. Love rejoiceth when the other is blessed. Don't say you love somebody, and then be green with envy if they drive to church with a new car next Sunday. Love does not envy when someone gets ahead of you. If you love someone, you are full of joy to see that God has blessed them. Check yourself. Are you jealous of your sister because she has a nicer home? Are you envious about her nice furniture? Do you envy her talents and ability to pray or preach or sing? If you do, you do not love her as you should. Love doesn't have to keep up with the neighbors. Love travels along at its own pace and is glad for what anyone else possesses.

"LOVE VAUNTETH NOT ITSELF: ...."

Love doesn't push itself in front. It is humble. It prefers others before itself. Love is not egotistic or boastful. In the Orient we are so used to the observance of the customs of the people. At a Chinese feast one must be very careful not to take the "head seat." Even if one is offered, one should seek to refuse this seat of honor. We have become so coarse and careless and "pushy" in our times that sometimes we act as if we were the only person that counted.

A great love is a very humbling experience. It makes you feel unworthy and gives you the desire to serve and be gracious to the one who loves you. You cannot be in love and keep your pride.

"LOVE IS NOT PUFFED UP: ...."

True love knows no shame. It will make a fool out of you. You would go around the world in search of the one you love. It will make you humble down to the dust, and do things that your pride would never have done. Love breaks the pride in your heart. Don't say you love someone if you are too proud to marry that one. Love made Jesus leave heaven and come to earth. Love will enable you to live at the level of society that is lower than you were accustomed to, if that is the price you have to pay. Jesus left the riches of heaven to live among the poor. He didn't even have a grave of His own. It was borrowed. It was His great love that gave Him the strength to die the cursed and shameful death of hanging naked on the cross.

Verse 5, "LOVE DOTH NOT BEHAVE ITSELF UNSEEMLY: . . ."

Where there is love, there is no unkindness or cruelty. Love is not coarse and vulgar. Love does not have cruel words in its mouth. Love has a tenderness, a gentleness and a beautiful flow of the Christlike spirit. Love doesn't nag and grumble all the time. Love doesn't boss around. When we have the spirit of love in us we should be easy to get along with.

Have you ever met someone who is very difficult to get along with? There is something wrong with that person. They may say they have the Christian experience, they may even profess to be filled with the Holy Spirit; but the true manifestation of a true and real experience with God is his love. It is possible to have the spirit of Christ within. When one has this constant Christlike spirit within, one has a beautiful nature that will unite the heart with others who have the same love for God.

Beloved, it is possible that we have met some who do not profess to be born again who have a more beautiful spirit than some Christians have. They never speak against anyone, they show kindness and give mercy. While we have also met so-called Spirit-filled Christians who are loud and boastful and obnoxious. One wonders what they were saved from, if they have not been saved from their old, miserable disposition. May God give us a complete salvation so that we will have the fruit of love that will keep us from behaving unseemly, or in a way that is not right or proper.

"LOVE SEEKETH NOT HER OWN: . . ."

The one who loves does not live for himself. He lives for the one whom he loves. In other words, love makes you a slave. As soon as you live for somebody else, that means you are going to work by the sweat of your brow to bring home money to feed and clothe and care for the ones who are under your care. Love seeks the other one's good. It doesn't grab the best seat for itself. It doesn't choose the most comfortable bed or keep for itself the last piece of chocolate cake. Love takes the selfishness out of you.

When husband and wife live together and one wants his or her way all the time, it brings sorrow. Some couples get along real well because one of them always defers to the other. This is not love, this is ruling by fear and strength. Where there is love, there must be give and take. When two people love each other, they will not seek their own way but rather the way of each other. That makes balance, and where there is balance there is equality, and where there is equality there is peace. And if there is no peace, it is because one of them is pulling everything over onto their side and forcing their own way through, and as soon as that is done there is chaos.

True love brings a spirit of giving, a spirit of sharing, a spirit of consideration of others. It removes all the selfishness and greed and thinking of self. When one has that kind of love, one shares the cross with Jesus Christ and does not let Him carry His cross alone.

"LOVE IS NOT EASILY PROVOKED: . . ."

We are so easily provoked. Little things can upset us much too easily. We get a cup of tea which is not hot enough and we are provoked, someone drives too slowly to suit us and we are provoked, someone doesn't notice us in church and we are provoked. When you have the love of God in your heart, little things won't make you grouchy. When your wife forgets to sew that button on your shirt, you won't have a fit. Love makes margin for another's mistakes because love remembers that one has his own mistakes. If only we could stop being provoked and irritated, how beautiful we would be! Some people live in a constant state of irritation and even enjoy being grumpy. They think they are having a good time when they make a little bit of hell for everyone else. They like others to take notice that they are out of sorts, so others better watch out for them! Some think they have the right to act that way. They say to themselves, "I have been behaving myself pretty good for about three weeks, it's about time I stick out my prickles!" And so they defend themselves in their iniquity and think they are doing something they have every right to do, not realizing that they are destroying themselves because they are lacking in love.

When you first fell in love you never saw your loved one's failures. The funny little things he did you thought were cute. But after a while, when he started to tell you how to push the toothpaste out of the tube, you began to wonder. Every time he found that you had pushed it differently than he had for thirty years and you were due for a lecture at every toothbrushing session, you began to get tired of it. At first you thought he would forget, but you soon found out you were wrong. "What is the matter with you, don't you know how to squeeze out the toothpaste?" he shouts at you. And you answer stupidly, "I didn't know there was a special way to squeeze it. You mean there is a special way?" He anwers back, "I thought you knew that by now. Aren't you old enough to realize that you're wasting the toothpaste when you do it that dumb way!" And before you know it, the squeeze is on you instead of on the tube.

Beloved, we have to learn to stop being children. Let us grow up! Commanders have no time to fiddle with little incidentals like toothpaste. It is children who fight over toys. Adults work together in a cooperation of wisdom and love. Love will enable us to look at a situation cooly and calmly. Love won't throw us off balance. Love will give us a sense of patience so that we won't be irritated if things are not always done exactly like we like to have them done. Love makes room for other people's mistakes, slowness, laziness, indifference, inefficiencies and whatever imperfections the other one has. We are guilty of all these, and more, yet God loves us and makes room for us in spite of our imperfections. Should we not do the same?

Love will give you the patience to wait for the other one who is slow and who is always late. Love gives you the ability to go the second mile. Love helps you to live the law of the Kingdom. Jesus said, "If someone says you should go one mile, you should answer, 'If you like my company that much, I will come another mile with you.' " Love will give you the grace when you are slapped in the face to say, "Here is my other cheek."

"LOVE THINKETH NO EVIL: . . ."

It is very natural for us to think negatively and to doubt people. We are full of negativeness. As soon as your husband is late at night, you begin to doubt and wonder. As soon as your wife seems to be acting a little strange, you begin to think negatively. Love will remove all negativeness. There are a lot of people who want to be loved. They complain, "Nobody loves me." But they never give any love either. To receive love, you must give love. It will just pour back on you. Love looks for the good thing in people and situations. Love knows that ALL things work together for good. Love can afford to be deceived because love knows that God will work it out for good.

"Great peace have they which love thy law: and nothing shall offend them" (Psalm 119:165). Love is not easily offended. Love is not ready to "pay back" for the grievances it has suffered. When you love someone, you do not rejoice to see that one hurt or fall or make a mistake. So many times we have admired a certain person whom God has used in a special way, and we were almost jealous of their place in the Kingdom; but when we heard they had fallen, there was almost a feeling of smugness. "Look how he made a mistake!" We have run to one another and published it abroad, "Have you heard the latest?" Love will overlook and cover another man's mistakes and love will not point them out to others, or even think about them too much. Love is grieved when the loved one makes any mistake or grieves the Lord. Love suffers for the loved one who is suffering. Love will even suffer for the stranger who is suffering. Love prays with concern for the people one reads about in the newspapers who have suffered tragedy.

Never allow anything but love and compassion to fill your heart. No matter how you are treated or dragged in the mud, you must be careful to feel only mercy and compassion for your enemy. And when tragedy comes to them, don't allow yourself to rejoice over it and think, "It serves him right! He had it coming to him!" God has called us to be a people of love who rejoice in the truth.

Why is it that God's children are always so negative? As soon as we meet one of His children, we turn on our "spirit of discerning." And we think, "They couldn't be perfect. There must be something wrong with them. I wonder what it could be!" And then we find someone just like ourselves, the two of us get together and say, "What did you think about that person? How did you feel about that person? Wasn't there something strange about that one?" And the next one says, "Yes, come to think of it, I did notice she was a little bit strange. It seems I remember I heard something about that person. . . ." Do you think that is love?

I admit there are wrongs in some of God's people and no one is perfect. If we were perfect, we would not be here. We would have been translated like Enoch was. Next time you start to criticize someone, please turn around and look to see if your wings are starting to grow. Until you find that you have wings, don't criticize one of God's children. Don't lay your tongue on them!

Verse 6, "LOVE REJOICETH NOT IN INIQUITY . . ."

Iniquity comes from a root word which means "lack of inner quietness or peace and righteousness with God." Here the Holy Spirit is saying that love does not rejoice when someone loses that deep, sweet quietness in God. When we think of the word "iniquity" we immediately think of about five or six different sins which are on the top of the list of our "chief sins." We okay anyone who does not commit any of those sins. But there are a lot of "little iniquities" which we overlook which rob us of our inner quietness and peace, creating little tempests in our souls.

There are some Christians whose spirit within them is like a little Sea of Galilee with a storm welled up inside of them, and they are always ready to turn somebody else's ship upside down and throw Jesus into the sea. When there is a lack of inner quietness within you, there is something wrong with your spiritual life. When you have love, you will have that inner peace. If you don't have love, you will have a storm wherever you go, because you will make problems wherever you go. Love rejoiceth not in iniquity. Love rejoiceth not in stirring up a storm. Love rejoiceth not in being a troublemaker.

Jesus said, "Blessed are the peacemakers" (Matthew 5:9). He said "they shall be called the children of God." If you are a true child of God you will not be a northwind, blowing up a storm. You are a pacifist. That word has almost lost its meaning today because some of our country's biggest troublemakers are calling themselves pacifists. But I refer to it in its original meaning, "one who opposes violence as a means of settling disputes." As a peace-maker, you will step into a situation where two people are at enmity and you try to make them love each other and understand each other. This takes wisdom and grace, but if love can do it and if Jesus says there is a blessing for us when we do it, then that means that, as members of His Kingdom, we will live under His rules and we will work at turning our enemies into friends. And this is the greatest victory. The best way to get rid of your enemy is to turn him into a friend.

"LOVE REJOICETH IN THE TRUTH: . . ."

Love can rejoice at Truth, because love understands Truth and sees Truth; Truth is revealed to Love.

A little story is told about Socrates. One day someone came to him and said, "I have something to tell you about your friend." Socrates answered, "Before you tell me about my friend, have you put it through the "three sieves?" The man asked, "What do you mean?" Socrates answered, "First of all, are you sure that what you are going to tell me is the truth?" The man said, "No, I am not sure if it's true." Socrates asked, "All right, the second one: Do you think this would be good news that you are going to tell me?" He answered, "No. In fact, it is the opposite." Socrates said, "Let us try the third. Do you think it will make me happy?" The man answered, "No, I am afraid it wouldn't make you happy at all." "Well then, don't tell me," answered Socrates.

There is something beautiful about Honesty and Truth. Jesus said, "I am the Truth!" God is love, and when you have God (love) in you, you will rejoice in truth, which is Jesus. The Father has always rejoiced in the Son. The Father in you will rejoice in Jesus in you.

As Jesus stood before Pilate, Pilate asked Him the question, "What is Truth?" He never waited to hear the answer. But Jesus had earlier said, "I am the Way, the Truth and the Life" (John 14:6). Pilate didn't realize he was looking straight at Truth, because he had no love. If he would have had love, he would have rejoiced at Truth. If God would have been in his heart, Pilate would have recognized Jesus, the Truth.

But there was something wonderful about Pilate's wife. She was an idolater and yet God could speak to her. She sent a message to her husband, "Have nothing to do with that just man. I have suffered many things in a dream last night because of Him." Not only did she suffer for Jesus, she suffered for her husband Pilate because she loved her husband and she knew that he would be tempted to do something that day that would cause him to lose his own soul. Maybe she couldn't put it into these same words, she didn't have this kind of scriptural language, but she knew something terrible would happen to her husband. History tells us that later Pilate lost his high position and was called to Rome to answer charges which had been brought against him for mis-government. Eusebius left this record about Pilate, "Wearied with misfortunes, he killed himself." One traditional story says that he sought to hide his sorrows by the Lake of Lucerne on the mountain now called Mount Pilatus in Switzerland. After spending years in the recesses of the mountain in remorse and despair rather than penitence, he plunged into the dismal lake at its foot. Pilate's wife became a believer and one of the saints in the early church. The Roman Catholics observe her day every year. This little woman had love, and that is why she could recognize Truth and suffer for it. When you have love, you will stand on the side of Truth, even if you have to stand alone. Love will give you the strength and love will take you through. It is better to stand alone on the side of Truth than stand with the whole world on the side of wrong.

Verse 7, " LOVE BEARETH ALL THINGS: . . ."

No load is too heavy to carry when Love inspires you. The love a nurse feels for her patient makes her burden light. The love a mother feels for her baby makes that baby light. When God puts a baby in its mother's arms, He doesn't weigh 22 pounds, because God knows that mother doesn't have enough love to carry such a heavy baby. But as the infant grows, the mother's love grows and she is made capable through love to carry the heavier load with each passing day. As the baby develops its own personality, he not only has cute, innocent ways but also some that are very provoking and irritating. He refuses his bottle, screams all night, throws his dinner on the floor, breaks your best vase, teases the new baby and about that time you would be ready to throw him out, if your love had not grown for your child so that you are now able to cope with his contrary ways and take the love and patience to train him.

It was love that qualified Simon to bear that cross of Jesus on the way to Calvary. Many other strong men were there and they could have done it, but they did not have the qualification of love that was needed. We all have a cross to carry, and you can't do it without love. It is your love for God that will enable you to deny yourself, take up your cross and follow Him. You cannot carry two crosses. You cannot carry the cross of God's will and your will also. That is why Jesus said that you have to deny yourself. You have to NOT LOVE yourself. Put yourself on the cross and ask God to crucify you there. And when you have died there, you will have the strength to carry His cross the entire Via Dolorosa.

"LOVE BELIEVETH ALL THINGS: . . ."

The reason that the religious people of Jesus' day could not believe in Him was because they did not love Him. It takes pure love to have the kind of faith that can believe God for the great things which He has promised to those who are His children.

It is through love that you can accept the promises of God in His Word and make them your own. This is the kind of love that takes the limits off God and permits Him to do the spectacular in our lives and the lives of those for whom we are burdened. The prayer of faith that is prayed in love will always receive its answer.

When one knows in the Spirit the promise of God which He has prepared for you, it is only because love has made the contact and touched the hem of the garment of the One who came to show this world true love.

Jesus could have faith for everything because His love was perfect. Nothing was too hard for Him. I think another way of quoting that tremendous statement of Paul's so that we can understand it more fully is, "Love believes in spite of all things." There can be no impossibilities which are big enough to hinder love. Love will find a way. It will reach its destiny and stand on its mountain peak.

Love believes that no matter how dark the future is, beyond tomorrow there lies another tomorrow, brighter and fairer than the morning sun. Love knows and is persuaded that neither death, nor life, nor angels, nor principalities, nor powers, nor things present, nor things to come, nor height, nor depth, nor any other creature, shall be able to separate us from the LOVE OF GOD, which is in Christ Jesus our Lord (Romans 8:38, 39).

"LOVE HOPETH ALL THINGS: . . ."

Love is positive. When people are not sure that SOMEBODY loves them, just ANYBODY, they feel that they have nothing to hope for and nothing to live for. When a person loses hope, he begins to live in a negative state that leads down into a dark, gloomy valley of negativeness and suicide. We need to introduce such a one to God. God will give him the strength and the love to survive all situations of despair. God is love and therefore hope will again flood that heart. As soon as he has that seed of hope in his heart, it will grow and push out the darkness and despair.

When you have hope you don't need to desperately hang on and "hope for the best." Love is a victorious thing, a flying-over experience. It is the loosening of self. It is positive. When you let God's love flood your heart, it will always give you a positive attitude that the best will happen because you know God loves you. You will live in a state of expectation of good things to come.

Love is one of the great fruits of the Spirit. Love hopeth all things." Hope cannot operate without love. Why does hope need a helping hand? Why does hope need inspiration and strength? Because hope is a vision. You cannot have a vision until you have love. That is why love gives you hope. How can a woman hope for a certain thing if she doesn't love or want it? It is only when you love a certain thing that you begin to hope for it. If you don't have a house and are content to live on the street, you will never hope for a house. If you don't want to go to Israel, then you'll never hope to go. If you hate children and can't stand them and have no love for them, you'll never hope for a child. If you don't want to see the Lord Jesus and be in His presence forever, then you'll never hope for it. You have to desire a thing, have a picture of it in your heart before it can be fulfilled. What is this hope really? It is the visionary picture of faith. When you begin to carry in your heart that vision of hope, then you begin to exercise faith that makes it come to pass. Without faith, there is no hope. Hope is the seed of faith. When you are sick, then don't keep in your mind that picture of being sick forever.

Don't keep that picture of hospital bills and treatments and tests. Rather keep a picture of yourself being well and strong. When you carry that picture in your heart and hope for it every day, that hope will produce healing and strength in your body. The power of the mind is very great and it can work toward bringing healing if we will hope in God through our love for Him.

There is such power in hoping because our mind is involved when we hope, and when our mind is working in a positive way (because hope is positive; there is nothing negative about hope), miracles will begin to happen. Sometimes faith can be negative. You can believe for the worst, but you can never hope for the worst. You will only hope for the best, so hope comes first.

You must make a picture in your mind of a beautiful, God-promised, love-inspired thing and keep that picture in your mind. I want to say now that your mind is a very powerful tool. What you think makes you, not what you say. Jesus said, "Out of the heart proceedeth all that is in a man's soul." He meant, "out of the mind." Because in your heart there is really nothing; it is only another part of your body like the lungs or liver. But the innermost part of you, the "heart" of you is your mind. And your mind is the key to all your life. That is why it's important that our minds are stayed on Christ Jesus. That is why we must cast down every imagination that is not right. The Word of God says, "Whatsoever things are true, whatsoever things are honest, whatsoever things are just, whatsoever things are pure, whatsoever things are lovely, whatsoever things are of good report: if there be any virtue, and if there be any praise, think on these things" (Philippians 4:8). God is giving us the key to perfection for our whole life. When your mind is full of beautiful things, you have a vision and whatever that vision is, it will be fulfilled as you hold it constantly before you.

"LOVE ENDURETH ALL THINGS: . . ."

Love endures all things—all the doubts, all the fears, all the faults, all the heartaches, all the pain—not only for five minutes but for as long as God gives grace. We need love to go through what is coming. It was the love that Jesus had that took Him to the cross. It was the love of the saints that took them through the persecution under the "Neroes" of yesterday and the "Stalins" of our time.

For love, Jacob endured seven years of hard labor twice. His love for Rachel made it seem like only a few days. He worked around the clock and around the calendar, in the hot sun and in the winter cold. He didn't come home every evening at 5 o'clock. Sometimes he was out in the field for months at a time. There would be many weeks when he would not be able to see his beloved Rachel because he had to take his sheep far out into the distance where he could find green pasture. There was loneliness and danger. Many times there were wild beasts and evil men. His wages were not paid him, not only once, but ten times, yet he endured it all because of the love he had for Rachel.

After all this hard work was finished, he had a terrible disappointment. When he lifted the veil from the face of his bride, he found that the woman who had lain in his arms was another one and not the one for whom he had worked those first seven years. So he had to work another seven years for Rachel. Most men would have said, "One woman is as good as another. I am not going to be Laban's slave another seven years. I'll take this one and forget about the whole thing." But Jacob's love was too great to forget his precious little Rachel. And so he labored another seven years to be able to get her for his wife.

We, too, are going to be called to go through testing in the next while. They will be hard years, many will have to leave their comfort and their homes, and others will have to share the homes they have in safer areas; all of us will have our love tested. There will be little to eat and we will have to share everything. But by the grace of God and His love in our hearts, we will be able to endure ALL things with the peace of God in our hearts.

Verse 8, "LOVE NEVER FAILETH: . . . ."

Love never gives up. It is easy for us to give up, but love doesn't stop loving. Love is faithful. It does not change with the wind. Love does not hand out plaudits one day and persecution the next day, nor commendation one day and condemnation the next day. Love reproduces itself and multiplies so it cannot dry up like a fountain or a well can. Love has its source in God and not in the earth.

Religion is not enough. Emotion is not enough. Excitement is not enough. The religious people of Jerusalem were very emotional and excited as Jesus came riding into Jerusalem on the donkey, but within a week this same crowd cried, "Crucify Him! Crucify Him!" Love will crucify no one but self.

Love does not fail even though you have to spend fifteen years in a Siberian slave camp. Many of our brothers and sisters behind the Iron Curtain have told how, even though they were separated for many years from their families, their wives or husbands, and evil men lied to them that their wives had forgotten them and had married someone else, still they knew it was not true, for love knew truth and love could wait until the day of release.

Love sees the beauty that there is in love, and love never fails even though the body grows old and the hair turns to silver. Neither does it fail when the loved one returns with scars on the body and marks of suffering have scarred the beauty of the face.

A true story is told of a young girl in one of the Iron Curtain countries who loved the little children in her village and so she taught them about Jesus. It was against the law for her to do this, but she wanted these children to know the love of God. Someone reported her to the communist authorities and they decided to arrest her. They waited until her wedding day. As she was celebrating her wedding with her bridegroom and friends, the police arrived and put handcuffs on her. Her husband cried, "Please wait until our wedding is over!" The family begged the police to please wait until the ceremony and the humble meal had been partaken together.

But they were only mocked and rebuked. The bride was dragged out of the building in her white dress and handcuffs. She kissed her handcuffs and said to her bridegroom who was weeping bitterly, "Don't cry about me. If we cannot have a wedding feast here, we will have one up there."

She was sentenced to five years in prison. She suffered much, lost her health, her teeth, her beauty. After serving her prison term she was released and came home. She did not know if her bridegroom still would love her when he would see how terrible she looked. She knew that she had aged decades.

When she arrived home, many did not recognize her. When her bridegroom saw her, he could hardly believe this was the same fair, young maiden who had stood so happily at his side five years before. She saw the shock in his eyes. She told him, "I release you from your vows to me. I cannot hold you to me. Look at me, how ugly I have become!"

He took her in his arms and said, "My precious one, you are more beautiful than ever to me, for you bear on you the marks of the Lord Jesus Christ."

Love did not fail!

AND NOW ABIDETH FAITH, HOPE, LOVE, THESE THREE; BUT THE GREATEST OF THESE IS LOVE.

More Life-Changing Books

GWEN SHAW'S AUTOBIOGRAPHY

UNCONDITIONAL SURRENDER. The life story of Gwen R. Shaw, lovingly known as "Sister Gwen" to thousands of people in over one hundred nations. You will laugh and cry with her as you feel the heartbeat of a great woman of God who has given all to Him, asking only for souls in return. Your life will be challenged as you walk with her through mission field after mission field. You will never be the same when you read how God pours out His Spirit and confirms His Word. Paperback ....#000101 $15.00
Video NTSC (North American format) ....#GSL-99 $20.00
Video PAL (European format) ....#GSLP-99 $20.00

DAILY DEVOTIONALS BY GWEN SHAW

DAILY PREPARATIONS FOR PERFECTION — This daily devotional comes to you exactly as the Holy Spirit spoke to the author's heart in her own private devotions. You will feel that Jesus is speaking to you every time you open it. It is loved by all. You'll read it and re-read it ....Paperback #000202 $12.50

DAY BY DAY— This daily devotional book based on the Psalms will give you an inspiring word directly from the Throne Room each day to fill your heart with praise to God. Starting each day with praise is the secret of a joy-filled life ....Softcover #000204 $9.95
....Hardcover #000203 $18.50
Also available in French ....Hardcover #000203FR $18.50

FROM THE HEART OF JESUS — This devotional book will take you back to Bible days and you will walk and talk with Jesus and His disciples as he ministered to the people, as He suffered and died and as He rose again from the dead. These words from the heart of Jesus will go straight to your heart, bringing comfort, peace, encouragement and hope! 923 pages ....Hardcover #000207 $29.95

GEMS OF WISDOM — *A daily devotional based on the book of Proverbs.* In the Proverbs you will find instruction for upright living, honesty, justice and wisdom. Every word in the Proverbs applies to today's problems as when they were first written. If you are going through great difficulties and facing problems which seem to have no solution, you will find the answer in these Proverbs. You'll have a Proverb and an inspired writing about it for each day of the year! A great gift idea for graduates and newlyweds! ....Hardcover #000209 $25.95

IN THE BEGINNING — *A daily devotional based on the book of Genesis.* The Book of Genesis is perhaps the most important book in the Old Testament. It is the foundation stone of all knowledge and wisdom. Deep and wonderful truths hidden in the pages of Genesis are revealed in this devotional book. You'll be amazed at the soul-stirring writings inspired by the well-known stories of Genesis. Hardcover .... #000211 $27.95

DEEPEN YOUR WALK WITH GOD WITH CLASSIC ANOINTED BIBLE STUDIES BY GWEN SHAW!

BEHOLD THE BRIDEGROOM COMETH! A Bible study on the soon return of Jesus Christ. With so many false teachings these days, it is important that we realize how imminent the rapture of the saints of God really is .... #000304 $6.50

 ENDUED WITH LIGHT TO REIGN FOREVER. This deeply profound Bible study reveals the characteristics of the eternal, supernatural, creative light of God as found in His Word. The "Father of Lights," created man in His image. He longs for man to step out of darkness and into His light .... #000306 $5.00

GOD'S END-TIME BATTLE-PLAN. This study on spiritual warfare gives you the biblical weapons for spiritual warfare such as victory through dancing, shouting, praising, uplifted hands, marching, etc. It has been a great help to many who have been bound by tradition. .... #000305 $8.00

 IT'S TIME FOR REVIVAL. A Bible study on revival that not only gives scriptural promises of the end-time revival, but also presents the stories of revivals in the past and the revivalists whom God used. It will stir your heart and encourage you to believe for great revival! .... #000311 $7.75

OUR MINISTERING ANGELS. A scriptural Bible study on the topic of angels. Angels will be playing a more and more prominent part in these last days. We need to understand about them and their ministry. Read exciting accounts of angelic help .... #000308 $7.50

POUR OUT YOUR HEART. A wonderful Bible study on travailing prayer. The hour has come to intercede before the throne of God. The call to intercession is for everyone, and we must carry the Lord's burden and weep for the lost so that the harvest can be brought in quickly..#000301 $5.00

 REDEEMING THE LAND. A Bible study on spiritual warfare. This important teaching will help you know your authority through the Blood of Jesus to dislodge evil spirits, break the curse, and restore God's blessing upon the land. ....#000309 $9.50

THE FINE LINE. This Bible study clearly magnifies the "fine line" of difference between the soul realm and the spirit realm. Both are intangible and therefore cannot be discerned with the five senses, but must be discerned by the Holy Spirit and the Word of God. A must for the deeper Christian...#000307 $6.00

 THE POWER OF THE PRECIOUS BLOOD. A Bible study on the Blood of Jesus. The author shares how it was revealed to her how much Satan fears Jesus' Blood. This Bible study will help you overcome and destroy the works of Satan in your life and the lives of loved ones! ....#000303 $5.00

THE POWER OF PRAISE. When God created the heavens and the earth, He was surrounded by praise. Miracles happen when holy people praise a Holy God! Praise is the language of creation. If prayer can move the hand of God, how much more praise can move Him! ....#000312 $5.00

 YE SHALL RECEIVE POWER FROM ON HIGH. This is a much needed foundational teaching on the Baptism of the Holy Spirit. It will enable you to teach this subject, as well as to understand these truths more fully yourself ....#000310 $5.00

YOUR APPOINTMENT WITH GOD. A Bible study on fasting. Fasting is one of the most neglected sources of power over bondages of Satan that God has given the Church. The author's experiences shared in this Bible study will change your life ....#000302 $5.00

In-Depth Bible Studies for the Serious Student of God's Word

FORGIVE AND RECEIVE. This Bible Study is a lesson to the church on the much-needed truths of forgiveness and restoration. The epistle to Philemon came from the heart of Paul who had experienced great forgiveness ....#000406 $7.00

GRACE ALONE. This study teaches the reader to gain freedom in the finished work of the Cross by forsaking works (which cannot add to salvation) and live by *Grace Alone*..............#000402 $13.00

MYSTERY REVEALED. Search the depths of God's riches in one of Paul's most profound epistles, "to the praise of His glory!" Learn the "mystery" of the united Body of Christ..#000403 $15.00

OUR GLORIOUS HEAD. This book teaches vital truths for today, assisting the reader in discerning false teachings, when the philosophies of men are being promoted as being the truths of God. Jesus Christ is the Head of His Body!......................#000404 $9.00

THE CATCHING AWAY! This is a very timely Bible study because Jesus is coming soon! The book of 1 Thessalonians explains God's revelation to Paul on the rapture of the saints. 2 Thessalonians reveals what will happen after the rapture when the antichrist takes over..#000407 $13.00

THE LOVE LETTER. This expository study of the letter to the first church of Europe will give the reader an understanding of Paul's great love for the church that was born out of his suffering. ....#000405 $9.00

Popular Bible Course

THE TRIBES OF ISRAEL. This popular and well-loved study on the thirteen tribes of Israel will show you your place in the spiritual tribes in these last days. Understand yourself and others better through the study of this Bible Course!
....................#000501 $45.00 • Set of 13 tapes #TGS1 $42.00

The Women of the Bible Series by Gwen Shaw,

opens a window into the lives of the women of the Bible in the style of historical novels. Their joys and heartaches were the same as ours today.

 EVE—MOTHER OF US ALL. Read the life story of the first woman. Discover the secrets of one of the most neglected and misunderstood stories in history .... #000801 $4.50

SARAH—PRINCESS OF ALL MANKIND. She was beautiful — and barren. Feel the heartbeat and struggles of this woman who left so great an impact on us all .... #000802 $4.50

 REBEKAH—THE BRIDE. The destiny of the world was determined when she said three simple words, "I will go!" Enjoy this touching story. .... #000803 $4.50

LEAH AND RACHEL—THE TWIN WIVES OF JACOB. You will feel their dreams, their pains, their jealousies and their love for one man. .... #000804 $4.50

 MIRIAM—THE PROPHETESS. Miriam was the first female to lead worship, the first woman to whom the Lord gave the title "Leader of God's people." .... #000805 $7.50

Other Books by Gwen Shaw

GOING HOME. This book is a treasure which answers so many questions and comforts so many hearts. It gives strength and faith, and helps one to cope with the pain of the loss of a loved one. This book is not really a book about dying, but about Going Home to our Eternal Abode with our loving Heavenly Father .... #000607 $8.00

 LOVE, THE LAW OF THE ANGELS. This is undoubtedly the greatest of Gwen Shaw's writings. It carries a message of healing and life in a sad and fallen civilization. Love heals the broken-hearted and sets disarray in order. You will never be the same after reading this beautiful book about love. .... #000601 $10.00

SONG OF LOVE. She was a heart-broken missionary, far from home. She cried out to God for help. He spoke, "Turn to the Song of Solomon and read!" As she turned in obedience, the Lord took her into the "Throne Room" of Heaven and taught her about the love of Christ for His Bride, the church. She fell in love with Jesus afresh, and you will too .... #000401 $7.50

THE FALSE FAST. Now, from the pen of Gwen Shaw, author of Your Appointment With God (a Bible Study on fasting), comes an exposé on the False Fast. It will help you to examine your motives for fasting, and make your foundations sure, so that your fast will be a potent tool in the hands of God......................................#000602 $2.50

THE LIGHT WILL COME FROM RUSSIA. The thrilling testimony of Mother Barbara, Abbess of the Mount of Olives in Jerusalem. She shares prophecies which were given to her concerning the nations of the world in our time by a holy bishop of the Kremlin, ten days before his death just prior to the Russian Revolution ....#000606 $5.50

 THE PARABLE OF THE GOLDEN RAIN. This is the story of how revivals come and go, and a true picture, in parable language, of how the Church tries to replace the genuine move of the Spirit with man-made programs and tactics. It's amusing and convicting at the same time ....#000603 $4.00

THEY SHALL MOUNT UP WITH WINGS AS EAGLES. Though you may feel old or tired, if you wait on the Lord, you shall mount up on wings as eagles! Let this book encourage you to stretch your wings and fulfill your destiny — no matter what your age! ....#000604 $6.95

 TO BE LIKE JESUS. Based on her Throne Room experience in 1971, the author shares the Father's heart about our place as sons in His Family. Nothing is more important than To Be Like Jesus! ....#000605 $6.95

POCKET SERMON BOOKS BY GWEN SHAW

BEHOLD, THIS DREAMER COMETH. Dreams and dreamers are God's gift to humanity to bring His purposes into the hearts of mankind. The life of Joseph, the dreamer, will encourage you to believe God to fulfill the dream He has put into your heart ....#000707 $2.00

 BREAKTHROUGH. Just like when Peter was in prison, sometimes you need a "breakthrough" in your life! This book reveals the truth in a fresh and living way! ....#000708 $2.00

DON'T STRIKE THE ROCK! When Moses became angry with the people's rebellion and disobeyed God's order to speak to the Rock, it cost him his entrance into the Promised Land. Don't allow anything to keep you from fulfilling God's perfect will for your life!..........#000704 $2.00

GOD WILL DESTROY THE VEIL OF BLINDNESS. "...as the veil of the Temple was rent...I shall again rend the veil in two....for...the Arab, so they shall know that I am God...." This was the word of the Lord concerning God's plan for the nations in the days to come. Join in with Abraham's prayer "Let Ishmael live before Thee!"................#000712 $2.00

HASTENING OUR REDEMPTION. All of Heaven and Earth are waiting for the Body of Christ to rise up in maturity and reclaim what we lost in the Fall of Man. Applying the Blood of Jesus is the key to *Hastening Our Redemption* ....#000705 $2.00

 IT CAN BE AVERTED. Many people today are burdened and fearful over prophecies of doom and destruction. However, the Bible is clear that God prefers mercy over judgment when His people humble themselves and pray...#000706 $2.00

KAIROS TIME. That once in a lifetime opportunity—that second, or minute, or hour, or year, or even longer, when a golden opportunity is sovereignly given to us by the Almighty. What we do with it can change our lives and possibly even change the world....................#000709 $2.00

 KNOWING ONE ANOTHER IN THE SPIRIT. Experience great peace as you learn to understand the difficulties your friends, enemies and loved ones face that help to form their character. "Wherefore henceforth know we no man after the flesh..." (II Cor. 5:16a)............#000703 $2.00

THE ANOINTING BREAKS THE YOKE. Learn how the anointing of God can set you free from your bondage: free to fulfill your destiny in the call of God on your life!...#000710 $2.00

 THE CRUCIFIED LIFE. When you suffer, knowing the cause is not your own sin, for you have searched your heart before God, then you must accept that it is God doing a new thing in your life. Let joy rise up within you because you are a partaker of Christ's suffering ....#000701 $2.00

THE MASTER IS COME AND CALLETH FOR THEE. Read about how the Lord called Gwen Shaw to begin the ministry of the End-Time Handmaidens and Servants. Perhaps the Master is also calling you into His service. Bring Him the fragments of your life — He will put them together again. An anointed message booklet ....#000702 $2.00

 THE MERCY SEAT. The Days of Grace are coming to a close, and the Days of Mercy are now here. And oh, how we need mercy! There never has been a time when we needed it more!................#000711 $2.00

Children's Books by Gwen Shaw

LITTLE ONES TO HIM BELONG. Based on the testimonies of children's visions of Heaven and the death of a small Chinese boy, Sister Gwen weaves a delightful story of the precious joys of Heaven for children of all ages ....#000901 $9.00

TELL ME THE STORIES OF JESUS. Some of the greatest New Testament stories of the Life of Jesus and written in a way that will interest children and help them to love Jesus............#000902 $9.00

Books About Heaven

INTRA MUROS — Rebecca Springer. One of the most beautiful books about Heaven is available here in its unabridged form. Read the glorious account of this ordinary believer's visit to Heaven. It brings great comfort to the bereaved ....#109101 $8.00

PARADISE, THE HOLY CITY AND THE GLORY OF THE THRONE — Elwood Scott. Visited by a saint of God who spent forty days in Heaven, Elwood Scott's detailed description will edify and comfort your heart. Especially good for those with lost loved ones. Look into Heaven!...#104201 $8.00

Prophecies and Visions

THE DAY OF THE LORD IS NEAR: Vol. I - IV. *"Surely the Lord GOD will do nothing, but he revealeth his secret unto his servants the prophets."* (Amos 3:7) A collection of prophecies, visions and dreams. This startling compilation will help you understand what God has in His heart for the near future. ....Each Volume $10.00 • Volumes I - IV with binder..#001000 $25.00

Books Published by Engeltal Press

ATTITUDES IN THE BEATITUDES — Esther Rollins. An instructor of the Word of God for 50 years, Esther taught this anointed course on the Beatitudes as a guest teacher at our School of Ministry. Both basic and profound, this dynamic teaching is full of insight for the Christian walk ....#098801 $5.95

BANISHED FOR FAITH — Emil Waltner. The stirring story of the courageous forefathers of Gwen Shaw, the Hutterite Mennonites, who were banished from their homeland and suffered great persecution for their faith. Republished with an index and epilogue by Gwen Shaw. ....#126201 $12.95

BECOMING A SERVANT — Robert Baldwin. Learn what is on God's heart about servanthood. We must learn to serve before we can be trusted to lead. If you want to be great in God's Kingdom, learn to be the servant of all..#006901 $2.00

FIVE STONES AND A SWORD — Gene Little. Read the true account of how Jesus is appearing to His lost children, and revealing Himself to these sons of Abraham. Your heart will leap with joy, and you will be encouraged, with new faith, that God will send a great revival among the Moslem people of the world..#072501 #1.50

FOOTPRINTS — Larry Hunt. A collection of poems and stories reflecting the hand of God upon this humble pastor during 35 years of ministry..#057901 $3.75

FROM DUST TO GLORY — June Lewis. The Lord intends more than just salvation for us. He is making vessels of eternal Glory if we submit to Him. Rise up from your dust!........................#072001 $7.50

HOLY ANN — Helen Bingham. This humble Irish woman moved the arm of God through simple faith and prevailing prayer. Read these modern miracles that are told like a story from the Old Testament. The record of a lifetime of answered prayer ....#010501 $4.95

IT WAS WORTH IT ALL — Elly Matz. The story of a beautiful woman whose courage will inspire you. Feel her heart as she tells of her starving father, the young Communist engineer she married, the villages mysteriously evacuated, the invading German army, the concentration camp where she was a prisoner, and her escape into freedom..#078001 $5.95

LET'S KEEP MOVING — Pete Snyder. Travel with Peter to Haiti where he struggles with the call of God to be a missionary. Identify with Peter's growth of faith through trials and tribulations as he travels on to China where new adventures await and faithful endurance is needed. A must for the called! ....#108801 $9.95

RULING IN THEIR MIDST — June Lewis. The Lord has called us to rule even in the midst of all demonic activity and Satan's plans and schemes. Sister June has learned spiritual warfare from the Lord Himself, *"who teacheth my hands to war,"* in the face of personal tragedy
....#072002 $6.00

Prices are subject to change.

For a complete catalogue with current pricing, contact:

Engeltal Press
P.O. Box 447
Jasper, ARK 72641 U.S.A.
Telephone (870) 446-2665
Fax (870) 446-2259
Email books@eth-s.org
Website www.engeltalpress.com